# The French Connections

*of*

# JACQUES DERRIDA

# The French Connections

*of*

# JACQUES DERRIDA

Edited by

JULIAN WOLFREYS
JOHN BRANNIGAN
RUTH ROBBINS

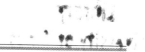

STATE UNIVERSITY OF NEW YORK PRESS

Published by
State University of New York Press, Albany

© 1999 State University of New York

For information, address State University of New York Press,
State University Plaza, Albany, NY 12246

Production by Laurie Searl
Marketing by Anne M. Valentine

**Library of Congress Cataloging-in-Publication Data**

The French connections of Jacques Derrida / edited by Julian Wolfreys,
   John Brannigan, and Ruth Robbins.
      p.   cm.
      Includes bibliographical references and index.
      ISBN 0-7914-4131-8 (alk. paper). — ISBN 0-7914-4132-6 (pbk. :
   alk. paper)
      1. Derrida, Jacques—Contributions in criticism.   2. Literature—
   Philosophy.   3. French literature—History and criticism.
   4. Oulipo (Association)   5. Difference (Philosophy)   6. Philosophy,
   French.   I. Wolfreys, Julian, 1958–      .   II. Brannigan, John.
   III. Robbins, Ruth, 1965–      .
   PN75.D45F74   1999                                          98-8450
                                                                  CIP

10 9 8 7 6 5 4 3 2 1

# Contents

# Abbreviations

Full bibliographical details are given in the Works Cited at the end of the collection.

| | |
|---|---|
| A | *Aporias* |
| Ai | *As if I were dead* |
| AL | *Acts of Literature* |
| ATRA | Of an Apocalyptic Tone Recently Adopted in Philosophy |
| Atvm | At this very moment in this work here I am |
| B | Biodegradables |
| C | *Cinders* |
| C | Circonfession / Circumfession |
| CP | *La carte postale* |
| D | *Dissemination* |
| Di | *La dissémination* |
| DRB | The Deaths of Roland Barthes |
| Ed | *L'Ecriture et la différence* |
| E | *De l'esprit: Heidegger et la question* |
| EO | *The Ear of the Other* |
| Fc | *Feu la cendre* |
| G | *Glas* |
| Gr | *De la Grammatologie* |
| Gra | *Of Grammatology* |
| GT | *Given Time: I Counterfeit Money* |
| HAS | How to Avoid Speaking: Denials |
| Hep | Un entretien avec Jacques Derrida: Heidegger, l'enfer des philosophes |
| JD | *Jacques Derrida* |
| K | *Khôra* |
| L'ac | *L'autre cap* |
| LDR | *Lecture de Droit de regards* |
| LOBL | Living On: Border Lines |
| LSSDS | Like the Sound of the Sea Deep Within a Shell |
| M | Mallarmé |

| | |
|---|---|
| *MA* | *Mal d'archive* |
| *MB* | *Memoirs of the Blind* |
| *MC* | My Chances / *Mes Chances* |
| *Mé* | *Mémoires, pour Paul de Man* |
| *MP* | *Margins of Philosophy* |
| *Mp* | *Marges de la philosophie* |
| *MPM* | *Memoires, for Paul de Man* |
| MRB | Les morts de Roland Barthes |
| NANN | No Apocalypse Not Now |
| No | Nombre de oui |
| *OH* | *The Other Heading* |
| *ONAATP* | *On a Newly Arisen Apocalyptic Tone in Philosophy* |
| *P* | *Parages* |
| *P* | Pas |
| *Pa* | *Politiques de l'amitié* |
| *PC* | *The Post Card* |
| *Pds* | *Points de suspension* |
| *pgpH* | *La problème de la genèse dans la philosophie de Husserl* |
| *PIa* | *Psyché: Inventions de l'autre* |
| PIO | Psyche: Inventions of the Other |
| *Pos* | *Positions* |
| *P. . .* | *Points . . . : Interviews, 1974–1994* |
| *S* | *Signéponge / Signsponge* |
| SIL | This Strange Institution Called Literature |
| *SM* | *Specters of Marx:* |
| *Sn* | *Sauf le nom (Post–Scriptum)* |
| *SNS* | *Spurs: Nietzsche's Styles* |
| *SP* | *Speech and Phenomena and Other Essays on Husserl's Theory of Signs* |
| *Sp* | Sauver les phénomènes |
| SPC | Shibboleth: For Paul Celan |
| SST | Some Statements and Truisms about Neologisms, Newisms, Postisms, Parasitisms, and Other Small Seismisms |
| *TP* | *The Truth in Painting* |
| TT | The Time of a Thesis: Punctuations |
| UG | Ulysses Gramophone: Hear Say Yes in Joyce |
| *VP* | *La Voix et le phénomène* |
| *WD* | *Writing and Difference* |

# Preface

nous avons dit les limites du commentaire et de l'interprétation
en nous limitant au commentaire et un peu (très peu)
d'interprétation. *Double bind* où notre fidélité absolue a été
l'infidélité même.

> —Geoffrey Bennington, "Envoi," *Jacques Derrida*

we have said the limits of commentary and interpretation in
limiting ourselves to commentary and a little (a very little)
interpretation. Double bind in which our absolute fidelity
has been infidelity itself.

> —Geoffrey Bennington, "Envoi," *Jacques Derrida*

. . . car enfin mais enfin que suis–je d'autre en vérité, qui
suis-je si je ne suis pas ce que j'habite et où j'ai lieu . . .

> —C, 279

. . . for after all but after all what else am I in truth, who am
I if I am not what I inhabit and where I take place . . .

> —C, 279

ceci est *une vie*, parmi d'autres, réelles, possibles, fictives ou
secrètes.

> —Geoffrey Bennington, "Actes (La loi du genre)," *Jacques Derrida*

. . . this is *one life* among others, real ones, possible ones,
fictive or secret ones.

> —Geoffrey Bennington, "Acts (The Law of Genre)," *Jacques Derrida*

As the title to this collection of essays might suggest
to you, this is very much an exploration of certain relationships and
inter-weavings—connections—between the writing of Jacques Derrida
and a range of mostly French writers and thinkers. The purpose of this
collection is to inform the reader of a variety of *connections*, to engage
with the text of Derrida in an original manner, and, finally, to throw
new light on Derrida's French intertexts (to borrow the phrase of one
of the book's anonymous readers). The word, *connections*, is given in
our title in its plural form, and this is wholly appropriate when one
comes to consider the multiple, diverse, highly singular range of connections, not only between Jacques Derrida and what is called French

thought or French literature, but also between the various writers and thinkers to whom Derrida (re)turns, in whom he has an *interest*, to cite that word which Laurent Milesi so forcefully and eloquently changes in the final essay of this collection, *The French Connections of Jacques Derrida*. The word *connection* has a number of meanings, provides a number of *connections* (numbers of *yeses*, we're tempted to suggest; responses to the responsible response always demonstrated so consistently by Derrida) with regard to the writing of Jacques Derrida. Its semantic riches can be seen to pertain, fortuitously, to Jacques Derrida, to his interests and concerns, and we hope you'll be patient with us if we advertise a few of these possible meanings.

Connection, the Oxford English Dictionary informs us, signifies the action or act of connecting, the state of being connected. It also suggests the making or connecting of an electrical circuit (Derrida's writings have sparked off or caused to spark numerous ideas, essays, books, articles, not least in his more recent publications which address technology and spectrality);[1] from the late nineteenth century onwards, the point in French writing with which we begin in this collection, with Mallarmé, with Baudelaire, connection refers—singularly appropriate in the case of considering Derrida—to "a linking by telephone connection." At the same time there is the sense of causal or logical relationship, interdependence, contextual relation, personal dealing, sexual relationship—so these, *can these*, not all be said to apply to the texts of Derrida, in one manner or another? There is also the less common sense of *connection*, of a person or acquaintance who has prestige or influence. In this case *the French Connections of Jacques Derrida* might well be understood to mean the influence Derrida has had, and continues to have, despite the grumblings of those such as Alan Sokal in the United States and Raymond Tallis in Great Britain, over a generation of thinkers, critics and academicians, who, by synecdoche—or even the contiguity of a metonym[2]—come to be figured through the collection of essays gathered here. The technological—and the metaphoric—rears its head again, when we consider that *connection* refers to the scheduled meeting of one mode of transport, one vehicle (recall the issues of transport and vehicle at the beginning of Derrida's essay, "Economimesis") with another. The OED even suggests as a definition the purchase of illegal drugs or the person or organization dealing in or supplying illicit substances (Avital Ronell's work has already made explicit such connections).[3] A Connector is a person or device for making connections, while connective tissue is that fibrous membrane or material connecting the more specialized tissues and organs of the body (the hymen?). As the very brief parentheses indicate, there is a connective network already at work, in place and taking place. Without pursuing these *connections* any further, it strikes us that any possible number of connections may be made in respect of Derrida's writings. What follows in this collection are only a few of the possible means of transport, a number of fibrous or textile strands that make the exploration of Derrida's thought available in given or assumed relationships with what is defined by the term *French.*

We consider this to be an exploration because, together, these essays constitute what is certainly a beginning of sorts, with regard to the various, innumerable "contexts" or intertexts of Jacques Derrida's huge output over the last thirty or so years. This is a multiple beginning; it doesn't start from any one point, and, indeed, it doesn't begin at all but turns back, unfolds, repeatedly, to Derrida and to those on whom he writes. In these acts of unfolding, we are not seeking to pin down a single Derrida, to decide upon him as definitely, *only,* a "French"—or even a *European*— thinker who emerges as part of a clearly definable cultural and literary tradition, even though such an assumption has an obvious, if limited "truth" to it. Derrida's own writing on the subject of identity should inform readers that there is no single identity that is not already marked by difference. Historical and biographical sources, hidden or otherwise, are not our primary concerns in gathering together and exploring certain perceived relations concerning Derrida's writing and that of the other French authors and thinkers such as Mallarmé, Baudelaire, Valéry, Artaud, Breton, Perec, Ponge, Paulhan, as well as the various groups or movements found in these pages. The (auto)biographical is to be found in most of Derrida's writings,[4] and if one were to construct a biography as cultural history from such traits (supposing such a thing were either likely or desirable), this would be a very different book indeed, and not one which we had ever intended. (It exists in the future as one of the possible specters of Derrida, waiting to be traced.) Furthermore, always supposing that such a biographico-cultural narrative had been our purpose, this would only have been to trace one strand among many possible others.

Instead, our shared interests might be expressed as the difference that is Derrida's, the difference and alterity within the writing that is signed "Jacques Derrida." This difference is also that to which Derrida has alerted us on numerous occasions concerning the language that he calls "his," French, and which, he has said, is the only language in which he addresses himself. Our interest is in opening up Derrida's writing to considerations that are other than the somewhat dominant

German-philosophical understanding which has been so visible in studies associated with Derrida's writing. Derrida's indebtedness to Hegel, to Kant, to Husserl, to Heidegger, is well documented, researched, considered, critiqued. Derrida's French identity is, in terms of critical works, somewhat more spectral, to use a suitably Derridean word, or less annotated, even though one could point to those studies of a certain French, if not Parisian, philosophical scene—a scene which through critical examination has become a seance—invoking the names of Merleau-Ponty and Levinas. We are interested in, and insert this collection of exploratory essays into the middle of a certain "French Derrida," if such a phrase is usable, and renaming Jacques somewhat abruptly; and recognizing all the while the suspension of definition which the quotation marks situate as the staging of a provisional range of identities or personae.

Who is this "French Derrida"? It is, obviously, one of the identities of Jacques Derrida, one of the many possible names by which we might know him. It might be an expression of perceived national identity (Derrida is French), or a colonial extension of France (like French Algeria). But it is rather, at least in this instance, a way of looking at Derrida within—what we call somewhat blithely for now—French contexts. This could have been a book of essays about what Derrida means in French, or what Derrida represents in France. But, instead, it is more exploratory, more adventurous than that, and each of the essays in this collection is an attempt to imagine how Derrida relates and associates with French literary, philosophical, and intellectual writings. How is Derrida connected in France? What are his connections? We are tracing some of Derrida's possible points of contact with French intellectual life, the lines and networks of communication which form and shape a certain Jacques Derrida (and which Derrida has in turn shaped, through, for example, his involvement with *Tel Quel*). French writers and thinkers have evidently been in contact with Derrida (on the phone, by postcard, etc.), but what is less clear is how their communications have been received, whether the line was disturbed or interrupted. It is not, then, a matter simply of tracing the links between Derrida and French writers, but of confronting an absence of tracing the links between them. Many of the essays place Derrida beside unexpected guests (Breton or Baudelaire), and eavesdrop on the fictive conversations taking place, inventing as well as finding French connections for Derrida.

There are of course, to reiterate the point, obvious discussions, interests that have surfaced on a number of occasions; for instance Derrida's readings of Mallarmé and his continuing study of Martin

Heidegger, as the latter philosopher's work has been interpreted by French philosophers or in what can be called a French or Parisian *milieu*. The critical appreciation and analyses of the French reception of Heidegger in relation to Derrida's part in that reception have largely been concerned with articulating a finite Derrida, a kind of limited liability with a knowable "context": Derrida Ltd. inc., perhaps. Blanchot is another French writer with whose texts Derrida has been associated (and whose name is connected to that of Heidegger),[5] but again in a more or less limited and limiting fashion, as if to acknowledge what happens, what gets lost in the translation from German to French of Heidegger as a "German" philosopher. (The proper names of languages as markers bearing cultural identities point to much more than the languages themselves, so that "German" or "French" imply supposedly definable cultures.) Whether those being cited are Heidegger, Nietzsche, Husserl, Blanchot, or Mallarmé, all serve to provide signatures which orient the reader to specific locations as the sites of Derrida's thinking. In turn, these signatures serve as ways of situating Derrida. Such situations are the places where a perceivable identity for Derrida—each time a different Derrida, Derrida differing from and deferring himself in the act of writing on the other—is seen to inhabit, to take place. These more familiar locations are the places from which this volume departs and to which it returns on occasion.

All of which is not to suggest that we are not returning here to some of those familiar sights (or sites). The collection begins and ends with two names with which all readers of Derrida will be familiar. Mallarmé cannot be ignored, any more than can Barthes (that is to say a certain Mallarmé, a certain Barthes). Derrida's repeated return to Mallarmé, his interest and indebtedness is acknowledged in this collection directly or indirectly in a number of places, especially in the essays by Michael Temple and Laurent Milesi, in the first and final chapters. Other already familiar conjunctions are also reexplored, opened up to fresh consideration, from other situations. One of the contributors to this current volume, Christopher Johnson, has already offered a sustained analysis of the relationship between Derridean thinking, the work of Lévi-Strauss, and scientific discourse in the context of French thinking in his impressive *System and Writing in the Philosophy of Jacques Derrida* (1993); here he pursues a reading of structuralism and the relationship between science and the linguistic model.

Despite a number of tantalizing and increasingly frequent comments on Derrida's part in interviews in recent years, and in a number of other texts, such as *The Other Heading* or "Circonfession," there remains a remarkable absence of critical material on Derrida in relation to or in (to use that problematic term once again) the "contexts" of French thought, whether literary or linguistic, philosophical or scientific. However, and to reiterate, this is still not a volume that seeks a specific identity for Derrida. As chapter 2, "In the Wake of: Baudelaire • Valéry • Derrida," by Ruth Robbins and Julian Wolfreys, sets out to explore, any consideration of identity, whether personal, national, cultural, or even spiritual, must always acknowledge, following Derrida, that there is no self-sufficient, homogeneous identity. Identity is written by difference, and difference is multiple. Each of the essays in this collection works to comprehend the difference of Derrida's texts within French, whether by this latter proper name we are identifying French language, literature, culture, philosophy, politics. Wherever and whenever Derrida writes with a specific knowledge of a particular and given Francophone "context"—whether that "context" be linguistic, literary, grammatical, institutional, structural—the figure of the other installed within the dominant discourse or form emerges. These essays acknowledge such otherness and look toward those situations where Derrida situates himself, those situations that interest Derrida and into which he inserts himself.

The fact that this collection should be so interested in the liminal, the marginal, difference, and otherness, as provisional markers for a range of heterogeneous concerns is perhaps itself a reason why this collection has no introduction other than this preface. After Derrida, it should no longer be necessary to justify the absence of the introduction, yet, more than ever, it appears necessary to do so, however briefly, and even if this preface may well turn out to be an introduction in disguise; recuperating ourselves into a position we seek to avoid is unavoidable; every denial is also, potentially, an affirmation. As we all know, following Derrida, the introduction is that convention, especially with collections such as this, with several different authors, in diverse hands, all with different concerns and interests, that, after the event, sets out to provide a reason for the collection's existence. The introduction serves a somewhat metonymic or synecdochic function re-presenting the argument of the whole in truncated and telegraphed form. This, of course, is the sleight of hand which defines the introduction, that which is so often written after everything else, yet presenting itself as having the key, setting the tone. The introduction behaves as though there were a program or methodology, a departure point. The introduction says, in other words, "get with the program," while telling you exactly what that program is, what you should tune into, what you should be looking for. So, no introduction, no program.

Instead of getting with the program ourselves or suggesting that you do the same according to some predetermined game plan which we might have set out (had there been an introduction), we're hoping that you "go with the flow." We want the reader to catch the drifts and currents of the various essays and their various rhythms, whether the concern is with poetics, literary language, polemics, the impossibilities of translation (see John Leavey's and Boris Belay's contributions), or a particular cultural moment or movement, as with structuralism, surrealism, or the Oulipo group, as in the essays by Johnson, John Brannigan, and Burhan Tufail. As the organization of the essays is intended to suggest, themes, interests, and concerns unfold themselves in particular ways during different cultural moments. Placing Tufail's essay against Johnson's for example, we wish only to indicate particular, heterogeneous flows during the mid decades of the twentieth century, which in and of themselves make it impossible to define a finite context for understanding the emergence of the work of Jacques Derrida. It is precisely the "between"—in this case that which is "between" poetics and scientific discourse—that allows for the constant reassessment of what we could, too easily, call Derrida's *oeuvre*. The absence of an introduction should suggest the absence of a predetermined heading (other than that most minimal of marker buoys known as the title), other than the headings chosen by the editors in the form of the essays that form *The French Connections of Jacques Derrida* and the possible heading(s) the reader chooses as an *other* heading, the *other* of a heading this preface avoids giving.

One word more about the title of this collection. The "connections" are all tentative, not prescriptive. These essays offer "connections" that are equally disjunctions, displacings, *contra-dictions*, in the sense of speaking against perceived wisdoms, beliefs about Jacques Derrida. And "French Connections": A *French* connection? Is such a thing imaginable? What constitutes the identity of such a link? What— or who—gives it its identity? Who does the defining, and on what authority? The issue of making connections, of tracing the connective tissue as, itself, a possible trace; all of this has to do with the impossible question of identity, tracing one narrative for that, and as that, identity, while recognizing that the identity is never totalizable, never discrete.

Julian Wolfreys, John Brannigan, Ruth Robbins

## NOTES TO PREFACE

1. See, for example, Jacques Derrida and Bernard Steigler, *Echographies de la télévision. Entretiens filmés* (1996).

2. This phrase is David Hearn's; we thank him.

3. See Ronell's *The Telephone Book: Technology, Schizophrenia, Electric Speech* (1989), and *Crack Wars: Literature, Addiction, Mania* (1992).

4. See, for example, the fine discussions of Nicholas Royle, *After Derrida* (1995) and Robert Smith, *Derrida and Autobiography* (1995).

5. See, for example, Timothy Clark, *Derrida, Heidegger, Blanchot: Sources of Derrida's Notion and Practice of Literature* (1992).

# Acknowledgments

This collection of essays was commissioned as a result of a conference, entitled "Applied Derrida," which occurred July 20–23, 1995, at the University of Luton. Two other collections of essays have already appeared: *Applying: to Derrida*, edited by the current editors (1996), and a special number of the journal *Imprimatur* (1:2/3; Spring 1996), edited by Julian Wolfreys. With this collection, nearly forty of the papers given at that conference, along with an interview with Derrida, will have appeared in print. In the present volume, all the essays (now much revised and expanded) were given as conference presentations, with the exception of those contributions by the editors.

We would like to thank Tim Boatswain, Dean of Humanities at the University of Luton, for his support for the conference. Others deserving mention are those students at Luton who helped with organizational matters before and throughout the weekend. A special debt of gratitude must go to Jacques Derrida whose enthusiasm for the conference and subsequent publications has been unwavering. James Peltz, Acquisitions Editor at SUNY, took over this project from his predecessor, and deserves thanks for staying with the project, having faith in it, and being supportive when there were times when it seemed it might never be finished. Laurie Searl and Alan Hewat both deserve thanks. We would also like to thank the various anonymous readers for SUNY who were insightful, helpful, and complimentary beyond the call of duty. Finally, we would like to thank Brian Niro, David Hearn, and Leah Wain for their tireless and good-humored copyreading and editorial efforts.

# CHAPTER 1

# "Mallarmé, par Jacques Derrida"

MICHAEL TEMPLE

> *peindre non la chose, mais l'effet qu'elle produit*
> [to paint, not the thing, but the effect it produces]

## MEETINGS

$M$y title is drawn from an encyclopaedic history of French literature published in 1974 and entitled *Tableau de la littérature française, vol. III: de Mme de Staël à Rimbaud*.[1] This may appear a strange place for the names of Mallarmé and Derrida to meet. Strange because one does not think of Derrida as a literary historian; strange because one does not think of Mallarmé as quite fitting into a history of French literature. He was either too late to be a Parnassian because of his age; or too advanced to be one because of his "poétique très nouvelle" [very new poetics].[2] He was too old to be a card-carrying Symbolist, although he seemed happy enough to patronize those of his young admirers who enjoyed such a label.[3] A century later, he was tardily rejuvenated by the *nouvelle critique*, structuralism, *Tel Quel*, and so on—diverse movements in which the name *Stéphane Mallarmé* has circulated with inconstant value and to differing effects. So Mallarmé is also a contemporary—living if paradoxical proof that:

> Unique fois au monde, parce qu'en raison d'un événement toujours que j'expliquerai, il n'est pas de Présent, non—un présent n'existe pas . . . (*Oc*, 372)[4]
>
> [One and only time in the world, because owing to an event always which I shall explain, there is no Present, no—a present does not exist . . .]

What we have in "Mallarmé, par Jacques Derrida" is a meeting of equals and opposites. A contemporary philosopher and a contemporary ghost.[5] Clearly, the encounter is governed by particular rules of engagement. Literary history makes assumptions about periods, meanings, movements, lives, etc.—in short, assumptions about representation—all of which we would expect Jacques Derrida to question and probably to subvert. This indeed is what he will go on to do (see next section on "mimicry"). And yet even this meeting of minds cannot quite escape the grasp of historical time—which is why I shall now say something about the occasion of "Mallarmé, par Jacques Derrida."

The meeting takes place in 1974. Now, whatever one might think of intellectual history as a discipline, it is clear that for the year 1974 the name, Stéphane Mallarmé, would have to be an object of its attention—perhaps even a privileged one at that. Moreover, this had been the case at least since the early sixties. The publication in 1961 of Jean-Pierre Richard's monumentally ambitious *L'univers imaginaire de Stéphane Mallarmé* had inspired the rereading of Mallarmé by (amongst others) Genette, Sollers, Kristeva . . . and of course Jacques Derrida.[6] If we focus on the last of these figures, we should certainly indicate the 1963 essay "Force et signification," which later opened *L'écriture et la différence* (1967). Although the direct target of the piece is Jean Rousset's *Forme et signification: essais sur les structures littéraires de Corneille à Claudel* (1962), the real force of Derrida's argument is an interrogation (not to say "deconstruction") of what had come to be known already as "structuralist" or "structural" criticism, and in particular its highly dubious assumptions about the unity or totality of a work, an age or, indeed, a universe. It is in this article that Derrida foreshadows the polite but devastating mimicry that in "La double séance" he will act out on Richard's world stage. Perhaps the sharpest signal of ulterior motivation appears at the epigraph to *L'écriture et la différence*:

> le tout sans nouveauté qu'un espacement de la lecture.
>
> [the whole without novelty other than a spacing out of reading.]

In its original context (the preface to "Un coup de dés"), the passage continues:

> Les 'blancs' en effet, assument l'importance, frappent d'abord; la versification en exigea, comme silence alentour, ordinairement, au point qu'un morceau, lyrique ou de peu de pieds, occupe, au milieu, le tiers environ du feuillet; je ne transgresse cette mesure, seulement la disperse. (*Oc*, 455)

[The "blancs" in effect take on importance, strike first: versification demanded them, as silence all around, ordinarily, to the point that a piece, lyrical or of few feet, occupies, in the middle, a third roughly of the sheet; I do not transgress this measure, only disperse it.]

Now, the epigraph often stands as a strategic indicator, but equally can function as a site of identification. *Dixit* Mallarmé, *ditto* Derrida. The difference and novelty marked *re* Richard (who is simply the best of all Mallarmean exegetes, and the only hermeneutician one could conceivably describe as "delicious") turns on the term *espacement*. In that "spacing out," unity falls for *différance*, and the totalitarian universe of meaning implodes into a virtual discontinuum of unpredictable "events." But also a printer's "space" where anything or nothing indifferently might happen or mean. A space in which *blanc* might also just be a blank.[7]

Were proof required that Mallarmé had remained on Derrida's mind between *L'écriture et la différence* (1967) and "Mallarmé, par Jacques Derrida," one need look no further than *Positions* (1972), the series of interviews published in the same year as *La Dissémination*. Mallarmé's name appears significantly on both the first and the last page of this collection. In response to Henri Ronse's bold opening question as to what Derrida's "system" might be—indeed what the organizing principle of the "ensemble de ses livres" ['entirety of his books'] might look like—the philosopher deflects the probing gaze toward the dead poet:

Ils (mes livres) forment, en effet, mais bien comme *déplacement* et comme déplacement d'une *question*, un certain système ouvert quelque part à quelque ressource indécidable qui lui donne son jeu. La note à laquelle vous faites allusion rappelait aussi la nécessité de ces 'blancs' dont on sait, depuis Mallarmé, qu'en tout texte ils 'assument l'importance.' (*Pos*, 11)

[They (my books) form, in effect, but indeed as a *displacement* and as displacement of a *question*, a certain system open somewhere to some undecidable resource which gives it its movement. The note to which you make allusion recalled also the necessity of these "blancs," of which we know, since Mallarmé, that in every text they "take on importance."]

The name unsurprisingly reoccurs throughout the eponymous dialogue with Jean-Louis Houdebine and Guy Scarpetta, the discussion returning repeatedly to *La Dissémination* and "La double séance" in particular.[8] For my present purpose, the philosophical details of what is said in those pages are less interesting than the insistence of the name as reference and authority, as kindred spirit or absent friend. To address the meeting of "Mallarmé, par Jacques Derrida," to calculate their relative positioning (or *gisement*) around this time, one need only examine the post-scriptum to *Positions*—a text that attempts precisely to situate or represent "Derrida" in relation to the literary-philosophical public:

> *P.S.* Et si nous donnions à cet échange, pour intitulé (germinal), le mot *positions*, dont la polysémie se marque, de surcroît, dans la lettre *s*, lettre 'disséminante' par excellence, disait Mallarmé? J'ajouterai, s'agissant de *positions*: scènes, actes, figures de la dissémination. (*Pos*, 133)

> [P.S. And if we give to this exchange, as (germinal) title, the word *positions*, whose polysemy is marked, moreover, in the letter *s*, an excellently "disseminating" letter, as Mallarmé used to say? I shall add, taking of *positions*: scenes, acts, figures of dissemination.]

I suggest, then, that at the time of the meeting in question Stéphane Mallarmé was, virtually speaking, Derrida's second hand—if it be true that writing is "une machine à deux mains" (*Ed*, 334 ["a two-handed machine"]). Before and after writing; in the title, in the text, in the seminar; even, it would appear, in the signature, since each time the philosopher wrote the "s" of "Jacques" he would sign disseminatingly the "s" of "Stéphane". . .

My own position here may seem a little extreme, so let me now examine the meeting in simpler, more straightforward terms. Time and place have been established, as have the names of those present. Remains the agenda. What was *to be done*? What did Derrida *want* from the meeting? And what did he *get*? The occasion of "Mallarmé, par Jacques Derrida" (perhaps no more than an accident of French publishing history) provided a place for the philosopher to "resume" a decade of his application to Stéphane Mallarmé—reading, writing, thinking. Twenty years on, it will allow me to schematize for you the *effects* (on Derrida) of "ce qui fut, par Mallarmé, écrit" (*Tableau*, 369 [what was, by Mallarmé, written]).

## MIMICRY

Before doing that, however, I should like to make some brief remarks concerning the way in which Derrida chose to negotiate the particular rules of engagement implicit in the *Tableau*; as well as the extent to which he might be seen to mimic Mallarmé's own approach to similar literary-philosophical contexts. I shall do this under the headings of *address*, *exposition*, and *representation*.

whole soul of the philosopher, and Luton and Cerisy and Cotonou will simultaneously cease to exist. Before such a disaster befalls us, however, let me turn to my final question, possibly the most practical in the eyes of the present audience. What did Derrida *get* from Mallarmé (in 1974)? What are the *effects*, on Jacques Derrida, of what was, by Mallarmé, written? I have arranged these effects into a Derridean portrait of Stéphane Mallarmé in seven brief *tableaux*:

1. *déjouer*
2. *événement*
3. *sens*
4. *opération*
5. *crise*
6. *blanc*
7. *salut*

## Effects

In 1995, the concepts I have just enumerated may sound to your ears more "Derridean" than "Mallarmean," and it is certainly not my intention to waste your time by explicating terms you know far better than I do. However, given Derrida's declared enthusiasm for the *greffe*, for citation, and for the problematics of "context" in general, I hope you will nonetheless *get* something from the ensuing "scholia," as Mallarmé would have called them. The very word *effect,* as a preliminary example, is one that Derrida has circulated throughout philosophy to great . . . effect. You all know "La philosophie en effet." But, *en effet,* you do not know "la philosophie." Is that what philosophy is ?— (With Gallic shrug) *En effet.* It is not my place here to mimic, nor certainly to mock, but rather to point out that there is another place where a writer—Stéphane Mallarmé—activated the *différend* between the thing (of philosophy?) and its effect. I refer you to Derrida's epigraph in the *Tableau,* the full text of which is:

> Pour moi, me voilà résolument à l'oeuvre. J'ai enfin commencé mon *Hérodiade.* Avec terreur, car j'invente une langue qui doit nécessairement jaillir d'une poétique très nouvelle, que je pourrais définir en ces deux mots: *Peindre, non la chose, mais l'effet qu'elle produit.* (Corr. vol. 1, 137)

> [As for me, here I am resolutely at work. I have finally started my *Hérodiade.* With terror, for I am inventing a language which must necessarily spring from a very new poetics, which I could define in these two words: *to paint, not the thing, but the effect it produces.*]

Might this not be the very motto of "La philosophie en effet"? With such a question in mind, here are my seven snapshots.

In the second paragraph of "Mallarmé, par Jacques Derrida," please note two terms in particular—*machiné* and *déjouer*:

> Près d'un siècle de lecture maintenant: nous commençons seulement à entrevoir que quelque chose a été machiné (par Mallarmé? en tout cas selon ce qui se passe *par* lui, comme à travers lui) pour déjouer les catégories de l'histoire et des classifications littéraires, de la critique littéraire, des philosophies et herméneutiques de tout genre. *(Tableau, 369)*

> [Almost a century of reading now: we are beginning to realize that something has been plotted (by Mallarmé? in any case according to what happened *by* him, as indeed through him) to confound the categories of history and of literary classifications, and of literary criticism, of philosophies and hermeneutics of all kinds.]

This is Mallarmé as troublemaker, breaking up or spoiling the deadly game of categories: "déjouer = cesser de jouer" [stop playing] *(Dictionnaire Robert)*. It is also Mallarmé as trickster or cheat, C.Auguste Dupin outwitting the plodding hermeneutics of Monsieur G-, the Parisian prefect of police: "machiner = former en secret (des desseins, des combinaisons malhonnêtes, illicites)" [form in secret (plots, intrigues, which are dishonest, illicit)] *(Robert Dictionary)*. From the interplay of these two attractive terms, one could spark off some thoughtful pyrotechnics: the dysfunctioning of Descartes's *machine*; the *machin* in relation to the *chose*; Mallarmé as linguistic virus in the thinking internet; and so on. If we develop this line of thought, the verb *déjouer* splits neatly into an imaginary noun *dé-joueur,* leading us unerringly to Mallarmé the *joueur de dés* [dice-player], the poetic player running the ultimate risk that maybe with "Un coup de dés" [a throw of the dice]— forerunner or fragment of the "Livre total," the Orphic song to order and harmonize the universe—his gamble might actually come off, bequeathing us the totalitarian nightmare—into which we would have already woken—of a world that really did make sense. We can sometimes be grateful that Mallarmé died mysteriously of a brain hemorrhage at the age of fifty-six. But when he showed young Valéry the proofs of "Un coup de dés," "il (lui) dit [according to the acolyte] avec un sourire admirable, ornement du plus pur orgueil inspiré à un homme par son sentiment de l'univers: 'Ne trouvez-vous pas que c'est un acte de démence?' " [he told him with an admirable smile, ornament of the purest pride inspired in a man by his feeling of the universe: "Do you not think that this is an act of folly?"] *(Oc,* 1582). And what if Derrida had been watching the scene, would it have been in silent admiration or passive denial?

In the third paragraph, the keywords are already underlined for us:

> On ne peut plus parler ici d'un *événement*, de l'événement d'un tel texte; on ne peut plus interroger son *sens* sauf à retomber en deça de lui, dans le réseau de valeurs qu'il a *pratiquement* remises en question; celle d'événement (présence, singularité sans répétition possible, temporalité, historicité) . . . (*Tableau,* 369)

> [One can no longer speak here of an *event*, of the event of such a text; one can no longer ask its *meaning* without falling short of it, back into the network of values which it has *practically* brought into question; the value of the event (presence, singularity without possible repetition, temporality, historicity) . . .]

The image of Mallarmé is again here essentially deconstructive. One effect of what Mallarmé wrote demands to be read as an "event," in the sense that he both provoked and diagnosed a "crisis in verse," the repercussions of which drowned out the anxious or liberating cries about the mere counting of syllables. He not only asked the question, "Sait-on ce que c'est qu'écrire?" (*Oc,* 481), or, "quelque chose comme les Lettres existe-t-il?" [Do we know what it is to write? . . . Does something like Letters exist?] (*Oc,* 645), but, as Derrida insists, he *practically* took apart the accepted values of reading and writing, in a way that seems utterly contemporary. The resulting paradox, however, is that the "avènement" [coming] of Mallarmé equally destroys the chances of a workable diachronic model for reading literature. Lastly, Mallarmé delivers a hammer blow to the text event as immutable object, the well-wrought urn, etc. The textual act for Mallarmé could always just as well have happened very differently, or indeed might never have happened at all; "rien n'aura eu lieu que le lieu" translates as "the paradigmatic axis is infinite," although I must declare a preference for the original. Beware confusion, however, at this point. Both Derrida and myself, I believe, would take on pugilistically any man or woman in the audience who claimed that Mallarmé either preached or practised *n'importe quoi*—some sort of random aesthetics of chance. Mallarmé could write an urn as well as the next poet, and my own private version of the final paroxysm imagines a Mallarmé lucid to the end ("cela devait être très beau" [it was going to be very beautiful])[14] regarding the true relation of the Work to the works, of poetic *oeuvres* (feminine plural) to the alchemical *Oeuvre* (masculine singular). It is the very impossibility of the notorious "Livre total" that both determines and liberates the "poèmes, ou études en vue de mieux" [poems, or studies with a view to something better], the "feuillets d'album" [sheets from an album], the "divagations" [divagations], the "cartes de visite" [calling cards], the "loisirs de la poste" [leisures of the postal system], the "vers de circonstance" [occasional verse] . . . That unwhole mess of *jouissifs* non-events is for me "resumed" in the opening line of the liminary sonnet to *Poésies*:

> Rien, cette écume, vierge vers (*Poé*, 3)
>
> [Nothing, this froth, virgin verse]

The keyword *sens* has already occurred in the passage cited above, but Derrida does not want to let it go:

> La valeur . . . de sens: Mallarmé n'a cessé de traquer la signification partout où s'y produisait la perte du sens, en particulier dans ces deux alchemies que sont l'esthétique et l'économie politique. (*Tableau*, 369)
>
> [The value . . . of meaning: Mallarmé unceasingly tracked down signification wherever the loss of meaning was taking place, in particular in those two alchemies which are aesthetics and political economy.]

The first trap to avoid here is called semantic richness, or polysemy in the Richardian sense of the term: the plenitudinous, unified, interminably coherent universe of the poetic imagination. Three times no. It is the fading or loss of meaning which Derrida's Mallarmé tracked down like a sleuth determined elegantly to reveal not whodunit but rather that nothing in effect happened at all: the purloined letter was a blank page. Ever since Mallarmé said "ayant appris l'anglais simplement pour mieux lire Poe" [having learned English better to read Poe] (*Oc*, 662), scholars have assumed he was referring to the poetry. This is hardly surprising, given that Mallarmé was the first to defy Baudelaire's challenge that the poems were untranslatable. But there may still exist an unseen role for Mallarmé in that academic psycho-soap of some years back, when Lacan and Derrida fought it out for the right to play C. Auguste Dupin. My second warning on Derrida's use of *sens* concerns the juxtaposition of aesthetics and political economy:

> Tout se résume dans l'Esthétique et l'Economie politique . . . (*Oc*, 656)[15]
>
> [Everything is summed up in Aesthetics and political Economy . . .]

One might be tempted to read the conjunction of aesthetics and politics as a belated effort to reactualize Mallarmé in the form of a *soixante-*

*huitard* radical; and no doubt in the early seventies he was occasionally employed in this capacity. If one reads more closely, however, the ensuing passage from "Magie" (a short text on Huysmans and alchemy), what emerges as more appealing to Derrida and to Mallarmé alike is the deconstruction of the apparent complementarity of economics and aesthetics. A genealogical maneuver reveals the former simply to be the metropolitanized country cousin of the latter; the alchemist's "pierre nulle, qui rêve l'or, dite philosophale . . . annonce, dans la finance, le futur crédit, précédant le capital en le réduisant à l'humilité de la monnaie!" [empty stone, dreaming of gold, known as the philosopher's . . . announces, in finance, future credit, preceding capital whilst reducing it to the humbleness of money!] (*Oc*, 399). Economics and finance are intriguing insofar as they deal in "empty" signs, circulating within a closed system of otherwise meaningless symbols, notes, and figures. Later in his portrait (*Tableau*, 376), Derrida carefully unfolds the multiple apparitions and significations *chez* Mallarmé of the word *or*, notably in the text of that name (*Oc*, 398). But if he does so, it is only the better to puncture the accumulated illusion of so many meanings, of so much *or*—thus mimicking the bursting of bubbles, the shock of financial disaster, in this particular case the scandal around the Panama canal:

> Le numéraire, engin de terrible précision, net aux consciences, perd jusqu'à un sens. . . . Si un nombre se majore et recule, vers l'improbable, il inscrit plus de zéros: signifiant que son total équivaut spirituellement à rien, presque. (*Oc*, 398)

> [Coin, a machine of terrible precision, clear in our consciousness, loses even a meaning. . . . If a number gets bigger and retreats toward the improbable, it inscribes more zeros: signifying that its total equals spiritually nothing, almost.]

The values of meaning may be wiped off the screen as easily and spectacularly as the exponential multiplication of market zeros.

In his theoretical speculations, Mallarmé gave to the simple word *opération* the kind of depth and scope that Derrida has invested in the equally banal term *écriture*. The manner in which the philosopher expresses his admiration for the poet's "takeover" of literature ("opération" in the financial sense) necessarily draws him back into the kind of historicism he would normally rather avoid. But the phrase "et si Mallarmé marquait une rupture . . ." [And if Mallarmé marked a rupture . . .] advances a historical hypothesis, which Derrida then curiously inflates into an almost apocalyptic hyperbole: "elle (la rupture) révélerait par exemple l'essence de la littérature passée comme telle" [it would reveal for example the essence of literature past as such] *(Tableau,* 370). The end of the word as we know it, all brought crashing down by the anonymous little name of *Mallarmé*? In truth, Derrida recognizes the paradoxical role of the *signature* in this comical catastrophe:

> La logique nouvelle . . . qu'on ne pourrait d'ailleurs attribuer à Mallarmé qu'en recourant à une théorie naïve et intéressée de la signature, celle– là même que Mallarmé, définissant justement ce qu'il appelait l'"opération," n'a cessé de dérouter. Un texte est fait pour se passer de références. A la chose même, nous le verrons, à l'auteur qui n'y consigne que sa disparition. Cette disparition est activement inscrite, elle n'est pas un accident du texte mais plutôt sa nature; elle y marque la signa- ture d'une omission incessante. *(Tableau,* 370)

> [The new logic . . . which by the way one could only attribute to Mallarmé by having recourse to a naive and motivated theory of the signature, the very one that Mallarmé, defining precisely what he called the "opera- tion," unceasingly undermined. A text is made so as to do without references. Even to the thing, as we shall see, to the author who con- signs to that place merely his disappearance. This disappearance is actively inscribed, it is not an accident of the text but rather the latter's nature; it marks there the signature of an incessant omission.]

My own past work on the "name of the poet" has thus far done little more than explore in scoliastic detail the "Mallarmean" side of this crucial strategic meeting point between the two writers. For develop- ment of the "Derridean" side, I refer you to the sections entitled "Le nom propre" and "La signature" in the excellent *Jacques Derrida* (1991).

At first glance, *crise* might look like a mere repetition of the his- torical "rupture" indicated above. In fact, Derrida teases out a quite distinct line of reasoning, which brings into a state of crisis the solid notions of criticism and decision.

> La *crise*, moment où la *décision* simple n'est plus possible, où le choix entre les voies opposées se suspend. Crise de la critique, donc, qui aura toujours voulu par un jugement *décider (krinein)* de la valeur et du sens, discerner entre ce qui est et ce qui n'est pas, ce qui vaut et ce qui ne vaut pas, le vrai et le faux, le beau et le laid, toute signification et son contraire. *(Tableau,* 370)

> [The *crisis*, the moment when the simple *decision* is no longer pos- sible, when the choice between opposite paths is suspended. Crisis of criticism, therefore, which has always sought by a judgment to decide (*krinein*) value and meaning, to discriminate between what is and what isn't, what has value and what doesn't, the true and the false, the beautiful and the ugly, all signification and its opposite.]

Criticism decides meaning, beauty, truth, etc., as long as to decide means to fix, to hold, to arrest:

> Philosophie du *sens*, du *mot*, du *nom*. (*Tableau*, 370)
>
> [Philosophy of *meaning*, of the *word*, of the *name*]

Ambiguity it can just about handle, providing that the relation between the two possible meanings itself remains stable and under control. But what happens if one goes firstly beyond the dual relation of the *double entendre* into an unstoppable slippage of signifiers? And worse, for the decider, if the relation between the terms forces him to suspend judgment?

> Or tout le texte de Mallarmé est organisé pour qu'en ses points les plus forts, le sens reste *indécidable*; dès lors, le signifiant ne se laisse plus traverser, il reste, résiste, existe et se donne à remarquer. (*Tableau*, 371)
>
> [Now Mallarmé's text is organized so that in its strongest points meaning remains *undecidable*; thenceforth, the signifier no longer allows itself to be traversed, it remains, resists, exists, and offers to be noticed.]

Is suspension, though, just another form of fixation? Is Mallarmé, like the sophist Zeno, simply hypnotizing the philosopher into critical paralysis? Derrida almost looks as if he is arguing himself into this position, but is saved by the dynamic Diogenes of Mallarmé's syntax, which simply gets up and *moves*:

> Ce qui suspend la décision, ce n'est pas la richesse de sens, la ressource inépuisable d'un mot, c'est un certain jeu de la syntaxe. (*Tableau*, 371)[16]
>
> [What suspends judgment is not the richness of meaning, the inexhaustible resource of a word, it is a certain play of syntax.]

Mallarmean syntax is "poetry in motion": it shifts words around and about the page, up and down and back and forth, so as to leave the arbiter not so much suspended as dismissed, *hors-jeu* according to what he presumed to be the rules by which he would arrive at (*arrêter*) his decision. "Je suis profondément et scrupuleusement syntaxier" [I am profoundly and scrupulously syntaxal], Mallarmé proudly declared. He was not merely playing with words, Derrida claims, but reworked the profound and scrupulous structures of *la langue* itself.

I have already mentioned the importance the *blancs*, for Mallarmé and Derrida, assumed. As the following passage will indicate, the *blanc* emerges from "Mallarmé, par Jacques Derrida" (and perhaps from the whole *Tableau de la littérature française*) as the emblem of what the philosopher has already named "la nouvelle logique" [the new logic]. Politely repositioning himself in relation to the aptly named Richard's polysemic universe, Derrida explains the double operation of the *blanc*:

> Par exemple le signe *blanc*, avec tout ce qui s'y associe de proche en proche, est un immense réservoir de sens (neige, froid, mort, marbre, etc.; cygne, aile, éventail, etc.; virginité, pureté, hymen, etc.; page, toile, voile, gaze, lait, semence, voie lactée, étoile, etc.). Comme par aimantation symbolique, il traverse tout le texte de Mallarmé. Et pourtant le blanc marque aussi, par l'intermédiaire de la page blanche, le lieu de l'écriture de ces blancs; et d'abord l'espacement entre les différentes significations (celle de blanc entre autres), *espacement de la lecture. Les "blancs" en effet, assument l'importance.* Le blanc de l'espacement n'a pas de sens déterminé, il n'appartient pas simplement à la plurivalence de tous les autres blancs. En-plus ou en-moins de la série polysémique, perte ou surcroît de sens, il replie le texte vers lui-même, en indique à chaque instant le lieu (où *rien n'aura eu lieu . . . que le lieu*), la condition, le travail, le rythme. (*Tableau*, 372)

> [For example, the sign "blanc" (white/blank) with everything which is gradually associated with it, is an immense reservoir of meaning (snow, cold, death, marble, etc.; swan, wing, fan, etc.; virginity, purity, hymen, etc.; page, canvas, sail, gauze, milk, seed, milky way, star, etc.). As if by symbolic magnetism, it traverses the whole of Mallarmé's text. And yet the *blanc* also marks, by the intermediary of the white page, the place of the writing of these *blancs*; and firstly the spacing between the different significations (that of *blanc* amongst others), *the spacing out of reading. The "blancs," in effect, take on importance.* The *blanc* of spacing out does not have a determined meaning, it does not belong simply to the multivalence of all other *blancs*. More than or less than the polysemic series, loss or overabundance of meaning, it folds the text back into itself, indicates at each instant the place within it (where *nothing will have taken place . . . but the place*), the condition, the work, the rhythm.]

I shall append to this brilliant exposition a merely technical point, pertaining to the word *rythme*. French versification is fundamentally different from English verse in that its basic rhythm is syllabic rather than accentual. To put it simply, the classic alexandrine (e.g., "Tel qu'en lui-même enfin l'éternité le change") must have twelve syllables, otherwise it is not an alexandrine. By contrast, an English pentameter (e.g., "Shall I compare thee to a summer rose?") may or may not have ten syllables; what makes it a pentameter is the beating of the five stressed syllables: shall/pare/to/sum/rose. Now, major fisticuffs have been known to break out over the finer details of comparative metrics, but my point here is to explain uncontroversially the consequences of the *numerical* base of French verse, especially as exploited by Mallarmé. Imagine you are going to compose an octosyllabic sonnet—What do you have before you on your page? Horizontally (left to right and vice versa), you have eight blank spaces to fill; vertically (up and down and vice versa) you have fourteen blank lines to complete. Now, even if we exclude some of the other pertinent factors such as stanza, rhyme, caesura (and naturally the whole history of the sonnet and its transitions), we can see that the poem, in its virtual or blank state, looks as much like an empty grid—a spatial object waiting to be constructed— as it does a silent song—sounds waiting to be articulated in time:

> A ce vitrage d'ostensoir
> Que frôle une harpe par l'Ange
> Formée avec son vol du soir
> Pour la délicate phalange
>
> Du doigt, que, sans le vieux santal
> Ni le vieux livre, elle balance
> Sur le plumage instrumental,
> Musicienne du silence. (*Poé,* 41)
>
> [In the glasswork of an ostensory
> Which a harp touches by the Angel
> Formed with her evening flight
> For the delicate phalange
>
> Of the finger, which, without the old sandalwood
> Or the old book she balances
> On the instrumental plumage
> Musician of silence.]

That spatio-temporal virtuality, which is also a collapsing of those dimensions, runs through French verse, French prose, French "effort au style"—and always already will have done so, *since* Mallarmé.

The word *salut* can mean in French either "hello" or "goodbye" according to the context. Mallarmé exploited this resource (the word has plenty of other meanings) by placing a sonnet so entitled at the head of his *Poésies*:

> Rien, cette écume, vierge vers (*Poé,* 3)
>
> [Nothing, this froth, virgin verse]

But the unfolding of the sonnet, as well as the actual context of its first public delivery (see note 3), render the speech act as much a valediction as a salutation. As I bring this chapter to a close, the question arises: How did Derrida (in 1974) say "salut" to Mallarmé? Greetings, compliments, exchange of gifts, even a degree of friendly mimicry: all these might be read as rituals of salutation. But what of separation? How do poet and philosopher go their separate ways? My first response is to suggest that, despite the relative fading of "Stéphane Mallarmé" from the Derridean corpus post-1974, the resuscitated figurehead of so much radical theory between 1960 and 1975 may have lingered on in phantomatic form, especially upon the backdrop to more recent debates about signatures and subjectivity, memory and anonymity. I now merely reiterate that hypothesis, and leave it in suspense . . . Turning now for the final time to "Mallarmé, par Jacques Derrida," in fact to the final paragraph of the piece, what can we represent as the *effect* of Derrida's parting glance? He dons briefly once more the literary historian's toque, and compares Mallarmé to the pre-Renaissance *grands rhétoriqueurs*—poets renowned for their ludic desires and dextrous experimentations. Flattering though this portrait may be, Derrida then steps back or aside from his canvas, and readjusts his thinking cap. Mallarmé's operation, he concludes, escapes the representational controls of classical, philosophical rhetoric, and demonstrates *practically* (his adverb, his emphasis) the impertinence of that whole tradition. "So where does that leave me?" (says Jacques). He reflects a while . . . then:

> Si au contraire on appelle rhéteur non plus celui qui soumet son discours aux bonnes règles du sens, de la philosophie, de la dialectique philosophique, de la vérité, non plus celui en somme que la rhétorique philosophique accepte en lui prescrivant ses règles de bienséance, mais au contraire celui que Platon—alors excédé—voulait *chasser de la cité comme un sophiste ou un anti–philosophe*, Mallarmé est peut-être alors un très grand rhétoriqueur; un sophiste, sans doute, mais celui qui ne se laisse pas prendre par l'image que la philosophie a voulu nous laisser de lui en le captant dans un spéculum platonicien et en même temps, ce qui n'est nullement contradictoire, en le mettant hors la loi. *On sait* que comme tant de lecteurs de Mallarmé, Platon doublait alors son *active méconnaissance* d'une *admiration déclarée*. (*Tableau*, 378; my emphasis)

> [If on the contrary one no longer calls a rhetor the person who submits his discourse to the appropriate rules of meaning, of philosophy, of philosophical dialectics, of truth, nor the person to sum up whom philosophical rhetoric accepts whilst prescribing him its rules of conventional behaviour, but on the contrary the person whom Plato—beside himself at this point—wanted to *expel from the city as a sophist or anti-philosopher*, Mallarmé is perhaps therefore a *grand rhétoriqueur*; a sophist, no doubt, but one who does not allow himself

to get caught in the image of him with which philosophy has sought to bequeath us, by capturing him in a Platonic speculum and at the same time, which is in no way contradictory, by placing him outside the law. *It is well known* that like so many of Mallarmé's readers, Plato combined his *active ignorance* with a *declared admiration.*]

The anonymity of "on sait" allows Derrida discreetly to slip away from the picture of "Stéphane Mallarmé," and quietly slip into the space left by "Platon." Thus he declares his admiration for the poet, whilst actively deciding to know him no more.

## NOTES

1. The article (hereafter referred to parenthetically as *Tableau*) is rarely referred to by Mallarmé scholars, although one exception would be John Llewelyn in his piece "Derrida, Mallarmé, and Anatole" (*Philosophers' poets*, ed. David Wood, 93–110). The encyclopaedia itself does not appear to have made its mark, and yet there are some other interesting encounters one could explore, for example "Léon Bloy, par Roland Barthes." For the full text *in English*, see Christine Roulston's admirable translation "Mallarmé" (*Acts of Literature*, ed. Derek Attridge, 110–127; thanks to Burhan Tufail for this information). In this article, however, the translations are my own, as are any mistakes. The reader will see that I have generally erred on the side of inelegant literalism. All bibliographical references are given in full in the Bibliography.

2. Derrida's epigraph to the article reads: "j'invente une langue qui doit nécessairement jaillir d'une poétique très nouvelle" [I am inventing a language that must necessarily spring from a very new poetics]. See section 3 below for fuller version of this extract from Mallarmé's correspondence. On the matter of Mallarmé's rejection from the Parnasse, see Henri Mondor, *L'Histoire d'un faune.*

3. As Mallarmé himself said, in a moment of rare arrogance: "Très affiné, j'ai été dix ans d'avance du côté où les jeunes esprits pareils devaient tourner aujourd'hui" (*Oeuvres complètes,* 664 [hereafter *Oc*] [Very refined, I was ten years ahead in that direction where similar young minds were destined to turn today]). In chapter 2 of *The name of the poet*, I comment upon Mallarmé's positioning relative to his youthful followers, in particular the sight of the senior poet standing at the "helm" of a literary banquet held in his honor and reading "Salut," a poem in which he ironizes precisely about the "youth" of his aesthetic advance and the "age" of his advancing years.

4. Derrida seems to have been especially fond of Mallarmé's denial of the "present." In the article I am discussing, the quotation "Unique fois, etc." is granted pride of place amongst the many citations from Mallarmé's writings. The passage is drawn from "L'action restreinte," and strongly echoes a similar dismantlement of presence in "Mimique," the text with which Derrida kicks

off "La double séance." I should add at this point that, to the Derrida specialist, much of "Mallarmé, par Jacques Derrida" may look like a bite-size rewrite of the double seminar of 1969. My aim is to inform that impression with some views from Valvins rather than Ris Orangis.

5. There is a great deal one might say about the pair's shared interest in ghosts. In addition to all the *hommages* and *tombeaux*, and plain journalistic obituaries, Derrida would surely have been familiar with Mallarmé's most evident piece of prosopopeia or ghost-speech, the sonnet entitled "Sur les bois oubliés . . . ," in which Mallarmé imagines the dead wife reassuring her grieving husband that "pour revivre il suffit qu'à tes lèvres j'emprunte/ Le souffle de mon nom murmuré tout un soir" (*Poésies*, 158 [hereafter *Poé*] [to live again it is enough that on your lips I borrow / The breath of my name murmured for a whole evening]).

6. See, for example, "Le bonheur de Mallarmé" in *Figures I*; "Littérature et totalité" in *Logiques*; and of course *La révolution du langage poétique*.

7. "Spacing out" is the dictionary translation of "espacement." Maud Ellmann follows it in her article "Spacing out: a double entendre on Mallarmé" (22–31). Regarding my use here of the word *totalitarian*, I should make it clear that Richard himself uses it to describe his project:

> Notre travail . . . se place dans une perspective que nous croyons nouvelle: nommons-la, si l'on veut, interrogative et totalitaire. Notre effort a été de comprendre Mallarmé globalement, de rejoindre en lui l'esprit à la lettre, le 'fond' à la 'forme,' et de réunir en un seul faisceau toutes les exaltations soulevées par cette oeuvre incomparable. A tous les niveaux où une même conscience poursuit un même projet d'être, il a voulu retrouver des lignes identiques de développement, des principes parallèles d'organization. La critique, croyons-nous, peut être à la fois une herméneutique et un art combinatoire. Elle déchiffre alors en réunissant . . . elle rêvera d'instituer entre toutes les oeuvres particulières, et tous les registres—sérieux, tragique, métaphysique, précieux, amoureux, esthétique, idéologique, frivole de cette oeuvre, une relation d'ensemble qui les oblige à mutuellement s'éclaircir. (1961, 14–15)

> [Our work . . . places itself in a perspective we believe to be new: let us call it, if you like, interrogative and totalitarian. Our effort has been to understand Mallarmé as a whole, to join up in him the spirit of the letter, the "content" to the "form," and to bring together in a single fasces (*sic*) all the exaltations inspired by this incomparable work. At all levels at which a single consciousness pursues a single project of being, it (our effort) has sought to find identical lines of development, parallel principles of organization. Criticism, we believe, can be at once a hermeneutic and a combinative art. It deciphers, then, as it brings together . . . it will dream of instituting between all the particular works, and all the registers—serious, tragic, metaphysical, precious, amorous, aesthetic, ideological, frivolous—of this work, an overall relationship which obliges them mutually to enlighten each other.]

I quote the passage at such length firstly because I believe it informs Derrida's rewriting of "force" and "forme," and secondly because it stands as an extraordinary illustration of the power and horror of totalitarian thought *circa* 1960. The nightmare or wet dream of reason lubricates the sheets of the harmless professor's magisterial tome. If Derrida in 1963 is marking out his space with regard to this mode of thinking, it is hardly surprising that five years later he was less than convinced by the promise of revolutionary transcendence.

8. See 58–59, 62–64, and 93–96.

9. On Mallarmé and "Monsieur Tout-le-Monde," see Gérard Genette, *Mimologiques*, 274. The anecdote about the bourgeois and his newspaper comes from the memoirs of René Ghil: "Il convient (dit Mallarmé) de nous servir des mots de tous les jours, dans le sens que tout le monde croit comprendre! Je n'emploie que ceux-là. Ce sont les mêmes mots que le Bourgeois lit tous les matins, les mêmes! Mais, voilà (et ici son sourire s'accentuait), s'il lui arrive de les retrouver en tel mien poëme, il ne les comprend pas!" [It is best (said Mallarmé) to use everyday words, in the sense that everyone thinks they understand! They are the only ones I use. The same words the Bourgeois reads every morning, the same ones! But there you are (and here his smile became more distinct), if he should happen to come across them in some poem of mine, he doesn't understand them!] (see Jacques Scherer, *Grammaire de Mallarmé* ).

10. The last word on Mallarmé's difficulty was said by Malcolm Bowie in *Mallarmé and the Art of Being Difficult*.

11. For discussion of the strategic roles of *Les dieux antiques* and *Les mots anglais*, see chapter 1 of *The Name of the Poet*.

12. For the *mise en scène* of the thinking subject, see *Discours de la méthode*, chapters 1–3.

13. See chapter 3 of *The Name of the Poet*, "Writing your name into history."

14. See the final note to his wife and daughter, Henri Mondor, *Autres précisions sur Mallarmé et inédits*, 250–251.

15. The phrase forms part of a supplementary note to Mallarmé's lecture "La Musique et les Lettres." The rest of Derrida's quotation comes from "Magie" (*Oc*, 399–340).

16. See *La dissémination* for a fuller expression of Derrida's admiration for Mallarmé *syntaxier* ("mot que je n'ai jamais rencontré ailleurs") (206).

# CHAPTER 2

# In the Wake of . . .
## *Baudelaire • Valéry • Derrida*

RUTH ROBBINS AND JULIAN WOLFREYS

> . . . this complicity with the "French" or "Parisian" context also meant conflict, opposition, rupture, estrangement, a certain uprootedness.
>
> —Jacques Derrida
>
> We are beginning to glimpse that the disruption of these categories is also the effect of what was written by Mallarmé.
>
> —Jacques Derrida

In our introduction we stated that historical and biographical sources, hidden or otherwise, were not our primary concern in gathering together and exploring certain perceived—and supposedly perceivable—relations concerning Derrida's writing and those of other French authors and thinkers. This holds particularly true for this essay. Recalling Derrida's opening gambit in his essay "Qual Quelle: Valéry's Sources," from *Margins of Philosophy*, we would say just now that we are not seeking to unearth various sources, tracing them back to their supposed origins or performing some kind of archaeological-historical act that "would chatter on about heritages, readings, borrowings, biographical inner springs" (*MP*, 275). To use Derrida's advertised phrase from the same passage, the "discourse of history" is not our concern. As the essay on Paul Valéry suggests, there is never a traceable source as such.

In this essay we will interest ourselves instead in what might be called a rhetoric of identity; if, by identity, we might also be allowed to suggest otherness, otherness within identity, the relation of otherness to identity, whether either alterity or identity refer to, directly or indirectly, personal, poetic, literary, or even national identity. The rheto-

23

ric in question is then one of uprootedness and disjunction, a rhetoric of disjointing which crosses boundaries, undoing the certainties concerning a certain identity, say for example between self and other, French and not-French. These sometimes clear, sometimes oblique, identities and *their* relationship to questions of place (*lieu*) and of what takes place (*a lieu*) in the name of such relationships—and in the relationship that literary critics sometimes explore between larger questions of identity (cultural, poetic, national) and proper names such as Baudelaire, Valéry, and Derrida—are what interest us here. In beginning the exploration of this complex and highly overdetermined rhetoric, we have in front of us questions asked by Derrida of Mallarmé which become our departure point, and which we paraphrase as the questioning and open-ended thesis of this chapter: is there *a place* for Derrida in a "history of literature"? Or, to begin with: does his text take place, take its place, in some overall picture of French literature? In a picture? of literature? of French literature (M, 111–112)?[1] By bringing together the three authors named in the title—and as the reason for this chapter—we hope to catch, in their wake, and after reading them in various ways, what, if anything, might be said either to haunt Derrida, Valéry, and Baudelaire, or traverse them, which disturbs any simple historical, personal, or national location, yet which has a certain bearing on the very question of French contexts and identities.

## Baudelaire—Looking/Writing: A Picture? of French Literature?

In many of his recent works, Jacques Derrida has written of the problematic of the relationship between differing orders of signification; of particular interest here is the relationship between literary and pictorial arts. In *The Truth in Painting*, for example, he discusses what might be called the ekphrastic impulse, that is, the will to submit pictorial representation to the signification of language, an act of appropriation that elides what *I see*—a representation of the other—with *what I write*—a representation (however mediated) of myself. The potential violence of such an act is particularly acute in French since *meaning* is always expressed as a "meaning to say" (*vouloir-dire*, to wish to say = to mean). Derrida writes:

> [B]y asking what art *means* (to say), one submits the mark "art" to a very determined regime of interpretation . . . ; it consists in its *tautology* without reserve in interrogating the *vouloir-dire* of every work of so-called

art, even if its form is not that of saying. In this way, one wonders what a plastic or musical work means (to say), submitting all productions to the authority of speech and the "discursive" arts. (*TP*, 22)

It is impossible absolutely to short-circuit this hierarchy of language over other forms of representation, since meaning appears to depend so utterly on utterance. But what if we were to approach the problematic from the other side? Is it possible, in other words, to conceive of a writing that submits itself to the visual—a writing that speaks (how could it not speak?) in visual terms?

In this context, Baudelaire presents an interesting case study. Before the publication of the *Les Fleurs du mal* (1857), Baudelaire, if he was known at all, was known primarily as an art critic. His primary impulse was ekphrastic. He judged the *vouloir-dire* of the Salons of the French Academy; he discussed the content and technique of the paintings he saw; and he submitted the visual to the authority of linguistic discourse by evaluating what he saw in his language practice.

In "Le Peintre de la vie moderne," one of his most famous essays, which combines artistic and literary theories, Baudelaire describes the works of the artist Constantin Guys. The nominal subject of the essay, however, is suppressed, Guys being named only by his initial. This virtual anonymity in discussing the works of a particular artist permits Baudelaire to use the visual metaphor at one remove, in order also to describe the methods of the poet. His attraction to Guys's work—the speed of execution, the outlines, his focus on contemporary life—renders also the methodology of the *poet* of modern life, who must equally rely on seeing whilst not being seen, on ghostliness and anonymity, if he is to be free to look at the world and to express what he sees. In the essay, Baudelaire describes Poe's story "The Man of the Crowd" as a picture ("*en vérité, c'est un tableau*"[It is indeed a picture]) (*OC*, 794).[2] The story tells of a man who is looking at a crowd in a city and identifying himself with it. "Un convalescent, contemplant la foule avec jouissance, se mêle par la pensée, à toutes les pensées qui s'agitent autour de lui." (*OC*, 794) [A convalescent, contemplating the crowd with pleasure, mingles himself in thought with all the other thoughts that swirl around him]. The man in the story rushes out into the crowd, impelled by curiosity about a particular face—anonymous and curious, adjectives which apply to both the narrator and his quarry. The mystery of the curious face remains intact in Poe's story. We are told merely that its meaning is one of those things "which does not permit itself to be read," a phrase also expressed in German: "*es lässt sich nicht lessen*," (Poe 1967, 179, 188) and its meaning in Poe's English and Baudelaire's French plays between readability and incomprehension—

a written phrase that is not immediately available to be read: it can be seen but not deciphered. The look of "The Man of the Crowd" cannot be read. His look impels curiosity but defers and defies significance. It is a look written but not read, with meaning playing merely on the borders between writing and reading, looking and seeing.

This episode, which Baudelaire translated from Poe's English, and to which he returned in his essay, is a kind of Derridean moment *avant la lettre*, if one is permitted to use such a phrase. "The Man of the Crowd" is a triple title, referring to the story "itself," to the narrator and to the man the narrator pursues. Identity is something at once bound up in the speaking self, the "I" of the narrative, and in the other "man of the crowd" whose meaning does not permit itself to be read, in the story, in the man himself, the men themselves. And the narrative is a picture ("en vérité, c'est un tableau") whose wish to say or meaning (*vouloir-dire*) depends on the *passe-partout*,[3] which in pictures describes an internal frame inside the frame, but which also implies the possibility of passing everywhere, and of allowing everything to pass through its borders (*passe-partout* = pass everywhere). It is a picture in (as well as of) French literature; and this, despite the fact that it was originally written in English, and contains a German phrase, "which does not permit itself to be read." It becomes French through an act of translation; and then through another kind of appropriation, when it is used as an example of the psychology of the French "painter of modern life" who leaks in turn through the *passe-partout* and is also a poet. The narrator's identity is mixed up with the "other" of the crowd. "The Man of the Crowd" is self and other, and most importantly, he is the *narrative* of that apparent opposition. He looked, he wrote; and the result is a picture in which illegibility is forever (and paradoxically) inscribed. The axis of looking and writing, and the will to depict, to render "picturesque,"[4] is the axis with which this part of the chapter is concerned. It depends for its force on the multiplicity, ambiguity, undecidability, of the word *look* ("regard") and its substitutes, in which the subject and object of verbal forms, the self and other of identity, exist in a necessary but sometimes terrifying symbiosis. As Derrida comments in *Memoirs of the Blind*, "*Aspectus* is at once gaze, sight, *and* that which meets the eyes: on one's side the spectator, and on the other, the aspect, in other words, the spectacle" (*MB*, 44).

Baudelaire's poetic persona habitually stands out against superior hierarchical positions in French culture—such as, for example, the values of "Frenchness,"[5] the family, the bourgeoisie, good sense, traditional moralities—and takes up the position of the *déclassé*: he writes, that is, his self as other, rendering that self ambiguous. He at once defines his own culture, and does so from a countercultural position. He is a man *looking at* and *writing of* the heart of the city from which he expresses his own alienation, and his desire to be elsewhere. He exemplifies the "conflict, opposition, rupture, estrangement . . . up-rootedness" observed by Derrida as being part of a "complicity with the 'French' or 'Parisian' context" (*P. . .* , 416). His is a voice that has its place, knows its own place, and yet refuses to take its place. What takes place in Baudelaire's work therefore, in Walter Benjamin's terms, is not straightforward description or statement of what is here or there, which might imply a single mimetic function for language; what takes place is invocation (Benjamin 1992, 164). The poet who invokes people and places and who is, in turn, invoked by his own words (his lan-guage speaks him) is a ghost or a trace, walking the Paris streets amongst (the) other ghosts and traces. We (he) cannot know his status. By implication he unsettles our own sense of identity too. It is as if he were dead, with all the implications of terror and the uncanny which Derrida has elaborated in a recent interview:

> The older I grow, the more I have to ask myself why we are fright-ened by death. . . . On the one hand, we are scared because we think we won't be there any more. So that would be the end of the world, not simply the end of *the* world, but the end of *our* world. But, on the other hand, what is scarier is the fantasy—and this is the origin of the fear—the fantasy that we are going to be present and to assist, to attend to this non-world, to our own death. We will continue to be dead, that is, absent, while attending the actual world, being de-prived of sharing the life of the survivors. That is even more terrible: dead without being dead. . . . What is absolutely scary is the idea of being dead while being quasi-dead, while looking at things from above, from beyond. (*Ai*, 216)

For Baudelaire there is no simple binary of self and other, which would, after all depend on a stable sense of self and other; there is only a recognition that the self is always someone else's other and that the other is someone else's self, making identity a state of flux. That rec-ognition comes through the eye: what is seen, what I see, what I look at, how it looks, how it looks back (at/to me)—how I look. The ex-changed look (what Derrida calls an "economy of the eye" [*GT*, 67]) has the potential to affirm identity and to deny it, since through the look, identity becomes something dependent on the other reflecting the self back to the self, rather than something intrinsic to the self. Like the ear, the eye is an organ of liminality.

Baudelaire seems then to write of a looking in which looking appears primary, and writing is merely a supplement that expresses what is already there. Except, of course, that "what is already is there" is "there" only because it is always already written. Writing appears therefore to have supreme status in seeking to express what looking might mean (to say). It has, however, only a disrupted authority because the discourse of looking, seeking to describe the act of looking in all its forms, is always already ambiguous. For writing, marking the paper, depends not just on what has been observed in the world "out there," but crucially on looking at the paper, as Derrida remarks on the difficulty of drawing in *Memoirs of the Blind*: "How can one claim to look at both a model and the lines [*traits*] that one jealously dedicates with one's own hand to the thing itself? Doesn't one have to be blind to one or the other? Doesn't one always have to be content with the memory of the other?" (*M*, 36–37).

Writing implies communication—at least a wish to communicate (something), an expectation of being read. Looking, however, might not communicate at all, as in an example discussed by Derrida from Baudelaire in *Given Time*, the prose poem "Les Yeux des pauvres." In one part of the poem *looking* speaks—the act of looking is a speech act. Three poor people—a man and his two children—look at the narrator and his mistress. Their look speaks to the narrator, requiring him to see the poor as figures of supplication (their eyes are "begging"), and to see himself and his mistress as grotesque and greedy. He looks at himself, that is, as by implication he must look to the poor in an exchange where the look of the other reveals the self—since the look renders the grammatical relationship between subject and object problematic. At the same time, however, the same look (if such a thing exists) provokes an obscurity (a darkness that troubles seeing, makes it impossible to see) which disturbs the relationship between lover and mistress. Under the scrutiny of the poor, they exchange a look, but they have each seen something different.

> Les chansonniers disent que le plaisir rend l'âme bonne et amollit le cœur. La chanson avait raison ce soir-là relativement à moi. Non seulement j'étais attendri par cette famille d'yeux, mais je me sentais un peu honteux de nos verres et de nos carafes, plus grand que notre soif. Je tournais mes regards vers les vôtres, cher amour, pour y lire *ma* pensée; je plongeais dans vos yeux si beaux et si bizarrement doux, dans vos yeux verts, habités par le Caprice et inspirés par la Lune, quand vous me dîtes: "Ces gens-là me sont insupportables avec leurs yeux ouverts comme des portes cochères! Ne pourriez-vous pas prier le maitre du café de les éloigner d'ici?"
>
> Tant il est difficile de s'entendre, mon cher ange, et tant de pensée est incommunicable, même entre gens qui s'aiment! (*OC*, 186)

[The songsters say that pleasure makes the soul good and softens the heart. The songs were right that evening, as far as I was concerned. Not only did I feel tender towards this family of eyes, but I felt a little ashamed of our glasses and bottles so much greater than our thirst. I turned to look at you, dear love, to read *my* thought in your eyes; I plunged into your beautiful, strangely sweet eyes, into your green eyes, touched by Caprice and inspired by the Moon, when you said to me: "Those people there are unbearable to me, with their eyes as wide as coach doors! Could you not ask the café-owner to send them away from here?"

That is how difficult it is to understand each other, my dear angel, and so much thought cannot be communicated, even among people who love each other.]

The passion with which the poetic persona describes the eyes of his beloved is entirely destroyed by her inability to see through those eyes, as he does, into the eyes of the poor. And if she saw through his eyes, in the idiomatic phrase, she would not have the eyes that impassion him. As Derrida comments on a different but related passage: "A beggar always looks threatening, incriminating, accusatory, vindictive in the very absolute of his demand" (*GT*, 139). It is a look that makes you look also at yourself. The other thereby informs identity—and threatens it. The threat of the look might be located in several different places: in the way the beggar looks at the poet; in the way he looks *to* the poet; in the way he makes the poet *look at himself*; in the way he makes the poet *look at his mistress*; in the *way the mistress interprets herself the look of the beggars* along all these axes. In the words of Hans-Jost Frey, this looker, like the painter, "does not paint what is, but what he sees. His object is not only what is seen, but also the seeing of what is seen, that is, *his own relationship to what is seen*." (Frey 1996, 64; emphasis added) It is the problematic of the *expression* (what it expresses, what it means [to say]) of the look and its effects on self and other which Baudelaire's poem calls into question, since thought, it would appear, is incommunicable through the medium of the look, even amongst people who love one another. The poet hopes to *read* his own thought in his mistress' eye, but it does not permit itself to be read. Looking and writing do not guarantee communication, reading.

In a prose poem entitled "Les fenêtres," the speaker asserts: "Celui qui regarde du dehors à travers une fenêtre ouverte ne voit jamais autant de choses que celui qui regarde une fenêtre fermée" (*OC*, 198) [He who looks from the outside through an open window never sees as much as he who looks through a closed window]. Thus, looking is inscribed as an action that takes place from the outside. At the same time, however, it is also internal, since what is seen is not the same as what is there to be seen. The narrator describes a woman he has seen through a closed window. Using the visible signs of her identity, "avec son visage, avec son vêtement, avec son geste, avec presque rien" [with her face, her clothes her movements, with almost nothing], he has remade (*refais*) her history (*son histoire*) and her story (*sa légende*);[6] it does not matter whether the (hi)story he has made is true or not, since its function has only been to reaffirm his own identity, and his own relationship to that identity: the (hi)story he has *made* "m'a aidé à vivre, à sentir que je suis et ce que je suis" (*OC*, 198) [has helped me to live, to feel that I am and what I am]. "*Ce que je suis*" is a poet. It is important therefore that the word chosen for the process of (hi)storytelling is derived from a word meaning "to make" (*refaire* = to re-make), since poetry (*poésie*) is literally a making (from the Greek *poeisis* = making). Looking becomes thereby an act of writing, though here, as with "The Eyes of the Poor," the looking/writing does not communicate in any simple sense; this poet only tells the woman's story to himself: "je me la raconte à moi-même en pleurant" [I retell it to myself whilst weeping]. The act of retelling takes over from the act of looking, because it generates an emotion that makes looking impossible—the eyes are filled with tears. The poet looks; he (re)makes and retells/recounts his story; he weeps; and he therefore feels *that* he is and feels *what* he is—looking, making (writing), weeping are the conditions of poetry and of the poet. But not even love can guarantee the communication of his looking/writing.

Writing and looking: they provide both affirmation and loss. What is at stake in the connection between them in Baudelaire's writing/looking is desire, in which the self is at once supremely affirmed and supremely dispersed into the other. In a prose poem entitled "Le désir de peindre" [The Desire to Paint], the narrator describes an ideal woman, the desire for whom tears him apart.[7] The poet speaks of burning (*je brûle*) to paint this woman, displacing an anarchic sexual longing onto the will to organize her image into an artistic totality. But he is poet, and he must write, not paint. Images must be *translated* from the visual (or imaginative) plane to the linguistic. He explores how writing cannot adequately recreate the image he sees in his mind's eye in the mind's eye of his reader. We do not see what he sees for two related reasons. Firstly we do not desire the same image—our ideal image is never the same. Secondly, he cannot make us desire the "same" image because of the inadequacy of his language to make us see the same image. He has a pressing *vouloir-dire* which can only be vaguely evoked, never spoken directly, because the meaning he wishes to communicate is also intrinsically a conflicted image, based on contradiction. He cannot say what his ideal woman is, only what he would like to compare her to, and what she makes him think of: her existence takes place entirely and overtly in the realm of *différance*—meaning deferred, different images:

> Je la comparerais à un soleil noir, si l'on pouvait concevoir un astre noir versant la lumière et le bonheur. Mais elle fait plus volontiers penser à la lune, qui sans doute l'a marquée de sa redoutable influence; non pas la lune blanche des idylles, qui ressemble à une froide mariée, mais la lune sinistre et enivrante, suspendue au fond d'une nuit orageuse et bousculée par les nuées qui courent; non pas la lune paisible et discrète visitant le sommeil des hommes purs, mais la lune arrachée du ciel, vaincue et révoltée, que les Sorcières thessaliennes contraignent durement à danser sur l'herbe terrifiée. (*OC*, 199)

> [I would compare her to a black sun, if it were possible to conceive[8] of a black star pouring out light and happiness. But she makes you think rather of the moon, which has doubtless touched her with its fearful influence; not the white moon of idylls which resembles a frigid bride, but the sinister, intoxicating moon, hanging in the depths of a stormy night and buffeted by flowing clouds; not the peaceful, discreet moon which visits sleep on the pure of heart, but the moon torn from the sky, vanquished yet defiant, who is forced to dance on the scorched earth by the witches of Thessaly.]

She is an unimaginable image—inconceivable and therefore only an image for and of writing, which cannot communicate her look.

The whole difficulty is in her eyes, her look, how he looks *at* her, how she looks *to* him. Her eyes are "comme deux antres où scintille vaguement le mystère, et son regard illumine comme l'éclair; c'est une explosion dans les ténèbres" (*OC*, 199) [her eyes are like two lairs where mystery vaguely glistens, and her look flashes like lightning; it/she is a burst in the shadows]. Her allure is violence and danger, and it renders the looker impotent and passive. His desire is not to approach (though he regrets her sudden disappearance or flight), nor to seize her. She provokes instead the desire "de mourir lentement dans son regard" [to die slowly beneath her gaze (look)]. Satisfaction comes, that is, not from her looking back, meeting his look, exchanging an "intercourse of gazes" that is impossible because she is only a painted/written imaginary image, a representation of desire—not desire itself—an image that would cease to function as either representation or desire once she is permitted to function as desiring/looking subject in her own right.

The aesthetic of looking therefore is an aesthetic of distance and deferral, which enunciates desire, but which keeps it at arm's length,

fearing above all the loss of focus in looking which is attendant on effacing the distance between self and other. Painting/looking are distancing
techniques, which fail, nonetheless to prevent the crossing of distance.
And when writing borrows their approach, or seeks to approach the
looked at, painted desired object, it can do so only by sacrificing the will
to intimacy in the act of representing a representation.

There is a section in *Les Fleurs du mal* that makes this clear—*Les
Tableaux Parisiens* [Parisian Pictures]—a title about which much might
be said.[9] In the poems of this section, Baudelaire writes through the
logic of a pictorial perspective of distance which renders intimacy
impossible. In part this is a function of the topology of Paris with its
crowded streets where one is never alone, but neither can one be
intimate with others: "Multitude, solitude: termes égaux et convert-
ibles pour le poète" (*OC*, 170) [Multitude, solitude: equal and inter-
changeable terms for the poet]. Through this section, the poet looks at
the city from afar, and then pans in—cinematically, one might say—to
look closely at specific instances of the city. At street level, he experiences a hyper-reality and a fantastic, macabre alterity, before he retreats again to a distance at the end of the section. Yet although there
is a sense of distance traversed, proximity to the citizens of Paris does
not entail intimacy. When the poet looks, in these poems, he is disturbed both when someone meets his gaze, and more acutely when
someone does not. He is a ghostly figure—*as if* he were dead—who
cannot decide whether he prefers to be seen or not to be seen. Thus,
the apparent certainty of looking and of writing what "I see" as an
affirmation "*that* I am" and of "*what* I am," in which the look is reflected
backward and forward, mediating between self and other, is painfully
dispersed into uncertainty.

Two poems placed side by side, "Les Aveugles" (The Blind Men
[a title that finds itself recalled as other than itself in the French title—
*Mémoires d'aveugle: L'autoportrait et autres ruines*—of *Memoirs of the Blind*])
and "À Une Passante" (To a [Woman] passer-by) (*OC, Fleurs du mal*
XCII, XCIII, 68–69) dramatize the importance of looking and writing,
of writing the look. In the first, "Les Aveugles," the speaker enjoins his
soul to contemplate "them," the blind, and finds them terrifying precisely because their condition makes it impossible for them to meet his
own look.

> Contemple-les, mon âme; ils sont vraiment affreux!
> Pareils aux mannequins; vaguement ridicules;
> Terribles, singuliers comme les somnambules;
> Dardant on ne sait où leurs globes ténèbreux.

Leurs yeux, d'où la divine étincelle est partie,
Comme s'ils regardaient au loin, restent levés
Au ciel; on ne les voit jamais sur les pavés
Pencher rêveusement leur tête appesantie.

[Contemplate them, my soul; they are truly dreadful! Like mannequins; vaguely ridiculous; terrible, strange like sleepwalkers; darting
their darkened eyeballs no one knows where.

Their eyes, from which the divine spark has gone, remain lifted to the
sky as if they were looking into the distance; you never see them lean
their heavy heads down toward the pavement.]

What is written into this poem is an appearance of looking without
seeing, akin to Freud's sense of the uncanny (and the blind men are
compared to mannequins), where it is the very undecidability of
what you are seeing—real or manufactured, life or a mere
simulacrum—which produces fear. The fear exists because there must
be an economy of the eye; an exchange between two or more people
looking at each other, rendering their own selves concrete through
the act of recognizing the other. Or, as Derrida puts it in "There is No
One Narcissism": "without a movement of narcissistic reappropriation, the relation to the other would be absolutely destroyed, it would
be destroyed even in advance. The relation to the other—even if it
remains asymmetrical, open, without possible reappropriation—must
trace a movement of reappropriation in the image of oneself for love
to be possible, for example" (P. . . , 199). What one looks for, what
one sees (and sometimes fails to see) is the image of the self reflected
back through the look of the other. Its absence renders the other
nonhuman; and that inhumanity reflects back on the self. In the poem
the voice is forced to require seeing precisely because seeing has not
occurred in any reciprocal way. He demands of the city itself that it
should see: "O cité! /Pendant qu'autour de nous tu chantes, ris et
beugles,/Éprise du plaisir jusqu'à l'atrocité,/Vois!" [O city, whilst all
around us you sing, laugh and bellow, carried away with pleasure to
the point of atrocity, see!].

What the city will see (if it obeys the invocation, and that is by
no means certain) is the poet, dragging himself through the city streets,
as dazzled as the blind men, and wondering to himself: "Que cherchent-
ils au Ciel, tous ces aveugles?" [What are all these blind people looking for in the sky (in Heaven) (my emphasis)]. The fact is that one
must be looking for or at something. The blind men disturb because
they look as if they are looking into the distance, in the hope of some
reciprocal exchange of looks. But because they cannot see, they are

in the anomalous position of being others without apparent (appearing) selves, since self depends on the reciprocated look, which they cannot find, and which they would not see even if it were there.

In "Les Aveugles" the failure of reciprocity is a threat to the self. But even when the look is reciprocal, as in "A une passante," its ability to guarantee identity is temporary and minimal. In a deafening crowd ("La rue assourdissante autour de moi"), the poet sees a woman, tall, slim, wearing mourning clothes and carefully holding up her skirt from the filth of the street. Her look arrests and intoxicates him.

> Moi, je buvais, crispé comme un extravagant,
> Dans son oeil, ciel livide où germe l'ouragan,
> La douceur qui fascine et le plaisir qui tue.
>
> Un éclair . . . puis la nuit!—Fugitive beauté
> Dont le regard m'a fait soudainement renaître,
> Ne te verrai-je plus que dans l'éternté?
>
> Ailleurs, bien loin d'ici! trop tard! *jamais* peut-être!
> Car j'ignore où tu fuis, tu ne sais où je vais,
> Ô toi que j'eusse aimée, ô toi qui le savais!
>
> [For myself, contorted like a madman, I drank in from her eye, that livid sky where storms breed, the sweetness that bewitches and the pleasure that kills.
>
> A flash of lightning . . . then night! Fleeting beauty whose look has suddenly made me be reborn, will I never see thee again except in eternity?
>
> Elsewhere, a long way from here! too late! Perhaps *never*! For I do not know whither thou art fleeing, nor dost thou know where I am going, o thou whom I might have loved, o thou who knew it!]

As Walter Benjamin writes: "The delight of the urban poet is love—not at first sight, but at last sight. It is a farewell forever which coincides in the poem with the moment of enchantment" (*I*, 166). Desire is heightened by its indefinite deferral into an impossible future. The whole experience takes place merely in the look—the exchange or intercourse of glances which takes place in a busy city street. From the look, the poet postulates that there has been a communication of love—that love has been written and read in the momentary look which shook the poet's body, communicated the woman's contradictions to him and his desire to her. This is what he has read, which is not the same thing as that which has been written in the way the woman looks (how she appears, how she sees). There may yet be something written here that does not permit itself to be read.

What Derrida calls the "fundamental presupposition" for the determination of meaning (*vouloir-dire*) depends on the assumption that "one can distinguish rigorously between the intrinsic and the extrinsic" (*TP,* 63), that one can know what one is seeing especially before setting out to discourse upon it. Looking is not so simple, however. No one—especially the Baudelairian persona—can believe his own eyes, since what they seek is a means to affirm identity: "that I am" and "what I am." The look can beguile and enchant; it can terrify in both its absence and its presence; but it can never straightforwardly be translated into the words "I am" since so often it does not communicate at all. There are no guarantees in looking, and whatever its various relationships with writing may be, the very liminality of the eyes as they mediate between self and other, deflects and defers communication. There is a writing on the wall—and one may see it. But it might not be read; it might be a form of writing that does not permit itself to be read. The picture of French literature with which we began is necessarily unstable, as Derrida has shown in the essay on Mallarmé from which we took our opening remarks. The visual metaphor cannot escape its linguistic function as metaphor. And because, in language, the word *look* suspends us between subject and object, self and other, any affirmation is also potentially a denial.

## Looking/Writing: For Example, Valéry?

> *Intérieurement, s'il y a voix, il n'y a pas vue de qui parle, et qui décrira, définira la *différence* qu'il y a *entre cette phrase même qui se dit* et *ne se prononce pas,* et cette *même phrase sonnante dans l'air?* Cette identité et cette différence sont un des secrets essentiels de la nature de l'esprit—et qui l'a signalée.[10]*
>
> —Paul Valéry, *Cahiers*

> [Within the subject's consciousness, if there is a voice, there is no sight of that which speaks, and who will describe, define the difference which is there between that very phrase which speaks itself and does not pronounce itself, and that same phrase sounds in the air? This identity and that difference are one of the essential secrets of the nature of spirit—and which has signalled there.]
>
> —Paul Valéry, *Cahiers*

> [In Algeria] . . . the source, the norm, the authority of the French language was elsewhere. And, in a certain manner, confusedly, we learned it, I learned it as the language of the

> other—even though I could only refer to one language as
> mine, you see! And this is why I say that it is not a question
> of language, but of culture, literature, history, history of
> *French literature*, what I was learning at school. I was totally
> immersed, I had no other reference, I had no other culture,
> but at the same time I sensed clearly that all of this came
> from á history and a milieu that were not in a simple and
> primitive way mine.
>
> —(emphasis added) Jacques Derrida
>
> La personne qui parle est déjà autre que moi
>
> —Paul Valéry, *Cahiers*
>
> [The person who speaks is already other than me]
>
> —Paul Valéry, *Cahiers*

If the picture or, at the very least, the subject of French literature *qua French* is destabilized in Derrida's wake (he being only the latest of a number of writers who disturb the certainty of French identity through the French language), then, tentatively, we might suggest that Derrida's thoughts on the subject, wherever they are encountered, are driven by that ekphrastic impulse—an impulse that is also a pulse, a rhythm—of which we have already spoken. The quotation given above locates importantly the situation of noncorrespondence and the manifestation of the other within the same, which divides identity and finds itself discussed wherever Jacques Derrida encounters Paul Valéry, whether directly or indirectly. Derrida gives us to see the limit of the transformation between a certain act of looking and a certain event in writing. This event occurs in encountering Valéry over the issues of the figure, the face, and the French language. It can also be intimated that Derrida's writing is never a reading as such, at least not in the sense that a reading brings to the text in advance of the encounter a program. Instead, this writing, we would argue, can be seen as a form of performative and transformative, radical ekphrasis, which in looking at the text of the other also views itself both as other and from other, equally destabilizing positions, breaking down—deconstructing?—the simple binary opposition of constative and performative utterance, discussed by Derrida (in his transaction with Ponge's "Fable") in "Psyche: Inventions of the Other" (PIO, 30–40).

What Derrida observes from that place of the other within French language and French literature in which he so often seeks to position himself in relation to a text, a thought, a subject, a painting, a poem, is the gaze of the other, the other writer, the other's text focused on that which is never absolutely interpretable because of its singularity and the necessity of its "internal" alterity. This singularity, which Derrida so frequently and faithfully traces in all its contours, denies the possibility of making an example of the given text, as an example that can be taken to offer an identity claiming to offer a universal model. Following Derrida, we can *see* the text in all its singularity, but this is not translatable into a written program for a general textual economy. This is equally the case whether Derrida is talking of an identity expressed through a poem or whether the subject is national or cultural identity. What Derrida thus sees—and offers to show us in his gaze, from his other location—is, to reiterate an earlier phrase of ours, a form of writing that does not permit itself to be read.

Such an impulse as the (re)generative rhythm(s) of Derrida's writing often means that we will encounter in Derrida's texts writers and *their* texts with which we believe we have some familiarity, yet who— in the wake of Derrida—strike us as never quite themselves, as somehow other than the signatures with which we assume ourselves to be on nodding terms, at least. If Derrida's Baudelaire is a certain less well-known Baudelaire than the author of *Les Fleurs de mal*, then the same may also be said, while acknowledging the singularity of the idiomatic example, of Paul Valéry. The Valéry encountered in Derrida's texts is not (simply) the poet Valéry, but an other Valéry—Valéry the political or philosophical essayist. This is not to say that the several Valérys are absolutely separate—this is to suggest an impossibility of the order of the supposed separability between constative and performative utterances—but that the Valéry whom we see through Derrida's eyes can never be read as quite the same as the writer we may have encountered before the event of reading in Derrida's wake. The affirmation of another Valéry, an affirmation of another identity *for* Valéry, is also potentially a denial of a Valéry whom we believed we had read. (The same might also be said for Baudelaire, Mallarmé, and, indeed, of Derrida himself, albeit all in highly different contexts.)

And it is Paul Valéry—this other Valéry within the familiar poet, side by side with himself, but never as quite himself—who dictates the triply remarked phrase in the opening of Derrida's essay "Qual Quelle: Valéry's Sources," given first as a lecture on the centenary of the writer's birth, in 1971. Three times, then, in different, differing and self-deferring, self-dividing ways, Derrida writes of the writing of the subject:

> I—mark(s) first of all a division in what will have been able to appear in the beginning. (*MP*, 275)
>
> —I mark(s) the division—(*MP*, 275)
>
> —again I mark(s) and multiply (multiplies) the division—(*MP*, 276)

These statements in their reiteration perform the division and dispersal of the subject, tracing a regenerative fragmentation of any possible identity (identities) even at that moment that appears to be the beginning of something so conventional as an essay or lecture. As Derrida puts it in the very same essay, the source is already divided (*MP*, 277), and this is as an acknowledgment of a certain "repetition of Valéry's" (*MP*, 278). If this is a repetition of Valéry's, something already installed in Valéry's own writing on the subject of the source, as Derrida intimates, then it is also in a certain way a reiteration and transformation of Valéry: a performance of Valéry's implied practice, as well as a précis of what Valéry does, *in other words*. We spoke just now of the (re)generative rhythm(s) of Derrida's writings. To claim this as a particular identity for Derrida, however, is to miss how such a movement or pulse "in Derrida" is also that similar—though never exactly the same—"power of regeneration," claimed by Derrida as Valéry's interest in "Qual Quelle" (*MP*, 278). In performing Valéry otherwise, Derrida displaces his own beginning *and his identity* in an essay on the impossibility of the source as a knowable single site, producing his own otherness.

The passage from which the claim concerning the "power of regeneration" comes is itself quite astounding in its opening, as are the subsequent folds of what is a very long paragraph. Derrida begins with a moment of return, a certain folding back upon himself in the section entitled "rebound":

> I had not reread Valéry for a long time. . . . [I]n going back to the texts I thought I knew . . . I asked myself in what ways a certain relationship had changed. Where had the displacement, which in a way had prevented me from taking my bearings, been effected? (*MP*, 278)

The act of rereading places a number of identities—a number of looks or gazes: the I who rereads now, the I who reread then, I asking myself—into a somewhat indeterminate relationship which disturbs and displaces the possibility of either a stable identity or any simple communication as the self-affirmation of an identity to itself. The look, looking back, looking at oneself as other than oneself, and asking oneself certain unanswerable questions, can never be represented straightforwardly as "I," the inscription of a self-presence (and this, of course, has been announced already at the beginning of the essay). Rereading already places the writing subject in a certain other relationship with/in himself, while partially erasing, denying, the possibilities of a first or original reading, forever displaced in the passage by that "first" redoubling verb. Doubleness, displacement, dislocation of the subject. "I" is prevented from "taking its bearings," and the source of that displacement can only be located in the unanswerable question, which leaves the subject all at sea.

Paul Valéry thus arrives and returns—*l'arrivant* as *le revenant*—to disturb identity. He turns up on a number of occasions in Derrida's writing, and often in a quite haunting fashion as the spirit at the wake of identity which Derrida has been rehearsing, certainly in later texts with regard to the question of national, spiritual, or cultural identity. From 1971 to 1991, Derrida returns to Valéry, even as the poet returns to Derrida. Between *Margins of Philosophy* and *The Other Heading*, the question is, specifically with regard to Valéry, never simply one, but is always a doubling and regenerative question of identities and the impossibility of location. He—Valéry—may well be everywhere, at every turn of the page, but the occasions to which we limit ourselves here are those involving discussion, citation, exegesis, passing reference, the deferral of authority. There is the essay, already briefly cited at the opening of this chapter (and immediately above), "Qual Quelle." There are also references in *Glas*, "Psyche: Invention de l'autre," *Specters of Marx, The Other Heading, Of Spirit*, and as a signature in a footnote to "Ulysses Gramophone." Many of the references to Valéry, and the citings (or sightings) of him, concern themselves with questions of identity and the spirit of identity, even with spirit or spectrality itself. In particular, and for the rest of this chapter, which has so far concerned itself with the problematization between discrete identities and between acts of seeing and writing as the movements between self and other, there is the question of Valéry's passing appearance on the stage of European identity in Derrida's *The Other Heading*. In this text, Valéry makes the kind of spectral appearance discussed in *Specters*, where Derrida situates Valéry in a "tradition" of spectral discourse tracing itself back to, and in the wake of, Shakespeare, via Karl Marx (*SM*, 5–6). Insistently, Valéry's text returns via some of Derrida's most extended endnotes, which endnotes serve to acknowledge the coming of the other as other and to do justice to the other.[11] Thus the structure of Derrida's text is doubled, as if in homage to Derrida's Valérian (dis)orientation in "Qual Quelle": arriving so insistently in the notes, the poet and essayist arrives in Derrida's wake, while Derrida acknowledges, both in the body of the text and, especially, in n.6 (*OH*, 118–122), that all he can do is to write on the subject of European cultural identity *after* Valéry, giving up commentary and giving himself over in this footnote and those that follow to extended quotation, thereby allowing Valéry's haunting trace to double his own text, to disrupt the certainty of its own European cultural identity. We will come back to *The Other Heading*, but for the moment must take a look at Valéry's spectral trace in "Psyché: Inventions of the Other."

As with all ghostly apparitions (*MPM*, 64), Valéry's appearance is swift though somewhat significant in "Psyché." This essay, which treats of inventiveness in the work of Paul de Man, and offers a sketch for a reading of Francis Ponge's "Fable," offers to confuse the identities of the constative and performative in language. The opening sentence of the essay is both *"used* and *mentioned*, as an example of an opening sentence," as Derek Attridge points out in his note to the text (*AL*, 311 n.1).[12] Following Derrida's argument in the essay, Attridge also alerts the reader to the French "original" of the opening sentence, "What else am I going to be able to invent?" (PIO, 25), which is: *Que vais-je inventer encore?* In its final word, the sentence is marked by a multiple ambiguity. *Encore* carries in it numerous identities, none of which are made any more certain in their meaning by the sentences having been framed as a question. The collapse of the use/mention binarism itself anticipates Derrida's comments on Ponge's text "Fable," a text that allows Derrida, typically, to recall yet one more anterior, other identity, in a seminar given at Yale. As Derrida recalls, remembering such a beginning allows him to mime a "starting over," which simultaneously calls up Ponge's text as a "myth of impossible origins" (PIO, 31), and which "presents itself . . . as the invention of language as the same and the other, of oneself as (of) the other" (PIO, 31). Although Valéry is not mentioned, there are clearly discernible in these statements some of the concerns of "Qual Quelle," especially in that phrase, "myth of impossible origins," which Derrida explores through Valéry's use of the word "source" and the homonyms "Perrier/Père y est."

Following this, Derrida continues to regard certain situations or relationships by recalling a possible line of Valéry's: "In the beginning was the fable" (PIO, 32). This is described as "miming but also translating the first words of John's gospel . . . a performative demonstration of the very thing it is saying" (PIO, 32). It is this—which, as we suggest, is Derrida's own practice/performance—which leads him to comment on that mark that divides "I," the 'invention of the other in the same" (PIO, 33). Ponge's text involves a particular narcissistic desire and the breaking of a mirror. Importantly, this figure of the mirror in Ponge's text offers us the sight of the possible gaze of the other, from the other to the other. We describe it as the figure of the mirror rather than the mirror simply because of Derrida's use of *figure* in the French text of "Qual Quelle," which means both a figure in writing and the face or visage (to which we shall return). Once again, the subject is marked by a division in identity between writing and the look, of which Ponge's inscription of the looking glass as poetic figure serves to remind us.

We can catch the doubleness of *figure* in the figure of the echo's relationship to identity elsewhere in "Psyché," where Valéry's echo finds Derrida in the wake of the poet once more. Derrida moves from the consideration of the invention of the other in the same to point out that Ponge's first line has no metalinguistic function (in this, Derrida's "first" sentence in "Psyché" has anticipated it). It is its own repetition and only that, an echo without origin (PIO, 34), the echo of Narcissus. Although Valéry, strictly speaking, is not mentioned throughout this essay, other than that brief memory of Derrida's already cited, nonetheless, and arguably, Valéry returns and retreats again and again as the other of Derrida's words in the narcissistic commentary. The line in question which haunts Derrida's words is from Valéry's notebooks: "It must be confessed that the self is nothing but an echo" (Valéry, cit. Lacoue-Labarthe 1989, 139).

It is worth a momentary digression here, into Philippe Lacoue-Labarthe's thinking on the subject of identity, in order to suggest the communication and displacement between word and image which is at work in Derrida's writing on/after Valéry. In his reading of Theodor Reik and Lacan's analysis of the subject, Lacoue-Labarthe comments on the "theoretical" consequence of thinking the subject at the limit of the theorizable that

> the figure is never *one*. Not only is it the Other, but there is no unity or stability of the figural; the imago has no fixity or proper being. There is no "proper image" with which to identify totally, no essence of the imaginary . . . the subject "desists" because it must always confront *at least* two figures (or one figure that is *at least* double), and that its only chance of "grasping itself" lies in introducing itself and oscillating *between* figure and figure. . . .
>
> Everything seems to point to the fact that this destabilizing division of the figural . . . [connects] it, as a result, with the autobiographical compulsion itself. (Lacoue-Labarthe 1989, 175; emphasis in original)

As we see from Lacoue-Labarthe's remarks, the situation of identity involves both writing and the gaze, as well as what is located by the gaze of the other, misrecognizing the image as itself. Identity's (self-) destabilization is caught up in, connected to this "autobiographical" compulsion: the desire to write oneself, to imagine and see oneself, but always seeing oneself from another place (a self-displacing situating of one's identity caught by Derrida in the term "autobio-photographies," from the title of an interview already quoted, a term that brings together the graphic, the figural and the look, the image).

The complex strands woven together here are clearly discernible in Derrida's writings on identity, and especially in those places where the issue of cultural identity—in relation, say, to a "French" writer or the French language—is at stake. We may even suggest then, following the subject of fragmented identity and the echo of the subject as the other within the same, the other which places the self-same (identity) under erasure, that the interview just mentioned—"There is no *one* Narcissism: Autobiophotographies" (a title that echoes Valéy's Narcissus fragments; *P. . . ,* 196–216)—is Derrida's clearest commentary on his otherness within French culture and within the French language, an otherness always being performed in every act of writing.

If otherness is not always or only the most appropriate word, exteriority might be. In response to a question concerning a certain Judaic-Greek-German traditional axis within his work, Derrida suggests that there is "certainly . . . a feeling of exteriority with regard to European, French, German, Greek culture. . . . I have the feeling that I am doing it from another place that I do not know: an exteriority based on a place that I do not inhabit in a certain way, or that I do not identify" (*P. . . ,* 206). Thus, there is, for Derrida, a constant sense of placing himself in certain ungovernable situations in relation to perceivable dominant identities, and allowing that "taking place" to dictate to him. Derrida's writing thus takes from Valéry's own texts (as it does with regard to Baudelaire, Mallarmé, Artaud, and others) the task of acknowledging the self looking at its other self within itself.

This is the very kind of "situating," of placing or letting take place, with which we interest ourselves with regard to the question of the instability of identities: a situation that is neither an exhaustible nor definable context, but one that, once comprehended as a possibilty, itself makes possible certain readings, certain writings (of Derrida's, our own), and certain ways of *seeing* involved with complicity *and* conflict, as the first epigraph to this essay announces. There is, thus, a relationship or situation marked by what Derrida, with reference to Mallarmé, has called *"suggestion, . . .* undecided allusion" (M, 120), which relationship, in remarking the place where something takes place, announces a certain liminality and, with that, a question of undecidability concerning identity. The question of the undecided allusion is not only a question posed by Derrida to cultural or spiritual identities writ large but, as we know, at a particular lexico-conceptual level also. When, in "There is no *one* Narcissism," Derrida comments that the word *deconstruction* imposed itself on him (*P. . . ,* 211), he is acknowledging his relationship to French; importantly, however, he also points out that the word "plays on several registers, for example linguistic or

pean through and through. . . . My cultural identity, that in the name of which I speak, is not only European, it is not identical to itself. . . . If to conclude, I declared that I feel European *among other things*, would this be, in this very declaration, to be more or less European. . . . It is up to the others, in any case, and up to me *among them*, to decide. (*OH*, 82–83)

Returning to the resistance that always lies at the heart of the autobiographical impulse, a resistance that is also the necessary tracing of affirmation and otherness, Derrida once more collapses the distinction between comment and performance, as he simultaneously marks the fragmentation of the I, locates himself in some other position, in the position of the other, and sees himself—me *among them*—among those European others, in the midst of European identity, as the other within the same.

Thus, Derrida always writes in Valéry's wake, seeing the poet as an other who returns in a ghostly fashion to disturb the (question of) identity of (in) Derrida's writing. Seeing the other, Derrida's writing performs that act of tracing the *trait* that divides the identity of the writer as a self who recognizes himself in his other. Clearly, this is the gesture in the early essay "Qual Quelle," where Derrida gives himself up to the other in the discussion, especially at those moments when he considers the dream or "lure of the I" (*MP*, 297) conjured by hearing oneself speak. One does not see oneself, one is blind to one's location; but the event of speech convinces us that we are present to ourselves, our identities complete and self-sufficient. As Derrida points out, "[w]hen I speak (to myself) without moving tongue and lips, I believe that I hear myself, although the source is other; or I believe that we are two. . . . [T]his [is] the possibility of a 'normal' double hallucination" (*MP*, 297). Yet it is possible to sight oneself otherwise, as the concluding comments from *The Other Heading* demonstrate. Instead of maintaining the "possibility of the double hallucination," Derrida's quasi-autobiographical gesture doubles the "'normal' double" in a movement, a rhythm that prohibits the European "we" speaking itself to itself.

All of which is to follow in Valéry's footsteps, to *see* in Valéry that which divides identity and thus holds itself up as other than itself, performing its own deconstruction. In seeing Valéry's blind spots, as Michael Naas puts it, (Naas, lv) in "Qual Quelle," Derrida displaces himself and, in encountering Valéry, transforming Valéry, transforms his own acts of writing also, performing as other than himself through acts of ventriloquization. In doing so, Derrida demonstrates what Naas calls "the irreducible singularity of Valéry's discourse [with which] . . . Derrida identifies himself, his situation, and his time" (Naas, lv). Hence, the frequent, though fleeting appearances of Valéry throughout Derrida's writing, as the haunting example that disjoints the notion of the exemplary, illuminating the return of the other and the impossibility of the source as an origin, explored in "Qual Quelle." For, as with the example of Baudelaire—as we mentioned earlier, in tracing Baudelaire in Walter Benjamin's footsteps—Valéry is, for Derrida, the figure whose texts make it impossible to know the status of the poet and, by implication, unsettle the identities of both Derrida and, in turn, the reader. In the wake of Baudelaire and Valéry Derrida performs that work that is the most necessary, seeing and situating identities against the most imposing dominant identities, those which are, in his own words "the most solid ones in some way, of the culture, the philosophy, the politics in which we live" (*P. . .* , 215).

## NOTES

1. In these questions we have replaced Mallarmé's name with that of Derrida. We understand the essay, with its self-problematizing position of Mallarmé in relation to *French* Literature (the very idea of such a possibility), to have an importance for understanding and exploring Derrida's own, often self-conscious positioning, in relation to *French* culture, *French* literature, *French* philosophy, *French* traditions in thinking and a certain *French* institutional location of a variety of poetic and nonpoetic discourses. Derrida's thinking on Mallarmé, and his essays in various places on Baudelaire and Valéry, offer interesting, if sometimes tangential, insights into the relationships we address in the opening paragraphs of this essay.

2. All references are to Charles Baudelaire *Oeuvres Complètes* (1980). All translations are our own.

3. See Derrida: "*Between* the outside and inside, between the external edge-line, the framer and the framed, the figure and the ground, form and content, signifier and signified, and *so on* for any two-faced opposition. The trait thus divides in this place where it takes place. The emblem for this topos seems undiscoverable; I shall borrow it from the nomenclature of framing: the *passe-partout*" (*TP,* 12).

4. Picturesque is an important word for Baudelaire, since he uses it in his dedication (to Arsene Houssaye) for *Les Petits poemes en prose.* His aim in writing the prose poems, he says, has been to mimic the technique of Aloysius Bertrand. In reading Bertrand's *Gaspard de la nuit,* "l'idée m'est venue de tenter quelque chose d'analogue, et d'appliquer à la description de la vie moderne, ou plutôt d'*une* vie moderne et plus abstraite, le procédé qu'il avait appliqué à la peinture de la vie ancienne, si étrangement pittoresque" (*OC,* 161) [the very idea came to me to try something similar, and to apply to the description

of modern life, or rather to *a* life, modern and more abstract, the process that Bertrand had applied to the painting of ancient life, so strangely picturesque.] His interest seems then to be more than the life "itself."

5. There are many examples of Baudelaire's disdain for what it means to be French. In one of the prose poems, the devil offers a man who has lost his soul in a card game the full range of worldly pleasures to make up for the loss. Amongst those choices is the ability to change nationality at will—and it is placed alongside worldly riches, wine, women, and song as a gift of similar proportions. See *OC*, 191, "Le Joueur généraux."

6. *Légende* is an interesting word in this context, since it can also be used to refer to the title of a painting.

7. There is a play on the approximate phonetic similarity between *désir* (desire) and *déchire* (to tear).

8. In French, *concevoir* contains within it also the verb to see—*voir*, reinforcing the strong relationship between the physical eye and the mind's eye.

9. Derrida has had much to say about the position of the title and its relationship to the text "proper." See, for example, "Before the Law," in *Acts of Literature* (181–220); see also his discussion of the title of Baudelaire's "Counterfeit Money," in *Given Time* (85ff.). The title, "Parisian Pictures," inscribes several layers of ambiguity, coming as it does, from a signature first associated with art criticism. Are these pictures of Paris (depicting Paris), or Pictures in Paris (hung, for example, in a Parisian gallery)? And what might it mean that these pictures are merely metaphorical, in the sense that they are poems, which though they have a spatial, visual existence, are not primarily read in those terms? Moreover, a picture might seem to fix what is portrayed; but here everything is in motion. One of the poems, "Le Squelette laboureur," describes literal pictures which are to be found quite literally on the streets of the city, for sale in street markets. These are written landscapes (or, more properly, cityscapes) and portraits. The fact of their having been written means, however, that they require a different kind of looking (reading) from the picture in the gallery.

10. There are a number of "untranslatables" in this passage, not least that opening word, which we have given as "Within the subject's consciousness," in order to provide the context of the passage from which this extract is taken. There is an elegance in the French, wherein what is being stated collapses into a performance of its propositions, which ties in with remarks made further on in this essay on the collapse between constative and performative utterance. As Valéry's passage makes clear, the voice, far from producing one's identity as a self-evident presence (to itself) instead is always already marked by a written difference in its self-dividing dissemination. This is strikingly marked in the doubling of identity and difference given by Valéry as *one* of the essential secrets.

11. On the ethical question of awaiting the other's arrival, see Derek Attridge, "Expecting the Unexpected in Coetzee's *The Master of Petersburg* and Derrida's recent writings," in *Applying: to Derrida* (1996, 21–40).

12. The pagination of "Psyché" referred to is taken from the first English language translation of the text by Catherine Porter, published in the collection of essays, *Reading de Man Reading* (1989, 25–65).

13. The reader is referred to *Of Spirit* (61 and 122–24 n. 2), in which Derrida offers a brief discussion of Valéry's thinking on spirit, European spirit in particular, during the interwar years, as a comparison in passing between Valéry's writing and that of both Heidegger and Husserl. In a number of ways other headings are being pointed out in this note and on the page to which the note refers, with the references in Valéry's writing to "Psyche," to ashes and to the revenant, to spectrality in general. Valéry's own references to Hamlet (which Derrida paraphrases and quotes) are themselves clearly anticipatory of *Specters of Marx*. As with the notes in *The Other Heading* (of which more in the body of the essay), in this note commentary gives way before more extensive citation, Derrida once again allowing Valéry to return as the other to his own text, as Derrida becomes the shadowy ghost behind Valéry and in his wake.

# CHAPTER 3

# "We have nothing to do with literature"
## Derrida and Surrealist Writing

JOHN BRANNIGAN

> Philosophy deviates from itself and gives rise to the blows that will strike it nonetheless from the outside.
>
> —Jacques Derrida, *The Archeology of the Frivolous*

> For those who will not fail to discover the sordid intentions of the author, the author will add these few simple words.
>
> —Louis Aragon, "Red Front"

> Do not read, look at the designs created by the white spaces between the words of several lines in a book and draw inspiration from them.
>
> —Breton and Eluard, *The Immaculate Conception*

"We have nothing to do with literature," it is stated in the "Declaration of January 27, 1925," of the surrealist movement, "but we are quite capable, when necessary, of making use of it like anyone else" (Nadeau 1987, 240). This declaration, issued by the *Bureau de Recherches Surréalistes*, is addressed to "the entire braying literary, dramatic, philosophical, exegetical and even theological body of contemporary criticism." It indicates, perhaps along with the widespread use of manifestoes, that the surrealists were more interested in the political sphere than in the literary or artistic, and that they saw themselves in opposition to the growing metadiscursive institution of criticism. To see the surrealists as having more to do with politics than with literature is hardly an original appraisal. Walter Benjamin argued this very point in his essay "Surrealism: The Last Snapshot of the European Intelligentsia." Benjamin argued that despite the reputation that surrealist writers and artists had attained for becoming "a pendant to art for art's sake in an inventory of snobbery," (Benjamin 1996, 76), surrealist uses of the irrational, the cult of evil, the anarchic, were political devices wielded in opposition to bourgeois "moralizing dilettantism": "To win the energies of intoxication for the revolution—this is the project about which Surrealism circles in all its books and enterprises" (Benjamin 1996, 78). Writing from Mexico in 1938, André Breton argued that "True art . . . cannot be anything other than revolutionary" (Breton 1995, 30). Breton's interest in using psychoanalysis as a means of developing oppositional political strategies, combined with his flirtations with revolutionary Marxism, make surrealist experiments a significant foundation for "postmodern articulations of subversion," as Margaret Cohen argues in *Profane Illumination* (Cohen 1993, 111). Cohen examines Benjamin's relationship to surrealism and argues that they share what she calls "Gothic Marxism," which is defined as Marxism "fascinated by the irrational aspects of social processes" (Cohen 1993, 1). Moreover, she finds that the revolutionary or subversive potential of surrealist thought detected by Benjamin has continued to have a "subterranean but vital presence" in subsequent French thinking, and she argues that the work of Deleuze and Guattari and of Michel de Certeau are examples of where surrealism continues to be an influence on how irrationality is exposed as a source of revolutionary potential (Cohen 1993, 13).

Cohen doesn't deal in any way with the significance of surrealism for the work of Jacques Derrida, but in identifying a genealogy of "Gothic Marxism" she traces the structure of influence in which we might think of Derrida and surrealism as having close affinities. Derrida has flirted with Marxism to the same extent as Breton, and perhaps also endured the same frustrations as Breton concerning pragmatic Marxism. Derrida has also been accused of obscuring his politics, even sacrificing politics in pursuit of philosophy, and not least when *Specters of Marx* (the very title places it within Gothic Marxism) was published (1993). John Lechte, in his *Fifty Key Contemporary Thinkers*, implies that there is no political element to Derrida's work. Lechte writes soon after the publication of *Specters of Marx*: "many are now waiting, perhaps wrongly, in anticipation to see if there is indeed a political element in Derrida's grammatology" (Lechte 1994, 105). Derek Attridge makes the same implication in addressing expectations of what *Specters of Marx* would contain:

> We extrapolated from various features of Derrida's earlier work, its glancing allusions to Marx and Marxism, its practices of reading, its political allegiances, and so on. One day, we said, Derrida will write a book on Marx, will fulfil his old promise to face, fair and square,

what he seemed for so long to be avoiding; and we inevitably tried to predict what it would be like. (Attridge ed. Brannigan et al. 1996, 21)

On reading *Specters of Marx*, Attridge says that "it seems a strange book, a book with passages of great clarity and passages of obscurity and inscrutability, passages of excess and tangentiality." Foucault's criticism of Derrida's work as "obscurantist terrorism" seems to be echoed here, and echo further the criticisms of surrealism as irretrievably offbeat and excessively poetic and obscure. Most interesting in such criticisms is the implication that strange or obscure writing is apolitical, an implication that I want to contest here.

In this essay I want to examine the relationship between Derrida and surrealism, not in terms of a historical link, or a conscious debt to the surrealists in Derrida's work, but as a series of intellectual and theoretical resonances. I will argue that the politics of surrealist writing have close affinities in the work of Jacques Derrida, and that surrealism and Derridean thinking share a fascination with the production of language which gives the space of writing over to the other. They share the same refusal of the programmatic (e.g., "We have nothing to do with literature" for the surrealists; Derrida's argument that deconstruction is not an analysis, nor a critique, nor a method, nor even an act, in "Letter to a Japanese Friend"), and they share too the strategic use of such media in attempting to use literature or philosophy or art to deviate from itself and expose its "oppositional unconscious," as Louis Aragon calls it in "Red Front."

This "oppositional unconscious" is an important concept in understanding the Gothic Marxist strategies adopted by both the surrealists and Derrida, and one that I'm going to focus on in this essay. Automatic writing, automatic drawing, the theatre of cruelty, the "possessions" or attempted simulations: these surrealist experiments and forms are attempts to release desires and dreams out of repression and into consciousness, and they are to that extent concerned with the unconscious. However, their concern is not in itself with this release, but in the effects that this release will have on sensibilities, and on the relationship between the individual and society. Artaud's theatre of cruelty is not an end in itself, but is intended to go beyond Western dialectical philosophy, to reach a new level of intellectualism by transforming the relationship between art and the body. "In our present degenerative state," writes Artaud, "metaphysics must be made to enter the mind through the body" (Artaud 1993, 77). Artaud's theatre pushes through the dualism of mind and body by making art perform in a ritual, magical relationship to the body, as gestural and vocal spectacle rather than as signification. In such a way, Artaud's theatre would produce oppositional acts toward the logos. It would, in fact, refuse the logos while simultaneously acting in relation to it. Derrida's position is somewhat similar. In "Freud and the Scene of Writing," Derrida writes:

> Despite appearances the deconstruction of logocentrism is not a psychoanalysis of philosophy.
>     These appearances: the analysis of a historical repression and suppression of writing since Plato. This repression constitutes the origin of philosophy as *episteme*, and of truth as the *logos* and *phone*. (WD, 196)

Derridean thinking is concerned therefore with the other of Western philosophy, the repressed, the unconscious, and "analyzes" the repressed, thereby bringing it to the foreground of a properly philosophical text.[1] It is oppositional to the extent that it appears to philosophy as its duplication, its repetition, as the pure presence of philosophy which is at the same time its pure difference.[2] Both Derridean thinking and surrealism can be conceptualized as the return of a presence to itself, the return of the repressed, not in the Freudian sense of a primal or libidinal motivated return, but in the sense of the repressed always present at the scene of writing, art, philosophy, thought. In this respect, the space of the unconscious is exactly that of the conscious, and the traces of the repressed are discernible at this scene, but only when the processes of representation and analysis are turned in on themselves. The theatre of cruelty must first be the theatre of theatre. Derridean philosophy must first be the philosophy of philosophy. Reflexivity is then the first condition of the "oppositional unconscious." In this respect, there is an affinity between surrealism and Derridean thinking, in that both manipulate the discourse in which they work to fold back on itself. Surrealist literature does not just create new works, and add a new trend to the history of literature, but makes literature turn back on itself:

> Swift is Surrealist in malice,
> Sade is Surrealist in sadism.
> Chateaubriand is Surrealist in exoticism.
> Constant is Surrealist in politics.
> Hugo is Surrealist when he isn't stupid.
> Desbordes-Valmore is Surrealist in love.
> Bertrand is Surrealist in the past.
> Rabbe is Surrealist in death.
> Poe is Surrealist in adventure.
> Baudelaire is Surrealist in morality.
> Rimbaud is Surrealist in the way he lived, and elsewhere.

Mallarmé is Surrealist when he is confiding.
Jarry is Surrealist in absinthe.
Nouveau is Surrealist in the kiss.
Saint-Pol-Roux is Surrealist in his use of symbols.
Fargue is Surrealist in the atmosphere.
Vaché is Surrealist in me.
Reverdy is Surrealist at home.
Saint-Jean-Perse is Surrealist at a distance.
Roussel is Surrealist as a storyteller.
Etc. (Breton 1972, 26–27)

Here Breton rewrites the history of literature so that the surrealism of the listed writers is exposed, just as Derrida revisits Hegel, Condillac, Freud, even Artaud, and reads deconstruction in(to) their writings. Both surrealism and Derridean thinking in this way fold back on the literary and philosophical genealogy from which they emerge, and both make, as Jacqueline Chénieux-Gendron argues about surrealism, "an unprecedented move towards annexation made by none of the European forms of Romanticism or Symbolism" (Chénieux-Gendron 1990, 12). This is a move away from the binary logic whereby Romanticism sets itself up against Neoclassicism or Symbolism sets itself up against Realism. It is not a dialectical logic that underwrites the surrealist and deconstructive attempts to situate themselves, but rather it is the recognition that each text contains its others and is defined only at the cost of excluding or violently suppressing those others. Neither Breton nor Derrida, in exposing the surrealism or deconstruction working at the heart of a text, insists that the text is absolutely and irrefutably surrealist or deconstructive. After Breton has listed the surrealism of the writers above, for example, he writes: "they are not always Surrealists, in that I discern in each of them a certain number of preconceived ideas to which—very naively!—they hold" (Breton 1972, 27). Derrida's readings, too, operate according to the logic that Heidegger, Hegel, etc., are not deconstructive in themselves, but the deconstructive and the aporetic can be read within their works. Both Breton and Derrida then, we might say, read the oppositional unconscious of a text, in that the surrealism and deconstruction which they read are oppositional toward the entire history of Western metaphysical discourse, and that they read this in the unconscious which is the pure presence of the text. In this reflexive turn on the genealogy of surrealism and Derridean thinking, Chénieux-Gendron sees "an essentially participatory way of thinking." (Chénieux-Gendron 1990, 12).

One of the most influential ideas that surrealism spawned was Artaud's "theatre of cruelty." Jean Genet, Fernando Arrabal, Ann

Jellicoe, and Peter Brook, to name but a few, all experimented with Artaud's "theatre of cruelty."[3] Derrida celebrates Artaud's theatre with enthusiasm in his essay "The Theater of Cruelty and the Closure of Representation," in which he argues that Artaud "wanted to explode . . . the very foundations of Western theater" (*WD*, 234). This is, then, an important intersection between Derrida and surrealism, and as such may yield fruitful lessons about what Derrida sees in surrealism, and perhaps also, how surrealism inhabits Derridean thinking. Derrida begins his essay by rejecting the idea that Artaud's theatre of cruelty is destructive or negative, although it may "ravage [everything] in its wake" (*WD*, 232). It is an affirmation of the force and life of the theatre and the theatrical. Artaud writes this himself in a letter "To J. P." in 1932:

> Cruelty is not an adjunct to my thoughts, it has always been there, but I had to become conscious of it. I use the word cruelty in the sense of hungering after life, cosmic strictness, relentless necessity, in the Gnostic sense of a living vortex engulfing darkness, in the sense of an inescapably necessary pain without which life could not continue. (Artaud 1993, 80)

Cruelty is a vital component of life for Artaud. It is desire. It is strictness, rigor. It is "relentless necessity." In the second manifesto of "The Theatre of Cruelty," he writes that it was created "in order to restore an impassioned compulsive concept of life to theatre" (Artaud 1993, 81). Artaud's theatre proposes to return to theatre a conception of life, and in effect to return life to the theatre, to join life and theatre together. In so doing, Artaud's theatre affirms the very impulse and essence of theatre, even though theatre is the very thing that must be put at risk in order to bring theatre back to itself. It is this relationship between life and theatre, between life of theatre and theatre of life, that concerns Derrida as much as Artaud. Artaud was expelled from the surrealists in 1926, according to Maurice Nadeau for having "acknowledged literary activity as a value" (Nadeau 1987, 135–136), and it is interesting to note that Derrida's reading proposes a view of Artaud's essays in *The Theatre and Its Double* as "more a system of critiques *shaking the entirety* of Occidental history than a treatise on theatrical practice" (*WD*, 235). Artaud's interest is not, then, primarily theatrical or literary, but profoundly political in the broadest sense. Derrida's Artaud is an exemplary surrealist, determined, as the "Declaration of January 27, 1925," which Artaud signed, promises "to show the fragility of thought, and on what shifting foundations, what caverns we have built our trembling houses" (Nadeau 1987, 240). Derrida's

Artaud "uses" theatre, not for its inherent value, whatever that might be, but as a tool.

For Derrida, the "shifting foundations" are those of the mimetic structures that inhabit the whole of Western culture ("its religions, philosophies, politics" [WD, 234]). The crucial issue in the relationship between theatre and life is the space of representation that comes between them. Theatre, by imitating life, "lets itself be doubled and emptied by negation" (WD, 234). Imitative theatre is negated in producing an appearance of creating which in fact merely reproduces the real. Imitative theatre "comports a passive, seated public," and "creates nothing" (WD, 235). Derrida argues that Artaud, however, questions and contests the imitative principle in art and theatre:

> The theater of cruelty is not a *representation*. It is life itself, in the extent to which life is unrepresentable. Life is the nonrepresentable origin of representation. "I have therefore said 'cruelty' as I might have said 'life' " [from Artaud's *Theatre and its Double*]. . . . Artaud wants to have done with the *imitative* concept of art. . . . Theatrical art should be the primordial and privileged site of this destruction of imitation. (WD, 234)

Artaud for Derrida refuses theatre as a representation, and in his "theatre of cruelty" produces theatre as life, and "announces the limit of representation" (WD 234). This constitutes a doubling of life, which affirms life, with an act of creation, which is nonrepresentable, nonimitative. The theatre of cruelty produces its own space as life, as pure presence which inhabits life as a pure difference. It interrogates and explodes theatrical representation. The space that it inhabits as theatrical nonrepresentation is that of "original representation, the archimanifestation of force or of life" (WD, 238). The theatre of cruelty returns theatre to its origin as representation, and Derrida tells us what the origin of theatre entails:

> The origin of theater, such as it must be restored, is the hand lifted against the abusive wielder of the logos, against the father, against the God of a stage subjugated to the power of speech and text. (WD, 239)

The theatre of cruelty is the return of the nonrepresentable, the unconscious as pure presence, to the stage, the conscious arena in which the unconscious appears as pure difference. And by working always against the "abusive wielder of the logos," adopting a strategy of always foregrounding difference, total creation, deviation, Artaud's theatre of cruelty acts as the oppositional unconscious of Western theatre, and by extension, of the theatrical imitation that inhabits Western culture and history to its roots. Here we encounter the second condition of the oppositional unconscious: to question and explode the limits of representation.

For Artaud, it is the formal aspects of theatrical production that will bring life to the theatre, as much as the subject matter. It is by elucidating theatrical technique on stage, by exposing the artifice at the surface, that Artaud's theatre of cruelty will have achieved the effect of "a total creation in *real terms*" (Artaud 1993, 71). What Derrida sees in Artaud can also be seen in his own work. *Glas* is a work that brings to the surface of the text the questions that permeate its content. It describes and comments on its own form:

> Two unequal columns, they say distyle [*disent-ils*], each of which— envelop(e)(s) or sheath(es), incalculably reverses, turns inside out, re- places, remarks, overlaps [*recoupe*] the other. . . . Each little square is delimited, each column rises with an impassive self-sufficiency, and yet the element of contagion, the infinite circulation of general equiva- lence relates each sentence, each stump of writing (for example, "*je m'éc* . . .") to each other, within each column and from one column to the other of *what remained* infinitely calculable. (*G*, 1b)

The text of *Glas* reflects on its own textuality, playing with two columns that face each other, sometimes becoming entangled, sometimes disrupted, sometimes interrupted by a third column. It plays too with borders and limits, the text spilling onto the first page as if from outside, and flowing outward from the last page: "Today, here, now, the debris of [*débris de*]" (*G*, 262b). The text comments on itself and refers outside of itself, demonstrating both the reflexivity of textuality, and that language speaks through the text. This structure invites to the surface of the text the technologies that inhabit it. *Glas* is a text that considers "what remains"—of Hegel, of Genet, of *Glas*—the remains of a text, the remainder of the text. Through the structure of the two columns, the interruptions into the columns, the different print sizes and styles, the parenthesized interjections and rem(a)inders, it is the textual surface, the textuality of the text, which becomes the subject of this text as much as Hegel, or Genet, or Derrida. As *Glas* invokes the space outside the text it also draws attention to the space that it occupies as a text. Its square shape, and the column structure of its print, figure the text as an architectural space, a space defined by its emptiness as much as its density, its blankness as much as its woven fabric of print, its margins and gaps as much as its squares and columns.

*Glas* is announcing the limit of representation. Derrida is not commenting *on* Hegel and Genet, as if in a metadiscursive relationship to their texts. At the same time as Derrida comments on Hegel's *Aesthetics*, he describes the texture of the text in which his comments appear. The columns define the architectural structure of the text, and the writing is "tattooed on the columns" (*G*, 3a). *Glas* occupies the same space as the tattoo, the writing on the body, the writing that cannot be separated from the body. Derrida does not write in a text called *Glas* therefore, but writes *on* Hegel's texts, *on* Genet's texts, over them, inside them, between them. And it is not Derrida who writes, but rather someone who signs in his name, or the name of another: the "Jean D." who appears in the commentary on Genet, or the "Derrière" in which "something inside me used to start to recognize there my father's name, in golden letters on his tomb, even before he was there" (*G*, 68b). This is a text without a proper author, the text without a beginning or end, the text through which textuality—the technology of the text—passes. Only when it has passed will we have known of its passing as text, as commentary:

> We do not await death, we only desire it as a past we have not yet lived, that we have forgotten, but with a forgetfulness that has not come to cover over an experience, with a memory more ample, more capable, older than any perception. This is why there are only traces here, traces of traces without tracing, or, if you wish, tracings that only track and retrace other texts. (*G*, 79b)

*Glas* traces and tracks other texts, or rather, other texts track through *Glas*. This is the structure, the technology, which prevents Derrida's text from behaving in a metadiscursive way toward Hegel's and Genet's texts. Each text is inhabited by another, by its others, and in turn, by contagion, inhabits other texts, such as this one. In other words, *Glas* incites its others to appear within it and simultaneously outside it, invoking the un-text of the text, the anti-logos. It is stripped of footnotes, references, bibliographical citations as these are metatextual structures which lay claim to mastery. Derrida/*Glas* is not the master but the subject of the borderless, limitless condition of the text. In short, *Glas* does not *represent* Hegel or Genet; it does not *represent* sexual difference, the family, love, marriage, the state; it does not *represent*, that is, in the sense of representation as an attempt to settle the "real" nature of the subject represented, as the production of a commentary that establishes the "real" for an inquiring reader. Rather, it questions its own status as a representation. It fills its representations with the real, and makes the text live the nonrepresentable origin of the text by invoking other texts within its own textuality. At every point that Derrida talks about the structure of other texts he talks also about the structure of *Glas*. At every point that he talks about his own name it becomes the name of another. This is the "oppositional unconscious" of writing, the erasure of the written name in order to make space for the other, the opening of the text outside of itself to invite otherness into its heart. What Derrida sees in Artaud as the theatre that is not representation but is life, can be seen at work in his own text, *Glas*, as the text that is also not representation. It is through the reflexive structure of the text that it comes to be inhabited by life, and this formal surfacing of the technology of representation is a "technique" that Derrida seems to share with Surrealist writers.

It is not just the textual surface of a work like *Glas* or *Cinders*, or the formal imitation of the post card in "Envois," that makes Derrida's work analogous to surrealist writings. It is not just that both Derrida and the surrealists expose the technology of representation, and explode the limits of representation, and therefore shake the foundations of Western philosophy. Derrida bears the single most important legacy of the surrealist projects in his attention to the word, to language, and to the freedom of language. Blanchot believes that we are all haunted by surrealism:

> There is no longer a school, but a state of mind survives. No one belongs to this movement anymore, and everyone feels he could have been a part of it. In every person who writes there is a surrealist calling that is admitted, that miscarries, seems sometimes usurped, but that, even when false, expresses a sincere effort and need. Has surrealism vanished? It is no longer here or there: it is everywhere. It is a ghost, a brilliant obsession. (Blanchot 1995, 85)

No one bears this ghost, this brilliant obsession, after surrealism to quite the same extent as Jacques Derrida. The desire to be automatic, to lose control, pervades the work of Jacques Derrida. Derrida signs his writings over to language, to the production of an immediacy that is analogous to surrealist automatic writing, but that, like surrealist automatic writing, is also a fabrication, a device which must, if nothing else, produce. Surrealist writing, like Derrida's writing, is the *production* of language. The obsession, even addiction, of Derrida and surrealist writers is with production, how language is produced, textually, performatively. This is the third condition of the "oppositional unconscious" that marks the affinity between surrealist writing and Derrida—that their obsession with the production of language gives the space of their writing over to language as unconscious determinant, and that this maneuver itself, the gift of textual space, is oppositional in its invitation of the other—the deviation, the multiple—into the space of writing.

Both in automatic writing and Derrida's writing it is not the content of what is written that serves as an invitation to the other but rather it is the very understanding of writing exhibited in the text itself which invites otherness, difference, into the place of logocentric presence. This is achieved by a radical break from Saussure, from the concept that every signifier corresponds to a signified. The word as written according to Saussure is always subordinate and secondary to a meaning which is manifest in a concept and/or an object. There is always then a system of meaning to which the word is subjected, and which must be comprehended prior to the signifier. Such a system demarcates an origin for language, for being and for theology. In *Of Grammatology*, Derrida outlines the presuppositions of such a system:

> The good writing has always been *comprehended*. Comprehended as that which had to be comprehended: within a nature or a natural law, created or not, but first thought within an eternal presence. Comprehended, therefore, within a totality, and enveloped in a volume or a book. The idea of the book is the idea of a totality, finite or infinite, of the signifier; this totality of the signifier cannot be a totality, unless a totality constituted by the signified preexists it, supervises its inscriptions and its signs, and is independent of it in its ideality. (*OG* 1976, 18)

Writing, according to Derrida, has always been understood as a secondary process of translating or recording speech or thought. It has been understood as the metaphorical manifestation of a system of meaning, which always bears witness to something outside of writing. Writing operates within Western discourse, then, under the law, to "underwrite" the existence or thought of something outside of writing, and as such, operates at a distance from being:

> The written signifier is always technical and representative. It has no constitutive meaning. This derivation is the very origin of the notion of the "signifier." The notion of the sign always implies within itself the distinction between signifier and signified, even if, as Saussure argues, they are distinguished simply as the two faces of one and the same leaf. This notion remains therefore within the heritage of that logocentrism which is also a phonocentrism: absolute proximity of voice and being, of voice and the meaning of being, of voice and the ideality of meaning. (*OG*, 11–12)

Speech emanates at the site of being, and this implicates speech in the authority of the word and the presence of being in language. In such a way being serves as the authority for speech, whereas writing must be presumed to take the place of speech or being, and to represent speech or being (at a remove).

The problem Derrida has in mind is that writing, by operating at a remove from the author(ity), from being, may not simply be the bearer of logic, the logos, but also may become subject to "play." Writing may deviate from "literal" meaning, and may pass "automatically" through the medium of a "writer," rather than emanating from an author. Such automatic writing, Breton explains, is the preferred method of the surrealist writer:

> After you have settled yourself in a place as favorable as possible to the concentration of your mind upon itself, have writing materials brought to you. Put yourself in as passive, or receptive, a state of mind as you can. Forget about your genius, your talents, and the talents of everyone else. Keep reminding yourself that literature is one of the saddest roads that leads to everything. Write quickly, without any preconceived subject, fast enough so that you will not remember what you're writing and be tempted to reread what you have written. The first sentence will come spontaneously, so compelling is the truth that with every passing second there is a sentence unknown to our consciousness which is only crying out to be heard. . . . Put your trust in the inexhaustible nature of the murmur. (Breton 1972, 29–30)

The speed of writing, of course, is the key for Breton to automatic writing—not the key to its significance or meaning, but the key to how it is produced. Speed is the trick a surrealist writer must employ in order to erase the self from the writing process. In Freudian terms, it is "an id no longer subservient to a super-ego" (Breton and Soupault 1985, 15). Writing must be a process of forgetting that it is literature, forgetting that it is "authored," forgetting narrative, plot, or development. Writing is the amnesia by which consciousness is made "unknown," by which preconception is erased. There is only conception, only spontaneity, and what is conceived, given up, by the unconscious of writing is not the "true self" or libidinal self of the id, but rather language. When self is erased through writing, "there is a sentence." Breton asks his surrealist writer not to trust psychology but to trust "the inexhaustible nature of the murmur," to give one's self over to language, to writing. This is why Breton and Soupault title two sections of *The Magnetic Fields* "The Hermit-Crab Says:," precisely because it erases the author(s) and places writing in the voice of a mythical "Hermit-Crab." Writing is clearly the product of *The Magnetic Fields*, writing as difference from meaning, writing as the presence of inscription without explication:

A policeman of the 6th arrondissement met a man who was coming out of a café and running. A notebook fell from his pocket but the man had disappeared. By the light of a high street-lamp, he read these few lines written in pencil:

The redness of twilight can scare only mortals. I have preferred cruelty.

Anatomical manufactories and cheap dwellings destroy the highest towns.

Through the glass of the portholes, I always saw the same faces: they were escaped waves.

*Fever is turning round gently in my breast: you might say it is like the more distant sound of towns about eleven o'clock at night.*

The man ran away fast enough to lose breath. He stopped only when he noticed a square. Hero of many a great expedition, he forgot all caution. But the pulings of a new-born child made him realize the gravity of the hour. He rang the bell of a little door and immediately the window he was watching opened. He spoke, waiting in vain for a reply. There was no longer anybody in the square. He recognized his friend and memories hit his ear. Superfluous comets, falsified eruptions, keys to dreams, obscure charlatanisms. He understood the gleam of symbols and the monstrous evocations. (Breton and Soupault 1985, 55–56)

A policeman appears in the novel to read the lines from a notebook dropped by a man running. The inscriptions are given in the novel without explanation and without significance. The policeman never appears again. The man runs, and is stopped only to notice a sign, to hear a baby's whimperings, and to speak without hearing a reply. The "characters," if they can be called such, appear and disappear, like fleeting images in a dream. Nothing is of relevance to a character. No attention is given to the interpretations such characters may produce. The important elements in the novel are the inscriptions, signs, and symbols which are produced endlessly throughout. Language is produced in the novel not with reference to "an ideality of meaning," not with reference to being, but to the possibility of meaning, to the possibility of the event of meaning.

There is sense in each sentence in the novel. In the inscriptions from the notebook quoted above, for example, there is meaning to be gained, but it is meaning outside of a narrative structure. It is not preconceived within the novel, within a totality. There is no chain of expectations and satisfactions marking the reading experience of the novel, which is to say that the novel is without a libidinal economy, without the desire, cathexis, or satisfaction that would define the novel as an object for consumption. For a novel to be consumed means that it has, in a sense, entered the economy of the body, in that it has satisfied desire. To refuse consumption, on the other hand, is to remain at a distance from the body, and from the achievement of comprehension. To refuse consumption is therefore to achieve the production of language at a distance from the body, for no purpose other than production. Automatic writing has achieved its own space, separate from, and different from, the economy of the reader. It is, of course, read, and forms meaning, but not according to a predetermined narrative structure. Meaning becomes an event in the surrealist novel because it is always experienced as difference from desire. This is where *The Magnetic Fields* can be seen most clearly to borrow from psychology in its achievement of a writing, a language, which has separated from the subject and has become the other of desire, the other that is desired.

In Lacanian terms desire is always desire for the other, the desire to be recognized by the other, and this is the dynamic that operates at the heart of *The Magnetic Fields*, the desire of the subject for the other of writing (Lacan 1977, 59, 166–167). Writing embodies in an entirely derived, entirely other form the unconscious desires of the id, and so there exists between the subject and writing an impossible desire, and a perpetual magnetism. This is not to place surrealist writing within an overdetermined psychoanalytic structure, but to understand that writing, as understood in the surrealist novel, produces its own field of attraction outside of a predetermined libidinal economy of the subject. Writing, contrary to its traditional secondary function of representing or witnessing a reality or a desire outside of itself, comes to produce its own space, and its own "magnetic field."

If this effect has been created as a result of the spontaneity and absence of a predetermined program in surrealist writing, we can say that Derrida isn't unfamiliar with the approach, albeit in a different context. In a number of interviews—in speech, that is, rather than writing—Derrida has employed this method of coming without a predetermined subject, without preparation, and without sufficient "time," to speak at speed, and in doing so to "improvise."[4] He explained his reasons for doing so in a recent interview at the "Applied Derrida" conference at the University of Luton:

> Now, if I accepted to come here tonight unprepared—I'm totally unprepared . . . why did I come here totally unprepared? Because I didn't want to apply something ready-made, let's say, I wanted to expose myself to the event, to the singular event, of being in front of

you, totally disarmed, totally exposed, totally vulnerable. . . . This is the condition of the event. (*Ai*, 213)

The act of arriving without preparation, of speaking, or writing, without preparation is for Derrida a way of exposing his self to the event, of allowing the irreducible singularity of the event to permeate his self. To arrive without preparation is, to a certain extent, to achieve the status of what Derrida calls the "absolute *arrivant*"(*A*, 33–34). The "absolute *arrivant*" disturbs the boundaries between home and foreign, between self and other, because s/he comes before any invitation, comes before a route or a border or a point of transgression is defined. Totally disarmed, totally vulnerable, Derrida comes in front of, before, the audience, the interviewers, and exposes his self to what will be defined or established, and, by doing so, subjects his self to the otherness of the event. We could doubt his lack of preparation, just as we could doubt the automatism of surrealist writing, but whether Derrida and the surrealists achieve spontaneity or fabricate spontaneity, it doesn't alter the significance of the idea of subjecting one's self to language. If language comes prior to being, if it is the condition of the event of meaning, of being, then it is not a secondary effect of being. It is not the instrument by which human society communicates. Rather, it is the very condition of human society.

Language in this sense fabricates and produces the space of the real, and this is an idea that is evident commonly in both Derrida's writing and surrealist writing. In this matter, according to David Wills, the affinities between Derrida and the surrealists represent the precedent that surrealism set for contemporary critical theory:

> [B]oth Surrealism and recent critical theory have set themselves comparable tasks, however important the divergences might seem from other points of view, namely to reassess the means by which language functions as a referential and representational system. (Wills 1985, 18)

The importance of surrealism for Derrida is its obsession with the production of language that operates at a remove from being, and this is why it is particularly significant that Derrida's tracing of the word *differance* articulates both spatial "differing" and temporal "deferring." In both cases there is a close affinity between surrealist writing and Derrida's writing in the temporal and spatial distance from being, from self. In Derrida's work the space of writing is given over to the other, to the voice of the other. This is clear in the way in which Derrida has "countersigned" for the other in his writing on Rousseau, Heidegger, Condillac, Artaud, etc.:

> [T]he only way to sign with a name-to-come is, or should be (this is
> my hypothesis), a countersignature; not a signature but a countersig-
> nature, countersigning with your own name, but countersigning with
> the names of the others, or being true to the name of the other. So,
> when I read another, something I do all the time and which I have
> been reproached for, for not writing anything in my own name but
> being content with writing on Plato, on Kant, on Mallarmé and oth-
> ers—or on Geoff Bennington for that matter—the feeling of duty which
> I feel in myself is that I have to be true to the other; that is, to coun-
> tersign with my own name, but in a way that should be true to the
> other. I wouldn't say *True* vs. *False*, but true in the sense of fidelity. I
> want to add something, to give something to the other, but something
> that the other could receive and could, in his or her turn, actually or
> as a ghost, countersign. (*Ai*, 215)

The countersignature is the application of one's self to the other, not
as a projection of one's self onto the other, but as a way of exposing
the self to the arrival of the other. It is the maneuver that we see in
both Derrida's writing and surrealist writing of allowing language to
pass through the body, which simultaneously requires being as presence and gives homage to the other as *differance*. They do not work in
the same media, generically speaking, nor do they give homage in
quite the same way—Derrida's homage is spectral throughout, whereas
surrealism is conscious of what will have been created with the surrealist spark—but they both share the inclusive, anti-ego maneuver of
deploying writing on its own terms, and producing the space of writing through the other will have passed. By their deferral of ego, and
their making writing the space the other may inhabit, surrealist writers and Derrida evoke language as the unconscious, which because it
invites the singularity and otherness of the event into meaning, into
writing, also makes it oppositional.

To act as the oppositional unconscious is to erode the stability of cultural and philosophical borders, to bring into play all the uncertainties
that exist at the limits of familiar definitions and divisions. This is the
role that both Derrida and surrealist writers adopt, the role of the
oppositional unconscious, writing into existence the return of the repressed. The repressed returns not as the bearer of hidden truths but
as the bearer of hidden doubts, hidden ambiguities. Both surrealism
and Derridean thinking act as the deviation from Western art and
philosophy that returns to incline Western discourse toward other
questions, and the questions of the other. Both have the historic function of changing the question, as David Wills argues of surrealism:

Speaking teleologically, one can say that for a time criticism deflected the question, and instead of asking what meaning means, sought to enquire, through by no means unsophisticated methods, as to what such and such a text, or author, meant. Even when confronted with language or texts which seemed not to mean much, nor to make much sense. By virtue of its persistence and insistence, writing like that which is historically called Surrealist, forces criticism to stop asking what it really means, and to begin asking what meaning means. Furthermore . . . Surrealism demonstrates that in order to mean something, language must first mean nothing, or must also mean nothing. By virtue of its being "unconscious," Surrealist writing is out of control, out of the control of its author, it is writing which has no author. And lastly, by virtue of the coincidence between its simplistic ideology and highly evocative poetic sense, Surrealism asks how language can mean one and also many things. (Wills 1985, 6)

Contrary to the surrealist declaration that forms the title of this essay, surrealist writing has everything to do with literature. It is writing that collapses the distinction between literature and a metadiscursive criticism, and asks questions of its own status as it unfolds. It is the production of literature not just for consumption, or as Chénieux-Gendron argues, "not only for pleasure but to understand" (Chénieux-Gendron 1990, 26). In this sense, surrealist literature crosses all boundaries between literature and philosophy, literature and science, literature and history, literature and myth. To bring these boundaries into question, and to ask the question "what is meaning?" or "what is literature?" is to question the very system of relations within which these questions occur. Derrida makes clear in an interview, "There is No *One* Narcissism," that deconstruction could be defined in very similar terms:

Deconstruction concerns, first of all, systems. This does not mean that it brings down the system, but that it opens onto possibilities of arrangement or assembling, of being together if you like, that are not necessarily systematic, in the strict sense that philosophy gives to this word. It is thus a reflection on the system, on the closure and opening of the system.(*P.* . . , 212)

It may be the case that surrealism anticipates not just Derrida but also what are broadly called poststructuralist theories, but Derrida's writing is where surrealist concerns have the clearest resonances. Tracing such affinities may be useful itself in breaking down the distinctions between literature and theory which prevail in the academy, where theory becomes a static body of ideas to be applied to a literature that becomes simply an object for the production of meaning. If we can say that in this relationship between Derrida and surrealism we have an exchange of strategies that preclude rigid academic and institutional distinctions, this may open up the possibility, perhaps even the necessity, of rethinking literary, philosophical, and theoretical history.

## NOTES

1. Derrida's idea of "democratic non-identification" is useful here too and has affinities with "oppositional unconscious." In *The Other Heading*, Derrida argues that it is our democratic responsibility to counter or undermine ego/Euro-centrism by identifying with the other/unconscious of Europe: "it is necessary to make ourselves the guardians of an idea of Europe, of a difference of Europe, *but* of a Europe that consists precisely in not closing itself off in its own identity and in advancing itself in an exemplary way toward what it is not, toward the other heading or the heading of the other" (*OH* 1992, 29).

2. Derrida articulates this concept of "pure presence as pure difference" in "The Theater of Cruelty and the Closure of Representation" (*WD*, 247). Derrida's thoughts on spectrality have perhaps developed from the idea of a presence without economy, return, or history and so appears as pure difference.

3. The purpose of such experimentation with Artaud's "theatre of cruelty" seems to have been in each case a desire to create the total experience of theatre through startling psychological effects on the audience. As playwrights, Genet, Arrabal, and Jellicoe deliberately chose themes from violent and grotesque situations, as suggested by Artaud, involving race, religion, sex, power, and street violence. The style of such experiments tends to be visceral and spectacular.

4. For examples of where Derrida has spoken in interviews of the need to improvise or the need to speak quickly or expediently, see "*Ja*, or the *faux-bond* II," "Choreographies," "Unsealing," and "Dialanguages," (*P . . .* , 32, 90, 115, 133.

# CHAPTER 4

## *Musique–rythme*
### *Derrida and Roger Laporte*

IAN MACLACHLAN

> Music can also, in certain situations, resist effacement to
> the extent to which, by its very form, it does not let itself
> be so easily dissolved in the common element of discur-
> sive sense. From this point of view, at any rate, music would
> be less "(bio)degradable" than discourse and even than the
> art of discourse.
>
> —Jacques Derrida, "Biodegradables:
> Seven Diary Fragments"

There is an untotalizable economy of debt at work
between Derrida's writings on "literary" works and those works themselves. Derrida has consistently been at pains to underline what he
owes to certain literary texts (*TT,* 34–50; *AL,* 33–75). There is also a
straightforward sense in which the objects of Derrida's attention are in
turn indebted to him: the work of Maurice Blanchot or Edmond Jabès
would probably not—unfortunately, it must be said—have reached
the audience it has in recent years were it not for Derrida's essays on
these writers; our reading of Mallarmé or Ponge is renewed by Derrida's
mediation. If the reorientation of our reading effected by Derrida's
essays on these writers constitutes a form of gift, then it is a gift that
can turn to poison; at worst, what is identified as Derrida's literary
"inheritance"—I deliberately choose a term that conveys a one-way
finality entirely at odds with Derrida's readings—risks being reduced
to a set of supposedly Derridean propositions. At best, however, returning to these writers after Derrida allows us to reread them in such
a way as to release further dimensions of their singularity, according,
we might say, to a logic of supplementarity which means that there is

always more to come of the singular; the momentum of the economy persists, as these works continue to indebt us. This economy in constant disequilibrium, driven by the persistence of a remainder that will never finally be absorbed, never written off in a balance-sheet of reading, is crucial to Derrida's conception of literature. In the discussion of the work of Roger Laporte that follows, I hope to shed a little more light on this conception of literature or, to translate the title of Derrida's essay on Laporte, on "what remains by dint of music."

But first, the work of Roger Laporte requires a few words of introduction for, like Mathieu Bénézet and Jos Joliet on whom Derrida has written pieces so far unavailable in English translation, the attention of Derrida—not to mention that of Blanchot, Foucault, and Levinas—has yet to secure for his work the wider readership it deserves. After three short *récits*, first published in literary journals in the 1950s, Laporte's first major work, *La Veille*, appeared in 1963. This was also the first of Laporte's works Derrida encountered, having been urged to read it by Foucault (*JD*, 330). The sense of being "on watch" in the work's title refers to the attitude of the first–person narrator to an anonymous other, known simply as *il*—the whole work revolves around this relationship between *je* and *il* and its effect on the writing being undertaken. Space precludes proper consideration of *La Veille* here, but one can say very cursorily that it comes as no surprise that Derrida should take an interest in a work in which writing is related to an anonymous other that eludes the grasp of that writing of which it is nonetheless the condition, an other with which the narrator says he has no direct rapport, although this other in some sense enters into the constitution of his own identity. The two other works published in the 1960s, *Une Voix de fin silence* (1966) and *Une Voix de fin silence II: Pourquoi?* (1967), are also concerned with the relationship between writing and an inaccessible alterity, the anonymous *il* of *La Veille* giving way now to an inspirational event which compels writing from an immemorial past or an ever-impending future; as the joint title of these works suggests, this alterity is also characterized as a silent voice which demands and yet defies the writer's response. For our present purposes, the crucial factor in the transition from the second of these works to *Fugue* (1970) is Laporte's reading of and correspondence with Derrida—*Fugue* is in fact dedicated to Jacques and Marguerite Derrida. *Fugue* and its successor *Fugue: Supplément* (1973) will be our principal focus, since they are the texts to which Derrida refers in his essay on Laporte. They were in turn followed by *Fugue 3* (1975), *Suite* (1979), and *Moriendo* (1983), all of the works named thus far being collected as *Une Vie* (1986).[1]

We shall consider the impact of Derrida on Laporte's writing in *Fugue* in a moment. However, this emerging relationship was also marked by a number of studies of Derrida by Laporte which are of interest to us here. In 1972, Laporte wrote three times on Derrida in the space of a year. The most substantial of these pieces is "Une double stratégie," which appeared in a collective volume on Derrida entitled *Ecarts*; it is also in a sense the most straightforward, consisting largely of very lucid expositions of Derrida's accounts of phonocentrism, *archi-écriture*, the trace, and *différance*. In an issue of *Les Lettres françaises* devoted to Derrida's work, Laporte contributed a short piece entitled " Les 'blancs' assument l'importance, " which addresses the consequences of Derrida's conception of writing for any writers who might imagine that their " 'literary experience,' *qua* experience, has no relation to philosophy and evades cultural codes." Laporte's observation in that essay that he had been just such a writer is amplified in the third piece, "Bief," which appeared in the issue of *L'Arc* on Derrida; it is this piece that sheds most light on the transition in Laporte's writing from *Pourquoi?* to *Fugue*.[2]

Laporte begins this essay by remarking that it is a risky undertaking to write a third piece on Derrida in the space of a year. However, he goes on, whereas Laporte the author of "fictions" was scarcely engaged in a study like "Une double stratégie," in "Bief" he proposes to acknowledge what his own writing owes to Derrida. In fact, Laporte is embarking here on a critical idiom that is characteristic of him, namely, to write on other writers in such a way as to highlight how his reading of them acted as an impetus to writing; many of the essays collected in *Quinze variations sur un thème biographique* and *Etudes* would attest to this, and in the afterword of the former volume Laporte observes that: "A pure reading, a reading which does not call for another writing, is something which is and doubtless always has been incomprehensible to me" (1975, 237). For Laporte, the break between *Fugue* and his earlier works appears so decisive at the time of "Bief" that he would go so far as to disown the earlier works. However, the relationship between the earlier and the later Laporte, and Derrida's part in that relationship, are more nuanced than this would lead us to suppose; later in the essay, Laporte goes on to state that "the *breakthrough* effected by Derrida reopened a path for me back to 'myself,' back to my 'archi-project' as a writer," and that "Derrida's reading of my earlier works allowed me to 'move on to something else,' an assertion which leads me to admit that, whether I like it or not, from a certain perspective there must be some connection between my past as a writer and my present" (*Bi*, 68). There is then, at the least, a doubling of Laporte the writer, distinguished already in "Bief" from Laporte the critic, such that *Fugue* is articulated with the earlier work by a *brisure*, a connective-disjunctive interval;[3] clearly, Derrida's part in this doubling, his role in restoring Laporte to himself by helping to open a distance that makes return possible—but precludes complete return— is more complex than any notion of one-way, one-off indebtedness.

In order to locate Derrida's impact on his writing more specifically, Laporte remarks that he has always striven to create a work that would pertain neither simply to literature nor to philosophy. Such is still his intention, he adds, and indeed it is an ambition regularly reiterated in his published notebooks (1979), as well as in *Fugue*, where we find numerous references to the goal of instituting a new writerly domain, described variously as the "critical poem or narrative," "scriptography," and most notably as "biography," a term that we shall consider in a moment. To return for now to "Bief," Laporte observes that the weakness in his earlier works, which Derrida has enabled him to identify, resided in his belief at that time that he could immediately place himself outside of the philosophical field; he cites a passage of a letter from Derrida where the latter remarks that "I don't believe in an inside and an outside of the history of philosophy. I feel myself to be as little within it as I believe you to be outside of it" (*Bi*, 67). With more particular reference to Laporte's earlier works, a passage from another of Derrida's letters commenting on *Une Voix de fin silence* is especially interesting: "I too feel I am heading, have always been and will always be heading towards that 'now I am writing' whose time does not exist. There is no *Fête* because there is no *now* of writing, because writing is the very rupture of the 'now.' A pure waiting for an Event which places itself in the past although it has never taken place, which promises itself whilst assuring that it will never take place. That is why your text is in fact the destruction of the words 'waiting,' 'event,' 'future,' etc. which invade your vocabulary and lay siege to your writing" (*Bi*, 68). Here again is the suggestion, which Laporte goes on to underline, that the movement beyond these earlier works is already contained within them. I would also want to draw attention to Derrida's emphasis on the question of writing and time, on what we might call with Blanchot the time of the absence of time of writing, for this is a key factor in the *brisure* in Laporte's work which led to *Fugue*. But before we can expand on this claim, we shall have to consider *Fugue* in a little more detail.

*Fugue* was distinguished from its predecessors by the appearance of the word *biographie* on its cover. All of Laporte's subsequent works

some past which might have been present, which might have been. (*PIa*, 103)

Derrida concludes his essay with a quotation from *Fugue: Supplément* in which the narrator suggests that

> écrire ne conduit pas à un pur signifié, et il se pourrait que la Biographie se différencie de la philosophie, et au contraire se rapproche de la peinture et surtout de la musique, pour autant qu'elle ne comporte sans doute jamais un véritable contenu. (*V*, 362)

> [writing does not lead to a pure signified, and it could be that Biography differs from philosophy, and by contrast comes closer to painting and above all to music, insofar as it doubtless never comprises a true content.]

The music of Biography is a rhythmic scansion, a movement of *poesis* which is irreducible to any propositional content; I do not mean by this that it is a pure *poesis*, for there is no *poesis* without propositional content, just as—from the point of view of reading—there is no pure poetics devoid of hermeneutics. But what is irreducibly literary in Laporte's texts evades the grasp of any hermeneutics.

It is in that irreducibility to any summary that the music of these fugues effect a re-marking of time. One must take care here, for the time of writing that is re-marked by the rhythmic scansion of these texts is a time that does not simply elapse. The remainder which persists by dint of the rhythm of self–cancellation—the differentiation and deferral at work between the variant repetitions of these fugues— *is* time, *is* the temporalization of writing's spacing, *is* the *giving* of the time of reading-writing which *takes* time.[7] But the time thus re-marked is not a time that was, is, or shall be present. It is the time of an event that is inseparable from the movement of these texts without being punctually present in them.

We are close here, as both Laporte and Derrida repeatedly are, to the work of Blanchot, and particularly to the famous distinction he draws between the novel and the *récit* at the beginning of *Le Livre à venir*. Blanchot argues that, in the novel, there appears to be, in essence, event followed by narration—broadly speaking, Blanchot has in mind the realist novel, in which it is a tacit component of the narrative contract that something has taken place which is then narrated. Thus, the conception of time underpinning the novel's narrative is fundamentally serial: the one after the other. The *récit*, on the other hand, characteristically relates one extraordinary event—Ulysses's encounter with the Sirens is the example that opens *Le Livre à venir*—that is not part of our familiar, human experience. As a consequence, in the

*récit* it does not appear as if an event has "really" taken place and is
then recounted, but rather the narrative appears to bear this event
with it, an event that has no reality outside of the movement of narration. This produces a reflexivity peculiar to the *récit*:

> This is one of the peculiarities, one of the claims, let us say, of the *récit*.
> It only "relates" itself, and this relation, at the same time as it is carried
> out, produces what it recounts, is only possible as a relation if it ac-
> complishes what is happening in this relation, for then it encompasses
> the point or plane at which the reality which the *récit* "describes" may
> ceaselessly join with its reality as a *récit*, guarantee it and be guaran-
> teed by it.[8]

We should take the utmost care to note that Blanchot is *not* saying here
that narration and event are absolutely coextensive. If this were simply another account of literature's performative dimension, its capacity to do what it is saying, then the event *would* take place within the
narrative, would be accomplished—we would be back to the seriality
of the novel. What takes place in the *récit* does not "really" take place,
and the movement of the narrative is the dimension of it not taking
place. Echoing Derrida's remark about the "not nothing" that persists
in Laporte's texts, we may say of the *récit*—and, in their ceaselessly
unaccomplished reflexivity, of Laporte's texts—that this is the place
where nothing *is happening* (Clark 1992, 81).[9]

The happening of this (not) nothing, its ceaseless persistence, is
the re-marking of time, for in the reading of this remainder which
both calls for and resists reading, time is demanded, and is given
without ever being finally surrendered. I should like to conclude by
suggesting that in this re-marking of time we are confronted with a
curious logic of *saving time*. Laporte's writing resists the saving of
time—the collapsing of duration—and by demanding that we take
time it saves time, restores the time of reading-writing; but, at the
same time, this is a time that cannot be saved, cannot be held in
reserve or preserved, for it is never accomplished.[10]

## NOTES

1. All the works referred to thus far by Laporte will be cited in this
edition. All translations from the French are mine unless otherwise indicated,
and all emphases are in the original unless likewise indicated. In the case of
*Une Vie*, I have given the original French text followed by my translation. The
following abbreviations will be used:

*V*: Roger Laporte, *Une Vie* (1986)

*Bi*: Roger Laporte, "Bief," *L'Arc*: 54 (1973), "Jacques Derrida": 65–70
*PIa*: Jacques Derrida, "Ce qui reste à force de musique," (*PIa*, 95–103)

2. "Une double stratégie" appeared in Lucette Finas *et al*, *Ecarts: quatre essais à propos de Jacques Derrida* (1973, 208–264), and "Les 'blancs' assument l'importance " *Les Lettres françaises* 1429 (1972): 5. Laporte has published two further pieces on Derrida: "Nulle part séjournant," in *Les Fins de l'homme: à partir du travail de Jacques Derrida* (ed. Philippe Lacoue–Labarthe and Jean–Luc Nancy, 1981, 201–208), and "S'entendre parler," in his *Etudes* (1990, 83–93). There is also a brief interview with Laporte conducted by Derrida: "Roger Laporte au bord du silence" in *Libération* (22 décembre 1983), 28.

3. I use the term *brisure* to allude to another link between Laporte and Derrida. The section of Derrida's *Of Grammatology*,(1976), entitled "The Hinge [*La Brisure*]" opens with an epigraph from a letter written by Laporte which suggests the term *brisure* to Derrida (65).

4. In their "Entretiens sur Roger Laporte," *Digraphe* 18/19 (1979): 175–203 (188).

5. Much of my discussion of the double time in which Laporte's text requires to be read relies on Derrida's "Psyché, Invention de L'autre"; in English, the relevant part of this essay can most conveniently be found in *Acts of Literature* (310–343).

6. I discuss this and several of the other features of Laporte's work mentioned in this paper in more detail in "Writing as Fugue," a chapter of my study *Roger Laporte: The Orphic Text* (forthcoming).

7. I am indebted here to Derrida's *Given Time: I. Counterfeit Money* (1992). For example, the following passage, in which Derrida is exploring the ramifications of the unlimitable possibilities of counterfeiting in Baudelaire's prose poem "La fausse monnaie," could well be applied to Laporte's texts (in which, for instance, the use of *copies non conformes* is also a form of undecidable counterfeiting): "This text, then, is also the piece, *perhaps* a piece of counterfeit money, that is, a machine for provoking events: first of all, the event of the text that is there, like a narrative offering itself or holding itself open to reading (this event has taken place and continues to take place, it gives time and takes its time, it apparently gives itself time), but also and consequently, from there, in the order of the opened possibility and of the aleatory, an event pregnant with other events that have in common, however, a certain propitiousness for this staging of a trap or a deception [*leurre*]" (96). I should also add here that, given what Derrida says about both the ontological status of the remainder in his essay on Laporte and that of time in *Given Time* (where he writes of "a time that is what it is *without being (it)* [sans l'être], that is not what it is and that is what it is not, which is to be it *without being (it)* [qui est de l'être sans l'être]" [28]), the word "is" in my sentence would require some qualification.

8. Maurice Blanchot, *Le Livre à venir* (1959, reprinted in collection "Idées"), 15. An excellent account of Blanchot's conception of the *récit* may be found in

Timothy Clark's *Derrida, Heidegger, Blanchot: Sources of Derrida's Notion and Practice of Literature* (1992, 84–87).

9. I owe this last formulation to Timothy Clark.

10. I intend to develop some of the ideas contained in the latter part of this chapter in a work in progress on time and literary value in contemporary French literature and philosophy. An excellent, succinct account of some of the issues at stake here may be found in chapter 4 of Steven Connor's *Theory and Cultural Value* (1992), especially the section entitled "Wasting Time" (89–95). In the same chapter, the section on Beckett's *Worstward Ho* (80–89) also contains a good deal of analysis that would be pertinent to Laporte's texts.

# CHAPTER 5

# Domesticated Reading
*Paulhan, Derrida, and the Logic of Ancestry*

MICHAEL SYROTINSKI

A few dates to begin with.

1. Shortly before his death, in a letter to Francis Ponge dated 14 March 1968, Jean Paulhan writes that he has been reading Derrida, no doubt at Ponge's suggestion. Although he only has a few months left to live, Paulhan's comment typifies his enduring support for all that is new and challenging in the literary world: "Oui, c'est un esprit gentil et fin: très attachant" [Yes, he has a nice, subtle mind: very engaging] (1986, Letter 697, 347).

2. In 1941, Blanchot first published his essay, "How Is Literature Possible?" on Paulhan's *Les Fleurs de Tarbes*. In the 1969 issue of the *Nouvelle Revue Française* commemorating Jean Paulhan, Maurice Blanchot in the opening lines of his article "La Facilité de mourir" [The Ease of Dying] returns to these first years of their encounter (1994, 122–142). Blanchot recounts the history of their friendship as a sequence of punctual events, a rhythm of coincidental moments: from their first meeting in May 1940, to their disagreement and subsequent falling out over the question of Algerian independence in May 1958, and finally their planned reconciliation in May 1968, a reconciliation that was thwarted by the distraction of the events that dominated the French intellectual scene that Spring.

3. In 1948, Blanchot publishes *L'arrêt de mort* [*Death Sentence*], a *récit* set during the days of the Munich crisis of 1938. Although the text begins with a series of very specific dates around October 1938, no mention is made of the historical events which presumably framed the action of the story. Derrida will publish a number of important essays

on Blanchot's writing, among them a long reading of *L'arrêt de mort* in *Living On: Borderlines*.

What we have, then, is a constellation of dates, or temporal dots, or punctual moments of reading and writing which, when connected, seem to point to a network of influences linking Derrida, Blanchot, and Paulhan. In several polemical and deliberately provocative texts, the critic Jeffrey Mehlman has fleshed out this network, and made a case for what he sees as the hidden historical and ideological roots of the thought of Blanchot and Derrida. His most recent contribution has been in the volume produced in response to the discovery of Paul de Man's wartime journalism, which he gleefully seizes upon as further confirmation that deconstruction's intellectual ancestry can be traced back to an ideology of collaboration, and a willful blindness to historical and political circumstances.[1] In this rather grandly orchestrated configuration, Mehlman sees Blanchot's privileging of an essential silence or nothingness at the heart of the literary enterprise in his writings of the 1940s (that is, after he had abandoned his career as a political commentator for *Combat*, during which time his sympathies were very markedly fascist in orientation) as a conscious forgetting or covering over of his guilty past (BC). Elsewhere, he points to Derrida's omission of any mention of the historical context of Blanchot's *L'arrêt de mort* in his reading of this récit in *Living On: Borderlines* as itself a form of consent to Blanchot's own effacement of the ideological origins of his thinking (DLH). The central figure of Mehlman's readings, a figure who is absolutely crucial in the genealogy he constructs, is the now rather neglected writer, theoretician of language and literature, and editor of the *Nouvelle Revue Française*, Jean Paulhan, who had earned for himself during the 1930s and 1940s the reputation as the "grey eminence" of French literature. Mehlman's most important article in this regard is his "Writing and Deference: The Politics of Literary Adulation," in which he makes the explicit claim for Paulhan as an unacknowledged ancestor of deconstruction. As he writes, "there has not perhaps been an adequate appreciation of the extent to which this 'grammarian's' obsession with the conundra of language was pregnant with future developments," and he goes on to call Paulhan's essay *Alain ou la preuve par l'étymologie* [*Alain or Proof by Etymology*] "a local instance of what might be called, before the letter, applied grammatology" (WrDe, 5). What I would like to do, rather than dismissing Mehlman's argument as fanciful or vengeful, is to take them seriously, and look more closely at the claims he makes for Derrida as an inheritor of Paulhan's thought.[2] Whatever one might think of Mehlman's conclusions, his reading raises a number of important questions, since it concerns not only Derrida's own "debts," but also the history of the reception of his thought—that is, our indebtedness to Derrida—as well as the forms and modalities of its *application*.

Mehlman's positing of a relationship of "ancestry" between the two writers is based on what he sees as three points of convergence between Paulhan's and Derrida's thought. First of all, Paulhan's call for a political amnesty of literary collaborators after World War II is said to prefigure Derrida's amnesic "forgetting" of history. Secondly, Paulhan's late interest in "homophonic antonyms" (words that can at the same time mean their opposite), inspired by Karl Abel's 1884 work *On the Antithetical Sense of Primal Words*, and Paulhan's related analysis in *Alain ou la preuve par l'étymologie* of the impossibility of telling whether an etymology in fact reveals a word's original meaning, or whether it is merely a pun, as an anticipation of Derrida's foregrounding of undecidable terms such as *hymen* or *pharmakon*. This provides the linguistic structure that allows Paulhan, in his polemic during the postwar literary purge in France, to read Collaboration and Resistance as two sides of a reversible chiasmus. And thirdly, Mehlman takes the admiration shown by Gerhard Heller, the German literary attaché in Paris during the war, for Paulhan (in his memoirs he refers to Paulhan as "Mon maître"—"My master") as an early paradigm of a generalized pattern of deference to charismatic French intellectuals by outsiders, with the American "adulation" of Derrida being the latest example.[3] Paulhan's work is said to lead irresistibly to Derrida's: "With the transcendental signified (or etymon) generated after the fact by a tension between signifiers, the problematic later to emerge as deconstruction was already broached" (WrDe, 12). The text of Paulhan's around which Mehlman organizes his argument is a little-known text published in 1947 entitled *De la paille et du grain* (*Of the Wheat and the Chaff*, but which I would translate, paying attention to the partitives, as *Some Wheat and Some Chaff*).[4] The one allusive reference to my knowledge that Derrida has in fact made to Paulhan is in relation to this text, in the course of his article on Paul de Man's wartime writing. Derrida is at this point very reluctant to engage with Paulhan's text, and confines himself to the comment: "My own thinking as regards Paulhan's discourse cannot be summed up in a few lines" (LSSDS, 138). While clearly not wishing to deflect attention too far from de Man's wartime writings, which are the focus of Derrida's article, his caution is in all likelihood not unrelated to his awareness of Mehlman's argument about his own writings. *De la paille et du grain*, written just after the Liberation, became something of a *cause célèbre* of the period. In it, Paulhan condemns the *Comité National des Ecrivains* (National Committee of Writers)—the most important literary organization in France after the war—for its moralistic stance in conducting its own purge of writers who collaborated with the Nazis during the Occupation. This was all the more shocking to people at the time given that during the Occupation Paulhan had himself been one of the pivotal figures of the literary Resistance, and his defense of collaborators seemed to be a betrayal of everything his fellow *Résistants* had fought for.

To summarize briefly, the thrust of Paulhan's argument was that the National Committee of Writers had no right to judge the patriotic loyalty of other writers, since they themselves were an interested party, and that the meting out of justice should, in a democratic society, be the task of an independent jury randomly selected from the general public. As Paulhan saw it, the main crime that the collaborators were accused of, in a strictly legal sense, was antipatriotism. Why, he asked, were the so-called antipatriots of 1939 any less tolerable than the antipatriots of 1914 or 1871 (he cites Louis Aragon and Arthur Rimbaud as two of the most anti-French of French writers)? Hence the argument about the reversibility of the terms of Resistance and Collaboration, which Mehlman summarizes accurately as follows: "The great paradox of World War II was that the national Resistance to foreign occupation was the achievement of an ideological group that had long been denigrating all national values with a view toward a future collaboration—*with* the Russians. In addition, the Collaborators with the Germans were a group that had long been training as future Resistance fighters—*against* the Russians" (WrDe, 6; my emphasis). Mehlman continues by pointing out that Paulhan's view of language—the discussion of homophonic antonyms—provides the context, and the frame, for his exonerating collaborationist writers. This is certainly how Paulhan's argument proceeds. I would like to suggest, however, that Mehlman does not take into account the subtlety and deceptive forcefulness of Paulhan's writing. While it is perhaps true that Paulhan, as many people felt at the time, was being politically disingenuous, any reading of his text also needs to take into account the sections that add to, and affect significantly, the explicit argument. If France was divided between Collaboration and Resistance, Pétain and de Gaulle, then these could be seen, according to Paulhan, as two halves of the *patrie*, which he defines variously as physical and spiritual, sentimental and intellectual, contingent form and inner essence, and carrying it across into the linguistic realm, words and ideas. Any "side" that claimed to be the unique representative of the *patrie* would, according to Paulhan, be indulging in partisanship, not patriotism: "Du simple point de vue de la *patrie*, ils se valent: c'est blanc bonnet et bonnet blanc" (From the simple point of view of the *patrie*, they are equivalent: it's *blanc bonnet et bonnet blanc*) (WC, 350). Now, anyone who has read Paulhan's early writings from his time on Madagascar will know that proverbs are not to be taken lightly, but in Paulhan's eyes have an unusual and enigmatic force to them. Indeed, much of his later interest in clichés and commonplace expressions originated in his work on Malagasy proverbs. The fact that Paulhan should, then, invoke a proverb at this point in his text is not a matter of indifference. It is in fact the crucial turning point of the text, a pivotal moment which will lead us either back out into Mehlman's historically overdetermined context, or further into the text's articulation of the questions it raises. It works as a rather neat summary of Paulhan's sets of parallels, and what it *means* is something like "It's six of one and half a dozen of the other," with the underlying notion of there being two equally acceptable ways of thinking of the same thing, the choice between them making no difference. In fact the problem of *translating* this proverb, as we shall see, is itself part of what is at stake. Why it works in French is, of course, that whether *blanc* precedes or follows the noun does not really affect the meaning. But any translation, even any approximately synonymous idiom in French, would not only diminish the specifically proverbial flavor of the original, but would also lose the symmetrical reversal of the syntax (the trope of hyperbaton), that is itself not only an example, but also an *enactment* of the reversibility that structures Paulhan's argument. It only works *within the context* of the essay, and as such it supplements the semantic or political argument with a kind of syntactical excess.

Whether or not we read the gap opened up by this textual performance of the proverb determines the way in which we read the rest of the text, which contains a number of other linguistic analogies or allegories. One such allegory is Paulhan's discussion of invented languages such as Esperanto, which claims to be a language that is unfailingly and universally comprehensible. Similarly—and this is where the allegory ties in with the "main" argument of the text—the kind of purge of French literature proposed by the CNE is an attempt to perfect and purify the *patrie*, to separate the wheat from the chaff, and in terms of language, to divide it into a part that is "essential" and a part that is "dispensable." Paulhan goes very much against the grain of the predominant ideology of the time (he critiques, among other things, the universalizing ideals of the UNO) when he states that "What attaches us to a language and makes us want to speak it is not that it is perfect" (WC, 324), and he argues passionately for a language that is rich with confusion, errors, baroque turns of phrase, and adopted foreign words, comparing it to a masked ball. The tolerance of antipatriots is, according to Paulhan, a sign of a healthy democracy, and a healthy *patrie* ("Anti-patriots are a *patrie*'s luxury" [329]). Just as there is no perfect language (in fact, he sees it as being constitutively imperfect), so there is no perfect *patrie*. Paulhan is determined to safeguard the mystery of differences between languages (and nations) since this mystery is also a guarantee of the existence of the difference within languages (and nations). Yet how can we read the difference within language (between exposition and performance, semantics and syntax, *blanc bonnet* and *bonnet blanc*), when this difference makes no difference, when it exemplifies the mystery of the reversibility of *indifference*? Perhaps the only way to read it is as the very mark of difference itself. It is precisely the proverb's point of resistance to any translation which could be said to underpin, at a microcosmic level, the larger political claim to a national linguistic identity, the difference within language that marks the difference between languages.

With this plea for a certain untranslatability as the condition of possibility of translation, it becomes clear that the text and its various analogies are not reducible to the rhetorical structure of a reversible chiasmus, a neutralization of opposites. The linguistic allegories are not just examples—in German, *Beispiel*, frivolous by-play to the serious body of the text—which would mean they would in effect be cancelled out, swallowed up by the apparent argument of political indifference, but they are themselves the primary evidence for the text's affirmation of linguistic and national difference. At this point we already find a number of echoes within Derrida's own writings on the structure of the chiasmus. As Derrida reminds us in *Positions*, and throughout *Dissemination*, the chiasmus is essentially *dissymmetrical*, "a kind of fork . . . moreover, unequal, one of the points extending its range further than the other" (*Pos*, 70). It would be analogous, therefore, to the structure of the hymen or the pharmakon, or *la différance*, to the extent that its doubleness is marked by a supplementary re-mark, which is neither inside nor outside, but is that which makes the chiasmic structure possible. This supplementary fold of the chiasmus might indeed, if we hear the fold of the *pli* in "application," point to the dissymmetrical chiasmus as the very figure of the "application" of deconstruction. It indicates, at any rate, how we might begin to think of Derrida "applying" Paulhan, or Paulhan "applying" grammatology before the letter. To put the question another way, we might ask how

Derrida "applies to" Paulhan, and the direction a more productive critical dialogue between their respective texts might take.

Paulhan's texts cannot, as I have argued, simply be reduced to their explicit polemical subject matter or themes, but must be read as a writing that engages and exemplifies the very problematic it elaborates. An inattentiveness to the narrative dynamic of the texts themselves prohibits a casually metonymic chain of associations leading from "reversibility," for example, as it operates in Paulhan's texts, to "applied grammatology," "undecidability," and "dissemination." Thus, for example, when Mehlman reads Paulhan's *Fleurs de Tarbes* as initiating the future of French criticism ("what Paulhan calls *clichés, what has been more generally thematized as écriture*"; my highlighting), he fails to take into account the more disruptive play of the text itself (BC, 12). To return to the questions raised by Paulhan's *De la paille et du grain*, for example, we saw that for Paulhan the postwar purge could be read at an empirical level as the necessity of the reduction of the duplicity or doubleness of France to a single essence. At the linguistic level this would function in a similar manner, insofar as most contemporary readings of Paulhan's texts are motivated by a tendency to efface the radical undecidability which is their very theoretical foundation. This act of effacement, whereby the contingent is expelled in order to consolidate the assumed priority of the essential, is itself not accidental, but is, as Derrida has argued in "Plato's Pharmacy," part of a long and well-established philosophical tradition (D, 61–171). Derrida's focus on the radical ambivalence of *pharmakon*, as a disruption of the Platonic privileging of presence, points to a more generalized disruptiveness occasioned by writing. According to Derrida, however, it is precisely the strange, ambivalent logic of writing that opens up and makes possible the very distinction between language and presence. Paulhan's ambiguity—which is quite different from a simple semantic conflict—is from a theoretical perspective of a similar order to the ambiguity of a term such as *pharmakon*. If anything, what Derrida's and Paulhan's texts have in common is precisely a skepticism toward, or an ironization of, intellectual history structured as a continuous sequence of influences, which Mehlman's argument relies upon (including, most pertinently, the claim of a direct thread linking Paulhan to Derrida). In his reading of the connection between Paulhan and Derrida, Mehlman is not wholly off the mark, but very precisely halfway off the mark. He effectively decontextualizes Paulhan by only reading the "wheat" of his text, not its "chaff," or reduces its "chaff" to its "wheat," and its radical doubleness to a single historically overdetermined essence, which allows him to project a hypothetical series of cause and effect. If we pay attention to Paulhan's textual performance we see how it undoes Mehlman's neat pattern of historical continuity, which he develops in his article on de Man as follows: "Between Paulhan, on the one hand, claiming his collaborators were originally resisters and his resisters collaborators, and Derrida, on the other, that Heidegger was a Nazi only to the extent that he was a humanist and Husserl and Valéry humanists only to the extent they were (Eurocentric) racists, the continuity seems to be so substantial as to be conclusive" (Per, 330). Mehlman's argument here relies on the very chiasmic structures that the writings of Paulhan and Derrida invoke, but which they do so precisely in order to *dis*articulate.

What is perhaps more intriguing about Mehlman's argument, however, is not just that it involves a decontextualized exposition, and a serious misreading of Paulhan, but that he inscribes himself as an important protagonist in the narratives he is constructing. His bemoaning of the fate of deconstruction would not be nearly so interesting if he did not also claim to be himself one of its chief advocates. In his rejoinder to Ann Smock's hard-hitting reply to "Writing and Deference," Mehlman states: "the person of Derrida, to whom my intellectual debt . . . should be obvious" (R, 163). While it is certainly true that he was one of the first critics in the United States to disseminate Derrida's thought and to assimilate his critical practises, he presents himself, rather hubristically, as a more faithful follower of Derrida than the legions of adulators who have "domesticated" Derrida's thought. As he says at the end of "Writing and Deference": "That my scenario—of Deconstruction as a forgetting of the perils engaged by Paulhan—requires a few vigorous intertextual leaps to achieve its coherence has seemed to me more to recommend than to invalidate the effort. My sense is that the discourse of difference will be able to make good its claims to heterogeneity only on the condition of running just such interpretative risks" (12). What he is saying, in other words, is that he is reasserting the original energy and purpose of deconstruction, which has been lost as it has been appropriated by its acolytes. The argument of "Writing and Deference," while intended as a critique of the fate of deconstruction, is thus at the same time proposed as an *example* of "applied Derrida."

What is deconstruction for Mehlman, then? It is "bricolage and/or the technique of reinscription," "vigorous intertextual leaps," "heterogeneity," and "interpretative risks" (R, 163). It seems that "applying Derrida" for him involves juxtaposing apparently disconnected texts and historical events, the more startlingly unlikely the better, and describing them in terms of analogies. In fact, his essay precisely reverses the process he describes as the inevitable shift from metaphor to metonymy, analogy to sequence ("that is, where the striking parallels between the different relations might be construable as part of a historical continuum" [R, 163]). By placing himself within the narrative he is setting up, and conceiving of this narrative in rhetorical terms, as an interplay between metaphor and metonymy, his own argument is caught in precisely the kind of chiasmic structure he sees as determining the relationship between Paulhan and Derrida (and Paulhan understood better than most that metaphor and metonymy are endlessly reversible tropes). If by claiming his text is a "purer" form of deconstruction because of its more vigorous intertextuality, its bolder interpretative risks, he appears to be blind to the effect of this metonymic reinscription of his own text into the narrative of deconstruction's supposed decline. He reads metonymy as metaphor (taking the example of his own contingent practise as the essential "truth" about deconstruction), just as he avoids reading Paulhan's (and Derrida's) texts by decontextualizing and thematizing them. A more perceptive reading of both these writers would reveal that they are in fact keenly aware of this very dynamic, as I hope to demonstrate in a little while by looking at one of Paulhan's short texts. The process of restoring a more authentic force to language is in fact a concern deconstruction is all too familiar with, and in Paulhan's critical writing it is described in terms of the Terrorist attempt to rid language of its clichés, its worn-out expressions, its impurities (all of which form the ever-increasing burden of Rhetoric's legacy), and as a nostalgic yearning for a kind of original expressiveness, which in its most extreme form would bypass language altogether.

Toward the end of his article "Writing and Deference," Mehlman locates another analogy as supplementary proof of his argument, and in doing so in fact pushes the polemic (perhaps unwittingly) beyond the personal or anecdotal (disguised as a serious reflection on history, politics, and ethics), and takes it on to more challenging theoretical territory. The discussion of Heller's admiration of Paulhan turns to the "lessons" in Cubist painting given by the latter to the former, and to Heller's descriptions in his memoirs of being taken by Paulhan to visit Picasso's apartment during the war. Heller was overwhelmed by the violent energy of the works he saw, but claimed that Paulhan gradually initiated him into mysteries of Modern Art by reading to him early drafts of what was to become his study on Braque, *Braque le patron* [*Braque the Boss*] (1970, 11–41). According to Mehlman, Paulhan's emphasis on the muted, mellowed lines of Braque's paintings in contrast to Picasso's more explosive use of form and color could be read as a form of domestication. He writes: "Paulhan's aesthetic, that is, allowed the *Sonderführer* to 'domesticate' the demonic reality of the situation, of the Nazi cause . . . " (WrDe, 11). This reference is too allusive to allow for any serious consideration of Paulhan's "aesthetic" (Paulhan was if fact one of the writers who did the most to promote Cubist and Modern art in France between the 1920s and 1950s), but there *was* a curious convergence of concerns of Paulhan during the war which seems to lend weight to Mehlman's argument. Paulhan wrote his most important texts on Rhetoric about the same time as his important studies of Cubist and Modern Art, that is, during the Occupation, and this dual interest would seem to confirm his willful indifference to the historical and political circumstances of the time, or his readiness to be distracted by such "frivolous pursuits," when more serious matters should have absorbed his attention. Yet his essays on Cubism and Modern Art are in fact inextricably linked to his other writings in ways that are not immediately apparent. Cubism is read by Paulhan as an artistic version of the "terrorist" impulse, a kind of revolutionary overthrow of classical perspective. One can see how such a reading would intersect his political and linguistic theories. In *Les Fleurs de Tarbes* [The Flowers of Tarbes], Paulhan talks of Terror's suspicion of Rhetoric's "beauty machine" [machine à beauté], in which aesthetic considerations were regarded as inessential, superfluous, in the same way that the "flowers of Rhetoric" were seen as the dispensable parts of language when compared to their more serious literal counterparts (1971). Rhetoric and Aesthetics are thus tightly interwoven in Paulhan's writing as part of a single problematic, and I'd like to sketch out how this is dramatized textually by reading a short piece written by Paulhan during the Occupation, called "Manie." This text will provide a focus for thinking about the relationship of aesthetics to domestication, within the context of a possible genealogy connecting Paulhan and Derrida.

"Manie" means "mania," but also describes an obsessive habit, or what one might call a kind of everyday repetition compulsion. The text, like the others in the collection in which it appears entitled *Les Causes célèbres*, is based on a paradox, which in this case is the freshness one can find in the routine of everyday life.[5] The text presents a domestic scene in the fairly ordinary life of a couple whom we take to be Paulhan and his wife, Germaine. The whole text illustrates a favourite theme of Paulhan, the renewal one can find *within* habits. This regeneration is in "Manie" a literal—albeit somewhat banal— *reawakening*, after a description of how the narrator and his wife now habitually *fall asleep*. Linguistically, the text thus subscribes to the "terrorist" project of giving back dead, or sleepy, metaphors their original force. This is phrased in the last paragraph as the importance, or wisdom, of naming modestly, appropriately, or *properly*. The last line— "Not to mention that it is wise to give things, and people, their most modest name" [Sans compter qu'il est prudent de donner aux choses, et aux personnes, leur nom le plus modeste]—is often quoted in the context of discussions of Paulhan's celebrated modesty, and the plain, everyday language appears to exemplify the very principle of modesty it advocates. The greatest pressure in the text to conform to its own linguistic imperative comes with the question of the name of the narrator's wife, Manie, whose "proper" name—Germaine—was in fact the name of Paulhan's wife. He gives "several reasons" [plusieurs raisons] for renaming her Manie:

> I have several reasons for naming her Manie. First of all, her name is Germaine, from which I got Maine. Then, it is true that love is a mania, I do not think of her with reason.

What are we to make of these reasons? It seems natural enough, to begin with, that since "it is true that love is a mania" [il est vrai que l'amour est une manie] and "I do not think of her with reason" [Je ne songe pas à elle avec raison], he should choose this name. But what kind of "reasons" are these if they depend on a fundamental *irrationality*? There is moreover no reason why Germaine should necessarily lead to Manie, since one could equally well come up with several other anagrams. These "reasons" thus reveal themselves on some level to be very unreasonable and destabilize the text's "modesty." In reading the text more attentively, its more disruptive features, which cannot be covered over for long, come to the fore. On a purely thematic level, there are the "cracks in the economic edifice," and the violent irruption of the tree into the couple's cozy interior. If we pause to reread the opening lines again—"After twenty years of marriage, we have all of a sudden adopted a new habit" [Après vingt ans de mariage, nous avons pris tout d'un coup une nouvelle habitude]—it dawns on us what is awry. Habit is not something that can be acquired "all of a sudden."

The paradoxical reversal of habit and sudden change brings into focus the principal rhetorical operation of the text, that is, metalepsis, or the reversal of cause and effect (which is also a kind of chiasmus). The naming of Manie can be read as a sort of metalepsis, and the term is often used, in classical rhetoric, to describe the inversion of the metonymic relation between name and thing, in which the thing (cause) would, once the inversion has taken place, be determined by the name

(effect). On one level her name is determined according to a logic of
predication ("love is a mania, I do not think of her with reason"), but
on the level of the letter it is possibly determined as a purely textual
effect. The reversal of the normal order—the name Manie as an ana-
gram ought to make sense only *after* it has been semantically motivated—is precisely the kind of inversion that metalepsis can account
for. It could likewise explain the reversal of habit and sudden change
that comes at the beginning of the text. The text is, however, also
marked by a proliferation of other names, such as the names of the
animals and of the oak tree, the polygamous Dessaulle and his five
wives, and a name we possibly gloss over too quickly, the "rapidex,"
which is the furniture polish the narrator uses:

> I woke Manie up to show her the tree. She was as surprised as I was.
> Before breakfast, she wanted to try the rapidex, which we bought
> yesterday. It's a furniture polish which will let us wipe away the marks
> I made on the table (Manie claims) when I put dishes down on it that
> were too hot.
>     The result was not conclusive. However, the marks seem to me
> more pleasant to look at.

All of the conflicting tensions of the text seem to come together in
the "rapidex." It both exemplifies the movement between proper and
common name, or between metaphor and metonymy (the brand name
of the furniture polish of the 1940s in France becomes the common
name "le rapidex," just as we often refer to all paper tissues as
"Kleenex," for example, and is infinitely reproducible, just as the
days and nights pass by, in an endless sequential series); likewise it
allows for the onomastic pun linking the proper name Manie to the
abstract noun *manie* and also—perhaps most importantly—serves as
a kind of domesticating force, covering over the marks left as a result
of the narrator's domestic accidents. The rapidex acts in fact like a
kind of aestheticizing of the marks, it makes them "more pleasant to
look at" [plus agréables à regarder]. An initial reading would therefore see rhetoric and aesthetics as recuperative, covering over the
discontinuities and the accidents of life, as one might cover over the
mistakes of one's past (this would in effect be Mehlman's reading,
that is, deconstruction covering over its guilty origins). But a more
persistent reading, one that attempted to account for this trace within
the text, would take these accidental marks, following Derrida, as
the very inscription of the text itself as historical event, the materiality of the letter as a supplementary but necessary re-mark, which
no amount of polishing could efface.[6]

The "proper naming" implied by modesty, in a gesture of recuperation and appropriation, would thus be doubled by a certain impropriety. Indeed, this is built into the very logic of "modesty," as Paulhan himself notes on several occasions. The moment the claim is made to modesty, he explains, the moment modesty names itself in other words, it is already something of a boast, it already takes the form of self-recognition, of self-congratulation, and is anything but modest. The claim to modesty is always necessarily excessive to what is being stated. Indeed, it is a hyperbole, or a "mania" of sorts. The text is thus always both deficient to itself (as a modest description) as well as always in excess of itself (as a kind of manic inscription), always both litotes and hyperbole, modesty and mania, but never able to coincide with itself, to be modest in the sense of adequate or proper. This textual noncoincidence, as it turns out, is precisely how Derrida describes the logic of the proper in *The Post Card*—as a necessary "disappropriation" or "exappropriation" which is built into the very possibility of the proper name, or of naming properly. *The Post Card* , and particularly the section "To Speculate—On Freud," is an extended reflection on structures of genealogy, specifically in relation to Freud's ancestry or legacy. The economy of genealogy is defined by Derrida as the restricted economy of the *logos* or *oikos*, what Derrida terms "the proper as domestico-familial" (*PC*, 300). It is perhaps no accident, in light of an "exappropriative" reading of "Manie," that Derrida's discussion of structures of "legation" should also pass through an analysis of the *fort-da* game as a repetition compulsion, or a kind of "manie." If, according to Derrida, the proper name underwrites the very possibility of ancestry, guaranteeing the metonymic repetition that structures relationships of genealogical descendence, then this is a logic Paulhan's text undoes (and indeed in "Manie" there is a disputed and very problematic inheritance, the one left by the polygamous Dessaulle, which interrupts the direct line of descendence).

What would this process of the text's undoing of its own linguistic logic imply for the relationship of ancestry that Mehlman traces between Paulhan and Derrida? If it is true that Paulhan could be said to "apply" Derrida "before the letter," as it were, this chronological impossibility is in fact quite easily recuperable both in Paulhan's terms (as a metaleptic reversal of cause and effect) and in Derrida's (as the back and forth movement, the fort/da of the "writing couple," Plato and Socrates, in *The Post Card*). This reversiblity would allow Derrida to "precede" Paulhan, in the same way that a translation can precede the original, program its reception, and so on. This inversion, however, would not simply be a reversible chiasmus, but would be radically dissymmetrical or heterogeneous, and one that would require not the economy of the proper name—in "Manie," as we have seen, there are "cracks in the economic edifice"—but rather the logic of *debt* as Derrida articulates it in *Specters of Marx*, what he terms, talking of Marx's legacy, "the radical and necessary heterogeneity of an inheritance" (*SM*, 16). This other logic of inheritance is one that has to pass through a kind of reading: "If the readability of a legacy were given, natural, transparent, univocal, if it did not call for and at the same time defy interpretation, one would never have anything to inherit from it (*on n'aurait jamais à en hériter*)" (*SM*, 16). The question with which we started out, then, could be formulated as a question of Paulhan's legacy. Not just "What is Paulhan's legacy?" but more importantly, "How do we read Paulhan's legacy?"

To return to Mehlman's own narrative of Paulhan's legacy as a debt squandered by Derrida and his followers, we might recapitulate as follows. According to Mehlman, Derridean deconstruction is *already* apparent in Paulhan's writings, particularly during and after World War II, an intellectual heritage that contaminates it by metonymic association with a politics of collaboration. This is said to take the form of an amnesic erasure of the historical specificity, and consequently of the ethical responsibility to the "time" and the circumstances of writing. My own reading of Paulhan, and of Mehlman's reading of Paulhan as a precursor of Derrida, has argued that any juxtaposition of the two writers has to take into account a far more radically disruptive heterogeneity than the thematized version Mehlman evokes in his various scenarios. This heterogeneity undoes the familiar economy of historical influences, and suggests instead that the singularity of a text's inscription is that which *remains*, to be read, in the sense of the text's irrecuperable though constitutive trace or re-mark, and which Derrida has, in his more recent meditations, variously referred to as "cinders," "shibboleth," "specter," and "archive." Mehlman's reading, in constructing an ingenious network of ancestry and mutual contamination, has the effect of domesticating and thereby effacing this irreducible singularity of the texts in question. One consequence of this is a form of literary history that blocks access to the deeper, hidden veins of energy circulating among texts, an energy that deconstruction has always sought to exploit. At the same time it covers over the possibility of a history that might be conceived of as a problematic, heterogeneous, nondialectical, nonmetonymic series of singular events of writing and of reading.

# NOTES

1. The texts in question are: "Blanchot at *Combat*," in *Legacies of Anti–Semitism in France* (1983; hereafter BC); "Deconstruction, Literature, History: The Case of *L'arrêt de mort*," *Proceedings of the Northeastern University Center for Literary Studies*, Volume 2, 1984, 33–53 (hereafter DLH); "Writing and Deference: The Politics of Literary Adulation," *Representations* 15 (Spring 1986): 1–14, 141–145 (hereafter WrDe); " 'Response' to 'More on Writing and Deference'," *Representations* 18 (Spring 1987): 162–164 (hereafter R); "Perspectives on De Man and *Le Soir*," *Responses: On Paul de Man's Wartime Journalism* (1989, 324–333) (hereafter Per).

2. I have gone into the complex relations between Paulhan and Blanchot elsewhere, in my "Noncoincidences: Paulhan in the text of Blanchot," forthcoming *Yale French Studies* issue on Blanchot, and my forthcoming book *Defying Gravity: Jean Paulhan's Interventions in Twentieth Century French Intellectual History*.

3. See Gerhard Heller, *Un Allemand à Paris* (1981).

4. "De la paille et du grain," in *Oeuvres complètes de Jean Paulhan, volume 5* (1970), 313–406 (hereafter WC). For a more extensive reading of Paulhan's text, see my "Some Wheat and Some Chaff: Jean Paulhan and the Post-War Literary Purge in France," *Studies in Twentieth Century Literature* 16: 2 (Summer 1992): 247–263.

5. "Manie," *Les Causes célèbres* (1982, 137–139, 1944 for original text). Present English translation by Christine Moneera Laennec and Michael Syrotinski. Full text of French original and English translation appear in Michael Syrotinski, *Defying Gravity* (1998).

6. At several points in his essays on art, Paulhan describes his aesthetics as just such a form of anti-aesthetics, an aesthetics of the trace, the remains, the leftovers. See, for example, Paulhan's writings on Cubist painting, collected in *La Peinture cubiste*, ed. Jean-Claude Zylberstein (1990). We might also read this text attentive to what Derrida says in *Schibboleth pour Paul Celan* (1986) about the singularity of a text's "datation interne" [internal dating], which is a kind of tracing in time that is *other* than the cyclical repetition of an anniversary.

# CHAPTER 6

# I Remember... (Points of Suspension)

JESSICA MAYNARD

> Writing denies itself to me. Hence plan for autobiographical investigations. Not biography but investigation and detection of the smallest component parts. Out of these I will then construct myself, as one whose house is unsafe wants to build a safe one next to it, if possible out of the material of the old one. What is bad, admittedly, is if in the midst of building his strength gives out and now, instead of one house, unsafe but yet complete, he has one half-destroyed and one half-finished house, that is to say, nothing.
>
> —Franz Kafka

## THE DEMAND FOR NARRATIVE

It is perhaps a similar act of reconstitution that Georges Perec attempts in *W ou Le Souvenir d'Enfance* (*W or the Memory of Childhood*, 3),[1] committing himself, for want of any better resource, to the "smallest component parts," and hoping, by such fidelity to the inessential—the trace, the fragmented recollection, the trivial—to reach the essential. But his text, like Kafka's house, turns out to be double. Or, as an author's note on the back cover tells us, the text is braided, two strands that, though they may seem disconnected, are nevertheless "inextricablement enchevêtres." This is not to say, however, that there is a metadiscourse lurking in the wings, ready to rescue this text from duplicity and self-estrangement. The two strands do not "resolve" themselves into a harmonious whole but remain, like the two versions of Kafka's house, insufficient in themselves; sufficient only perhaps in the *activity* of building and unbuilding that exists between them.

Perec begins:

> *J'ai longtemps hesité avant d'entreprendre le récit de mon voyage a W. Je m'y resous aujourd'hui, poussé par une nécessité impérieuse, persuadé que les évènements dont j'ai été le témoin doivent être révélés et mis en lumière.* (WSE, 9)

> [*For years I put off telling the tale of my voyage to W. Today, impelled by a commanding necessity and convinced that the events to which I was witness must be revealed and brought to light, I resolve to defer it no longer.*] (WMC, 3)

With these words, the writer surrenders to a kind of narrative compulsion, an obligation that has long been evaded and which must now, finally, be honored. This seems to be no voluntary undertaking, no spontaneous production; it is, he says, the reponse to "une nécessité impérieuse" or what Derrida calls the *"demand for narrative"*:

> When I say *demande* I mean something closer to the English "demand" than to a mere request: inquistorial insistence, an order, a petition. To know (before we know) what narrative is, the narrativity of narrative, we should perhaps first recount, return to the scene of one origin of narrative, to the narrative of one origin of narrative (will that still be a narrative?), to that scene that mobilizes various forces, or if you prefer various agencies or "subjects," some of which *demand* the narrative of the other, seek to extort it from him, like a secret-less secret, something that they call the truth about what has taken place: "Tell us exactly what happened" (LOBL, 260)

There is a violence inherent in such a "putting-to-the question," which can serve as "an instrument of torture working to wring the narrative out of one." Even in its most innocent, nonauthoritarian guises, the dynamic of question-and-answer carries within it traces of this violence, even in those liberal "refinements for making (and even letting) one talk that are unsurpassed in neutrality and politeness" (LOBL, 261). In Perec's case, the scene is of one of self-interrogation, and the task an autobiographical one.

*W ou le Souvenir d'Enfance* attempts to meet the demand for narrative, the demand that Perec remember his childhood. It is a demand that Perec has long evaded. For a long time, he tells us, he has settled for history with a capital H, the history of school textbooks: the war, the camps. For a long time he reduced his early years to one curt paragraph: "Je n'ai pas de souvenirs d'enfance. Jusqu'à ma douzième année à peu près, mon histoire tient en quelques lignes: j'ai perdu mon père a quatre ans, ma mère à six; j'ai passé la guerre dans diverses pensions de Villard-de-Lans. En 1945, la soeur de mon père et son mari m'adoptèrent" (*WSE*, 9) [I have no childhood memories. Up to my twelfth year or thereabouts, my story comes to barely a couple of lines: I lost my father at four, my mother at six; I spent the war in various boarding houses at Villard-de-Lans. In 1945, my father's sister and her husband adopted me (*WMC*, 3)].

Or then again, in 1970, in a short piece published as "Je suis né" (Jse 1990), he finds himself at that familiar point of departure, a sticking point—"I was born in 1936." The question, he says, is not so much why continue, as how. He toys for a moment with the journalist's six–point formula: what, who, when, where, how, and why?:

> Quoi? Je suis né.
>
> Qui? Je.
>
> Quand? Le 7 mars 1936.
>
> Plus précisement? Je ne sais pas l'heure; il faudrait (faudra) que je regarde sur un bulletin d'état civil. Disons 9 heures du soir. Il faudra aussi que j'aille un jour à la BN prendre quelques quotidiens de ce jour et regarder ce qui s'est passé. (Jse, 12)
>
> [What? I was born.
>
> Who? I.
>
> When? March 7th, 1936.
>
> A bit more precisely? I don't know the exact time; I'd have to (will have to) consult an identity document. Let's say nine o'clock at night. I'll also have to go to the Bibliothèque Nationale one day to take down some background details about that day and see what happened.]

The problem is already apparent. The answers to these questions do not supply fixed limits to identity, but send this writer chasing after documentary support, state authentication, to the archive, prompting him to think about what must be done *in future*—what I will have to do—in order to secure knowledge of the past. How *would* it be possible to recover that one moment, when it falls under so many jurisdictions? This is Derrida pressed on a similar point in an interview:

> You go as far to say: "it is up to you [*il vous revient*]" to say when you are born. No, if there is anything that cannot be "up to me," then this is it, whether we're talking about what you call "biological birth" transferred to the objectivity of the public record, or "true birth." "I was born": this is one of the most singular expressions I know, especially in its French grammatical form. . . . I would prefer, instead of answering you directly, to begin an interminable analysis of the phrase "*je, je suis, je suis né*" in which the tense is not given. Anxiety will never be

dispelled on this subject, for the event that is thereby designated can herald itself in me only in the future: "I am (not yet) born," but the future has the form of a past which I will never have witnessed and which for this reason remains always promised—and moreover also multiple. Who ever said that one was born just once? But how can one deny that through all the different promised births, it is a single and same time, the unique time, that insists and is repeated forever? (*P.* . . , 339–340)

Derrida here draws attention to how the syntactic necessity of "I am born" gives rise to the semantic paradox of a subject who, by the very sequence of words on page, precedes his own birth: the subject who is "not yet" born. "I am born" asserts a seemingly impossible chronology which must also, at the same time, be the condition for the subject's possibility. The French grammatical feature of a perfect tense formed by the auxiliary verb in the present tense ("Je suis né" as both "I was born" and "I am born") presents an oddity. What lies ahead, says Derrida, is expressed in terms of the past—a past that, as Perec also suggests, will be constituted of things "I will have to do," a past or a subjectivity that may well be multiple and inexhaustible, and not confined to one point of origin.

This takes us to Derrida's understanding of anamnesis, not the act of remembering what was lost or buried and is now recovered, but the act of construction whereby the past is only present through the future. This past, indeed, cannot strictly be said ever to have been present, as Freud maintained of "screen" memories:

Our childhood memories show us our earliest years not as they were but as they appeared at the later periods when the memories were aroused. In these periods of arousal, the childhood memories did not, as people are accustomed to say, *emerge*; they were *formed* at that time (1899, 322).

Such a distinction is also apparent in Hume's earlier attempt to theorize self-identity, an attempt that incidentally left Hume in a state of bewilderment, "involv'd," he said, "in such a labyrinth" that he was unable to provide a final, satisfactory account. Hume's position is that memory is not so much the receptacle for identity, as part of a dynamic interplay between causality and identity. In any attempt to affirm unitary identity, he argues, an appreciation of causality compensates for lapses of memory. In other words, where recollection falls down, inference makes good the shortcoming. Identity for Hume is partly constituted by necessary fictions:

For how few of our past actions are there of which we have any memory? Who can tell me, for instance, what were his thoughts and actions on the first of *January* 1715, the 11th of *March* 1719, and the 3d of *August* 1733? Or will he affirm, because he has entirely forgot the incidents of these days, that the present self is not the same person with the self of that time? In this view, therefore, memory does not so much *produce* as *discover* personal identity, by showing us the relation of cause and effect among our different perceptions. 'Twill be incumbent on those, who affirm that memory produces entirely our personal identity, to give a reason why we can thus extend our identity beyond our memory. (Hume 1978, 262)

By "produce," Hume can be taken to mean "produce from somewhere," the assumption being that identity is already present and can be located in the form of perceptions, experiences, ideas which merely need to be unearthed. Anamnesis does not refer to this form of memory, as Derrida would assert; it does not stand as a corrective for or preemptive action against forgetfulness.[2] This latter would be memory as systematic application, as the proliferation of records and archives associated with writing, and not memory as seemingly magical conjuration, a faculty that has the power to summon up the genie of the past, as Proust does, from present fragments.[3] Memory as prosthetic enhancement, as the "bad" drug of writing, poses a threat to transcendental truth, being regarded, says Derrida in "Plato's Pharmacy," as "the substitution of the mnemonic device for live memory . . . the passive, mechanical 'by heart' for the active reanimation of knowledge, for its reproduction in the present" (*D*, 108). In this sense of involuntarism, this notion of an act of unforgetting that is not the product of the will but something more in the nature of a visitation, there are certain correspondences to be drawn between what Beckett has called the "intellectual animism" of Proust's world, and the "active reanimation of knowledge" proposed in Derrida's discussion of Plato (Beckett 1980, 17). It might be said that the difference between this kind of "live" memory and the "archival" variety is that between repetition of the thing itself and the repetition of the repeater, which is whatever stands in for or represents this thing; between the immediacy of the object, and the object held at one remove (Beckett 1980, 111).

Hume's own privileging of the term *discover* over "produce" casts memory as more of an active, exploratory principle, creating connections and filling in gaps, hypothesizing on the basis of existing knowledge and so on: a metonymic facility working on association and contiguity, rather than a metaphoric one working on substitution. The preference is for movement and production over the stasis or rigid systemicity of the depth model. This might be a way of linking Hume's thoughts to the question of deconstruction itself. If philosophy, says Derrida, has essentially been taken up with anamnesis—the attempt to go back to origins, to recover ideality—then philosophy cannot but be infinite, "an interminable operation" which will always be concerned with what is "other" than itself:

> [F]or if there is anamnesis, it is because the memory in question is not turned towards the past, so to speak, it is not a memory that, at the end of a return across all the other anamneses, would finally reach an originary place of philosophy that would have been forgotten. The relation between forgetting and memory is much more disturbing. Memory is not just the opposite of forgetting . . . .To think memory or to think anamnesis . . . is to think things as paradoxical as the memory of the past that has not been present, the memory of the future—the movement of memory as tied to the future and not only to the past, memory turned toward the promise, toward what is coming, what is arriving, what is happening tomorrow. (*P.* . . , 381)

And yet, the narrative of identity inaugurated by "I am born" may seem to demand some form of codification, the ratifying power of "un bulletin d'état civil" which will confer on the subject a place in society, history, chronology. Perec's narrative doesn't and cannot work like this. The fascination that photos, certification, and inscriptions seem to hold in *W* can perhaps be put down to their bounded nature—a boundedness that is consistently compromised or breached. This is true of the photograph of Perec's father discussed in chapter 8, where an imperfect recollection of the photograph and the circumstances in which it was taken gives rise to a thoroughgoing series of amendments. The photo, Perec tells us, was given to him after the war, in a leather frame (*WSE,* 42). A footnote then explains: "C'est à cause de ce cadeau, je pense, que j'ai toujours cru que les cadres étaient objets précieux." (*WSE,* 50) [It's because of this present, I think, that I've always thought frames were precious objects (*WMC,* 34)]—precious perhaps because they enclose what so obviously militates against enclosure in his own text. Here is a photograph that can be said to spill out far beyond its frame, as the several pages devoted to its history and its contents testify. The reassurance that such a framing device might appear to give recurs a little later, too, when Perec visits his father's grave, finding there, in the symbolic power of the space and the inscription of his father's name and regimental number on a cross, an actuality that has previously found to be lacking, "comme si la découverte de ce miniscule espace de terre clôturait enfin cette morte que je n'avais jamais apprise, jamais éprouvée, jamais connue ni reconnue" (*WSE,* 54) [as if the discovery of this tiny patch of earth had at last put a boundary around that death which I had never learnt of, never experienced or known or acknowledged (*WMC*, 38)].

But though this memorial may seem to supply the shortfall of memory, the writer's task in *W* can never be a simple matter of reconstruction, of research, of confirming details (*préciser* is a word used frequently), of organizing information. Admittedly, Perec's vocabulary is saturated with words of almost bureaucratic circumspection; in his striving for exactitude, as Philippe Lejeune observes, he is tirelessly and even tiresomely noncommittal (Lejeune 1991, 21).[4] He displays the pedant's zeal for accurate citation (something he parodies elsewhere, in *Cantatrix Sopranica L.*), subjecting the text to a neverending procedure of factual verification, to an infinite recession of authority. There are affinities here, perhaps, with the Proust whose "proofreading habits," according to Benjamin, "were the despair of the typesetters":

> The galleys always went back covered with marginal notes, but not a single misprint had been corrected; all available space had been used for fresh text. Thus the laws of remembrance were operative even within the confines of the work. For an experienced event is finite—at any rate, confined to one sphere of experience; a remembered event is infinite, because it is only a key to everything that happened before and after it. (Benjamin 1992, 198)

Perec did not in fact alter his proofs very much; the comparison here is stylistic rather than methodological. He is an obsessive annotator, a cataloguer, apparently a neurotic seeker after precision. Each textual inaccuracy is mercilessly interrogated, each interpretation subjected to reinterpretation and so on, *ad infinitum*. There is no single pathway, no one destination for this writing, which as soon as it is written must be read and then rewritten. As a guarantee of authenticity, for example, Perec institutes a series of footnotes in order to gloss and where necessary amend an account of his parents that he wrote some years before; the effect is not to dispel inaccuracy but to breed further questions, further doubt. He remembers how he mistakenly believed his father's first name to be André—"un nom sympathique"—but later discovered it to be Icek Judko which, to him an alien denomination, something clearly un-Francophone, "ne voulait pas dire grand chose" (*WSE*, 43). What could this name mean to him, since whatever threads joined him to race and religion were to be broken? One footnote investigates the family name, Peretz, with typical efficiency dealing with matters of orthography and pronunciation; it even, economically, maps European diaspora. But the point that stands out is that even this attempted naming erases itself: it seems that Peretz, in Hebrew, means hole. After all, as Perec will say himself in an interview, "In fact, Jewishness was the mark of an absence, of a lack (the death of my parents during the war), and not of an identity (in both senses of the word)—being oneself and the same as others" (Perec 1993, 82). Or, even more briefly, "What is proper to the Jew is to have no property or essence. Jewish is not Jewish," which are Derrida's words in *Shibboleth* (*SFPC*, 37). What Perec's writing of childhood enacts but can never say—and this is the point—is that these scruples, this scribbling in the margins, far from settling "points of information," only disperse them, endowing on them new possibilities, new contexts. The laws of remembrance cannot be accommodated by the "confines of the work;" as Perec's perverse insistence on factual decorum shows, they breach the boundaries of the page, by the endless bifurcation of the footnote, its capacity always to take a new turn, a detour.

These memories resist any rationale of autobiographical organization; they are not necessarily those episodes, those moments of significance and wholeness—epiphanies—that, according the autobiographer's art, may be lined up to illustrate the evolution of a character, to establish continuities, genesis, history. In fact, the memories are almost dull, inspiring the reader with impatience. They are not necessarily the "ore" of meaning; rather, they are what is always contiguous to something else, as Freud says of shams: "[T]hey are not made of gold themselves but have lain beside something that is made of gold. The same simile might well be applied to some of the experiences of childhood which have been retained in the memory" (1899, 301–32). What was important here for Freud was the act of bridging, stepping across from sham to gold itself, from inessential to essential. Like Hume, he emphasized the importance of an associative mechanism.

## NARRATIVE SEQUENCES

The typography of *W* announces two narrative sequences. They are presented alternately, and the reader must vacillate, uneasily, between them. There is no reassuring rhythm of reading here, only dislocation, tiresome discontinuity, a certain sluggishness, even, in execution. This is no territory for Derrida's "bad" reader, the one who has already "decided upon deciding" in advance. But it is also, as Lejeune admits, quite difficult not to be the bad reader, at least at first. Lejeune talks of these interleaved typographies as going against the grain of the "plaisir romanesque," as imposing on the reader a pun-

a comic book illustration featuring Charlie Chaplin in a parachute and Perec with a broken arm in a sling. "Un triple trait parcourt ce souvenir," Perec writes:

> parachute, bras en écharpe, bandage herniaire: cela tient de la suspension, du soutien, presque de prosthèse. Pour être, besoin d'étai. Seize ans plus tard, en 1958, lorsque les hasards du service militaire ont fait de moi un éphémère parachutiste, je pus lire, dans la minute même du saut, un text déchiffré de ce souvenir: je fus précipité dans le vide; tous les fils furent rompus; je tombai, seul and sans soutien. Le parachute s'ouvrit. La corolle se déploya, fragile et sûr suspens avant la chute maîtrisée. (*WSE*, 77)

> [parachute, sling, truss: it suggests suspension, support, almost artificial limbs. To be, I need a prop. Sixteen years later, in 1958, when, by chance, military service briefly made a parachutist of me, I suddenly saw, in the very instant of jumping, one way of deciphering the text of this memory: I was plunged into nothingness; all the threads were broken; I fell, on my own, without any support. The parachute opened. The canopy unfurled, a fragile and firm suspense before the controlled descent.] (*WMC*, 55)

Perec's descent is no easy course; in fact, he falls into a void, that is, until he finds the "fragile et sûr suspens" of writing.

After all, it is an absence or what may euphemistically but also, for want of a better word, be termed a "disappearance" about which Perec is writing. The only memory of his mother that Perec retains is her seeing him off into evacuation at the Gare de Lyon. It is presumed that she was murdered at Auschwitz, but there is no grave and she is only officially declared dead on 13 October 1958, some fifteen years after the event, all of which suggests how inappropriate it may be to think in terms of a precise "moment" of death. So it is perhaps for these reasons that this disappearance is best indicated by those punctuation marks that separate, or join, or both, the first half of *W* from the second. These "points de suspension" are not a poor substitute for speech, a lesser, baser form of expression; in fact it may only be writing—and in particular a mark the very meaning of which is that it has no phonic life at all—which in this instance can enact the impossibility of doing justice to the unspeakable.

The voyage to the island of W, in thrall to an Olympian ideal, a society whose only law is a systematically administered injustice, where caprice is written into the rules, does not take much deciphering, especially as the chapters in italics intensify in their horror. But what is most striking is what Bernard Magné has called the "suturing" between this dystopian vision and the autobiographical fragments that accompany and interrupt it. Magné is referring to certain thematic, incidental, and lexical correspondences between the alternating texts, a sort of seepage of words and associations. One particular area in which these sutures are most apparent at a lexical level is that concerned with balance.[7] Perec recalled he was a rickety child. So too are those inhabitants of *W* who, incapable of achieving sporting triumph, are turned into a travesty of athleticism, made to perform a series of child's races:

> [L]e 200 mètres se court à cloche-pied, le 1500 mètres est un course en sac, la planche d'appel du saut en longueur est souvent dangereusement savonnée, etc . . . .Un novice faiseur de grimace, ou affligé de tics, ou légèrement handicapé, s'il est par exemple rachitique, ou s'il boite, ou s'il traîne un peu la patte . . . .risquera fort . . . d'être affecté a l'équipe du pentathlon ou du décathlon. (WSE, 116)

> [The 200 hundred metres is run three-legged, the 1,500 metres is a sack race, the take-off board in the long jump is often dangerously slippery, etc . . . A novice who pulls faces, or suffers from a tic, or has a slight handicap he may be rickety, for instance, or have a limp or be slightly lame . . . runs a real risk . . . of being put into the pentathlon or decathlon team. (WMC, 86)

"Cloche-pied" is translated three-legged, though it may mean something closer to "hopping on one leg." Either way, it takes us to "clocher": to be cockeyed, to be defective, or, more rarely, to limp. According to the dictionary, too, "Qu'est-ce qui cloche donc?" means "What's up with you?" a question that may very well take us back to Perec himself. It should be added that, as chance would have it, the college in Turenne which Perec attended was known as le Clocher, the Belltower.

A further memory has Perec causing a bobsled accident—again, the texts seem contaminated with one another—by leaning to the left when he should have leaned to the right. The cause of this erring, this deviation to the left? A "gaucherie contrariée" or frustrated lefthandedness, he says, which was suppressed at school. This now accounts for an inability to distinguish left from right, and indeed all manner of other binaries, including metaphor and metonymy, paradigm and syntagm, Montagu and Capulet, Whig and Tory (WMC, 183).

## "GAUCHERIE" AND TESTIMONY

*W* is an experience of both "gaucherie" and testimony, and it may be significant that this is also an association encountered elsewhere.[8]

In his essay "Des boyteux" (On the Lame), Montaigne spoke approvingly of the high skeptical tone of Roman law: "Le stile à Romme portoit que cela mesme qu'un tesmoin deposoit pour l'avoir veu de ses yeux, et ce qu'un juge ordonnait de sa plus certaine science, estoit conceu en cette forme de parler: 'Il me semble" (Montaigne 1969, 241; 1991, 1165)[9] [In Rome, the legal style required that even the testimony of an eye-witness or the sentence of a judge based on his most certain knowledge had to be couched in the formula, "It seems to me that . . . "]. This was also Georges Perec's formula, and his constraint. He too was a witness who—in the absence of any final proof—could only say "perhaps," and "it is possible," and "I'm not entirely certain but . . . ," caveats that Montaigne welcomed:

> On me faict hayr les choses vray-semblables quand on me les plante pour infallibles. J'ayme ces mots, qui amollissent et moderent la temerité de nos propositions: *A l'avanture, Aucunement, Quelque, On dict, Je pense,* et semblables. Et si j'eusse eu à dresser des enfans, je leur eusse tant mis en la bouche cette façon de respondre enquesteuse, non resolutive: "Qu'est-ce à dire? Je ne l'entens pas. It pourroit estre. Est-il vray?" qu'ils eussent plustost gardé la forme d'apprentis à soixante ans que de representer les docteurs à dix ans, comme ils font. (246)

> [You make me hate things probable when you thrust them on me as things infallible. I love terms which soften and tone down the rashness of what we put forward, terms such as "perhaps," "somewhat," "some," "they say," "I think," and so on. And if I had had sons to bring up I would have trained their lips to answer with inquiring and undecided expressions such as, "What does this mean?" "I do not understand that," "It might be so," "Is that true?" so that they would have been more likely to retain the manners of an apprentice at sixty than, as boys do, to act like learned doctors at ten.] (1171)

Hesitancy became a virtue, a certain awkwardness permissible, if perhaps it could avert the danger of unjust accusation, unsafe conviction, the kind of certainties that produced the witchhunt.

This may point toward a way in which Perec's writing round and through an absence could become some manner of survival, a form of evolution that did not have to be rigidly determined, but, rather, came to depend on what was out of kilter (see Derrida's "My Chances/*Mes Chances*"). Every system of constraint must have a bit of give, Perec believed. "It mustn't be rigid, it has to have some play, it has to creak a bit; the system mustn't be entirely coherent . . . the world works because there was an imbalance at the start" (cit. Magné 1993, 112). Not a clockwork universe, then, driven by the laws of causality, but a universe perpetuated by creative deviation. This is not so far from

Derrida, for whom the "clinamen" of Epicurean atomic theory, the swerving away or declination of atoms from a vertical course, is just such a chance event emerging from necessity, and crucial to life itself. As Christopher Johnson indicates, it is tempting to suggest an analogy between this process of dissemination, and Darwinian natural selection (Johnson 1993). For Johnson this may imply an "indeterminate telos," rather than the various forms of fatality—theological, scientific, historical—posited in Western thought.

This need not necessarily mean an irresponsible, freewheeling autonomy that abandons facts in favor of airy speculation and, at worst, revisionism, but the opening up of possibility, of ethical freedom, a snapping, as Lucretius put it, of "the bonds of fate." "Again, if all movement is always interconnected," he asked, "the new arising from the old in a determinate order—if the atoms never swerve so as to originate some new movement that will snap the bonds of fate, the everlasting sequence of cause and effect—what is the source of the free [will]?" (cit. Marx 1975, 416). It is a form of advancement that Derrida, along with Montaigne and Perec, writing of the back and forth motion, the writing oneself between the beams that W is all about, chooses to describe in terms of an uneven, halting gait:

> Fort:da. The most normal step has to bear disequilibrium, within itself, in order to carry itself forward, in order to have itself followed by an other one, the same again, that is a step, and so that the other comes back, amounts to [revienne] the same, but as other. Before all else limping has to be the very rhythm of the march, unterwegs. Before any accidental aggravation which could come to make limping itself falter. This is rhythm.

> If speculation necessarily remains unresolved because it plays on two boards, band contra band, losing by winning and winning by losing, how can one be surprised that it advances painfully [que ça marche mal]? But it has to advance painfully in order to advance; if it has to, if it has to advance, it must advance hesitatingly. It limps well, no? (PC, 406)

This is true of autobiography as it is dealt with by Perec and of writing as conceived by Derrida. Autobiography must "advance hesitatingly" because it cannot have a preordained destination. Instead, it is infinitely divisible, infinitely of the future, always "promised," always "unterwegs" or under way. A date, a mark, a word, says Derrida, is at once singular and repeatable, unique and endlessly reproduced, and this is how it is enabled to *mean* or signify in the first place:

A date gets carried away, transported; it takes off, takes itself off—and thus effaces itself in its very readability. Effacement is not something that befalls it like an accident; it affects neither its meaning nor its readibility; it merges, on the contrary, with reading's very access to that which a date may still signify. (SPC, 22)

This activity, whereby word, mark, date, in order to mean anything, must also erase themselves, is *différance*. It is the same as saying that "Je suis né" enacts the past only through the future, that the moment must already be in the past in order to be formed and made intelligible, and that destination, when it comes, is always after the event (Johnson 1993, 170). This parasitical folding in on itself of experience is variously referred to as playing upon "two boards, band contra band, losing by winning and winning by losing," as a double bind. It is, strictly speaking, neither transcendence nor a materialist denial of transcendence, neither necessity nor chance, but the play between the two, the "ligament that holds together fatality and its opposite" (Johnson 1993, 23). This is a breaching of the limit that has important implications for conceptions of identity, since, if all this is experience, continuation, and, as Johnson suggests, survival, there will no place for linguistic, personal, and national determinations as they have been traditionally understood. In Johnson's own words:

Deconstruction is evolution. It is survival itself, the continual filtering of virtualities, of our infinite, immemorial descent. (Johnson 1993, 187)

## Notes

1. Henceforth referred to parenthetically as *WSE* and *WMC*.

2. Beckett, invoking voluntary versus involuntary memory, says a similar thing in relation to Proust, that "[t]he man with a good memory does not remember anything because he does not forget anything" (Beckett 1980, 17).

3. See the distinction also in "Plato's Pharmacy" between "*hypomnesis* (re–memoration, recollection, consignation) . . . and *mneme* (living, knowing memory)" (D, 91).

4. This essay is indebted to Lejeune's discussion of *W* and the complex publishing history that goes along with it.

5. Hannah Arendt has much the same observations to make on totalitarianism's privileging of historical/natural movement: "In a perfect totalitarian government, where all men have become One Man, where all action aims at the acceleration of the movement of nature or history, where every single act is the execution of a death sentence which Nature or History

has already pronounced, that is, under conditions where terror can be completely relied upon to keep the movement in constant motion, no principle of action separate from its essence would be needed at all" (Arendt 1979, 467).

6. In his discussion of *W*, Philippe Lejeune refers to the Holocaust as "un grand naufrage," a great shipwreck (Lejeune 1991, 61).

7. Bernard Magné, "Les Sutures dans *W ou le Souvenir d'Enfance*," *Cahiers Georges Perec* No 2, textuel 34/44 1988.

8. Carlo Ginzburg points out a link between myths concerning seasonal imbalance and lameness, taking in, amongst others, the stories of Oedipus and Jacob. See *Ecstasies: Deciphering the Witches Sabbath* (1989), trans. Raymond Rosenthal (1992).

9. As is typical procedure for Montaigne, the essay presents a field of ideas that, though they may only seem incidentally linked, are more closely related. The discussion opens with the idea of temporal imbalance, with the transition to the Gregorian calendar and the foreshortening of the year by ten days. This question of calendrical time then leads Montaigne to consider the accuracy of historical records, and from there, to the issues of testimony and verification. Though he only makes very passing reference to lameness itself, it can be seen that Montaigne is pulling together ideas of imbalance or errancy that also extend to problems of knowledge, belief and proof. His final shift— a very deconstructive one—is to claim such vagaries or oscillations as a integral part of our understanding: "Il n'est rien si souple et erratique que nostre entendement; c'est le soulier de Theramenez, bon à tous pieds." (246) [There is nothing so supple and eccentric as our understanding. It is like Theramenes' shoe: good for either foot (1171)].

# CHAPTER 7

# Oulipian Grammatology

## La règle du jeu

BURHAN TUFAIL

A text is not a text unless it hides from the first comer, from the first glance, the law of its composition and the rules of its game. A text remains, moreover, forever imperceptible. Its law and its rules are not, however, harboured in the inaccessibility of a secret; it is simply that they can never be booked, in the *present*, into anything that could rigorously be called a perception. And hence, perpetually and essentially they run the risk of being definitively lost. Who will ever know of such disappearances? The dissimulation of the woven texture can in any case take centuries to undo its web.

—Jacques Derrida

Now it is actually in the passage from the *rule* to the *constraint* that the stumbling block appears: people accept the rule, they tolerate technique, but they refuse constraint. Precisely because it seems like an unnecessary rule, a superfluous redoubling of the exigencies of technique, and consequently no longer belongs—so the argument goes—to the admitted norm but rather to the process, and thus is exaggerative and excessive. It is as if there were a hermetic boundary between two domains: the one wherein the observance of rules is a natural fact, and the one wherein the excess of rules is perceived as a shameful artifice.

It is precisely this boundary, wholly arbitrary, that must be challenged in the name of a better knowledge of the functional modes of language and writing?

—Marcel Bénabou (Motte 1986, 41)

## COUNTRY COOKING . . .

The law of composition, the rule of the game, constraint, potentiality: one can find evidence of a certain sharing of terminology, but are the words translatable, from one writing to another, can one play with the play of terms? The linking of the Oulipo with Jacques Derrida seems an unlikely, if not willfully spurious, conjunction: on the one hand, a group of writers, mathematicians, and philosophers whose collective activity, that of writing under formal constraint, has been little recognized in the Anglo-Saxon world (although individual members have gained some renown, their link with the Oulipo is often ignored or underplayed), and on the other hand, one of the foremost thinkers of our time, whose influence is perhaps beyond calculation. What could possibly justify this? There are superficial connections at first glance: the Oulipo was formed in 1960, almost contemporaneous with Derrida's first major papers and publications (" 'Genèse et structure' et la phénoménologie" was given as a lecture in 1959, his "Introduction à 'L'Origine de la géométrie' par Edmund Husserl" appeared in 1962), both the Oulipo and Derrida have been accused of a certain *frivolity*, and endured a degree of marginality,[1] both in their own way challenge Romantic notions of literature and literary production. These "facts" however, and their implication of temporal or "thematic" connections, might easily be countermanded by others. The review *Tel Quel* was also founded in 1960, and has a more obvious claim to an association with Derrida, who was published in its pages; *Tel Quel*, as a group, were much more overtly connected with the question of theory, whereas the Oulipo have resolutely resisted theorizing their project; some of the founder members of the Oulipo could perhaps be seen as part of the French literary and cultural establishment in a way that those involved with *Tel Quel* were not; the *Tel Quel* group manifested themselves publicly during the sixties, whereas the Oulipo's first major collective public statement did not appear until 1973.[2] So, why insist on a more oblique, less arguable connection? Firstly, there is perhaps a question of propriety: what is *proper* to philosophy, or to literature, and what is it to break the rules of the game, the law of genre? Why are certain texts deemed monstrous and excessive, or, alternately, infantilizing and trivial? Furthermore, is there a tenuous connection to be drawn between the Oulipian concentration on the practice of writing, and texts such as *Glas* and *La Carte Postale*, where Derrida's formal invention is most apparent? And how to account for Derrida's increasing insistence *not* to be theorizing, his refusal of the desire to produce a methodology, the stress placed on the unavoidable *demand* of the work of writing, of reading?

In terms of *literary* contexts, always multiple and tentative, there might be ways of locating aspects of Derrida's work by means of other genealogies of French writing, *brisées*[3] that might trace or mark out unexpected affinities. This is not to imply either that the Oulipo in any way require the legitimation of a theoretical articulation, or that Derrida *should have* read or commented upon certain writers, but rather to suggest that questions of, for example, structure, law, and chance, of the pun and translation, of writing and memory, may be tracked through wider and stranger trajectories of French writing.[4] A series of literary-historical *puns* perhaps, pseudo-trails that lead across arbitrary boundaries, or, to situate this more closely, an attempt at bringing together two bodies of work that happened to be read, by chance, at the same time and began to generate a series of possibilities and questions. If, on the one hand, Derrida asks "What is literature?" with the recognition that the concept "literature" radically unsettles the "what is . . .?"[5] then, on the other hand, the Oulipian *play* with formal structures, sometimes eliciting from critics the cry of "This is not literature!" perhaps submits the more restricted or limited question of formalism to the same unsettling scrutiny. The multiplicity of formal constraints bring the Oulipian text into the realm of the act, the event, the signature; although the idea of the "formal constraint" already presupposes a crude opposition between form and content, the Oulipo utilizes techniques of constraint to resist and complicate such concepts.

## L'ARBRE (THE NOVEL AS HISTORY)

We could start with Alfred Jarry (1873–1907), author of, most famously, *Ubu Roi*, that monstrous creation whose epenthetic cry of *"Merdre!"* signalled a literature that utilizes puns, neologisms, and anagrams, that deforms words, ruptures genres, and marshals recondite reference and complex symbolism. Jarry's genius marks the twentieth century: as a *lycéen* in Rennes, he was introduced to Nietzsche by a philosophy teacher (before Nietzsche's works had been translated into French); at the Lycée Henri IV in Paris he studied under Bergson, and pursued his own idiosyncratic studies in literature, classics, and the cabbala; later he attended Mallarmé's *mardis*, where he became acquainted with the symbolists.[6] Admired by Apollinaire and the

Surrealists,[7] Jarry's influence may be seen in Antonin Artaud's founding of the Théâtre Alfred Jarry with Lugné-Poé, and in the activities of the Collège de 'pataphysique (founded in 1948).[8] Jarry's Gestes et opinions du docteur Faustroll, pataphysicien (published posthumously in 1911) was the principle source for Jarry's elaboration of the "science of 'Pataphysics," which is variously described as "the science of the particular, of laws governing exceptions," "the science of imaginary solutions," and as "the science of the realm beyond metaphysics" (Shattuck 1984, 102–106); at least one writer on Jarry has linked 'Pataphysics with deconstruction.[9] The College of 'Pataphysics, misunderstood or misrepresented often by commentators, has published texts by, for example, Jarry, Artaud, Max Jacob, René Daumal, and Alphonse Allais, and counts among its members many major literary, artistic, and academic figures: Raymond Queneau, Boris Vian, Joan Miró, Marcel Duchamp, Max Ernst, Michel Leiris, Francis Ponge, and many others.[10] Raymond Queneau, one of the founders of the Oulipo (originally a sub-committee of the College of 'Pataphysics), was also the editor of Kojève's lectures on Hegel (1947), which he had attended alongside Bataille, Lacan,[11] Merleau-Ponty, and Klossowski, and even, on occasion, André Breton. Kojève's lecture series, which ran from 1933–39, is one of the key events in twentieth-century French intellectual history.[12] Jean Hyppolite, who taught Derrida in the 1950s, was a "distinguished and influential commentator on Hegel," before moving toward the work of Heidegger (Johnson 1993, 201–202 n.12) Hyppolite and Kojève both translated Hegel's The Phenomenology of the Mind (WD, 334 n. 9). Hegel, in Kojève's reading, addressing, for example, the question of the relationship between madness, reason, and wisdom, sustains not only French philosophy of the period, but also the literary/theoretical aesthetics of writers such as Queneau and Bataille. Vincent Descombes points out that the same writers (Bataille, Klossowski, et al.) who attended Kojève's lectures "were to supply most of the ammunition for the 'generalised anti-Hegelianism' which Deleuze observed around him in 1968" (1980, 14). Derrida, across many of his texts, writes repeatedly on Hegel, but also on Bataille and Nietzsche. What is the relevance of this brief and unsatisfactory history lesson? Certainly not in any way to give a strict context or sociohistoric placing that would too reductively frame the works at hand (although I have unavoidably done just that), but rather to stage the possibilities of a series of encounters, coincidences, juxtapositions which might illuminate the ways in which Derrida and the Oulipo not only ask the question "What is literature?" but also choose certain linguistic strategies to do so: what I want to suggest is that these questions and strategies, as a recurrent feature in a particular and constructed genealogy of French writing, offer means by which the Oulipian project may be seen as a strange and distant relation of some of the issues at stake in the work of Derrida.

## Rats Who Must Build the Labyrinth from Which They Propose to Escape . . .

> Exclusively preoccupied with its great capitals (Work, Style, Inspiration, World-Vision, Fundamental Options Genius, Creation, etc.) literary history seems deliberately to ignore writing as practice, as work, as play. Systematic artifices, formal mannerisms ( that which in the final analysis, constitutes Rabelais, Sterne, Roussel . . . ) are relegated to the registers of the asylums for literary madmen, the "Curiosities": "Amusing Library," "Treasure of Singularities," "Philological Entertainments," "Literary Frivolities," compilations of a maniacal erudition where rhetorical "exploits" are described with suspect complaisance, useless exaggeration, and cretinous ignorance. Constraints are treated therein as aberrations, as pathological monstrosities of language and of writing; the works resulting from them are not even worthy to be called works: locked away, once and for all and without appeal, and often by their authors themselves, these works, in their prowess and skilfulness, remain paraliterary monsters justiciable only to a symptomatology whose enumeration and classification order a dictionary of literary madness?
>
> —Georges Perec (Motte 1986, 98)

The Oulipo, or **Ouvroir de Litterature Potentielle**, was founded in 1960 by Raymond Queneau and Francois Le Lionnais,[13] contemporaneous with the formation of Tel Quel. The name is usually translated as "Workshop of Potential Literature," although the word *ouvroir* has a complex etymology barely rendered by the term *workshop:* of its range of meanings, the one most favored by the group is that of a "sewing circle." Warren F. Motte Jr. ends his discussion of the word's etymological links thus:

> [O]uvroir is etymologically related to the verb *ouvrer*, "to work," in the sense of working a given material: wood, copper, stone, and so forth. It is also related to the noun *ouvrier*, "worker". . . . Last, it is related to *oeuvre*: herein, one can detect the final level of Oulipian taxonomic play. For *oeuvre* has strayed from the etymon in a striking manner:

applied to an individual literary text, for instance, it connotes far more than a mere "work"; applied to a body of texts produced by an author, it suggests completion, consecration, canonization if you will. When Perec, for instance, criticizes the literary establishment for its disdain of writing "as practice, as work," he is implicitly opposing *ouvroir* to *oeuvre*, labor to inspiration, collective effort to individual genius, the artisan to the artist. (Motte 1986, 9–10)

The implicit opposition to the notion of completion is important, as is the link to the third term of the title, *potentielle* (potential), given the importance of *process* to the Oulipian project, both in writing and reading. The simple and ingenious *Cent Mille Milliards de poèmes* by Raymond Queneau is perhaps the inaugural example of an Oulipian text, ten sonnets with similar rhymes, syntax, and semantic ambience, in a book whose pages are horizontally cut into strips in order to allow any line to be combined with any other, resulting in potentially one hundred trillion poems. To read these exhaustively would take more than a million centuries, and the combinations represent "a quantity of text far greater than everything man has written since the invention of writing, including popular novels, business letters, diplomatic correspondence, private mail, rough drafts thrown into the wastebasket, and graffiti" (Motte 1986, 3). This poem functions as a mathematico-literary *proof* of an inexhaustible text, beyond closure, always potential, rupturing any possibility of a total reading, and this occurs not only with regard to a "classical" notion of inexhaustibility, of the infinite, but also with regard to the *gaps* that make such multi–articulation possible. Derrida, in "Structure, Sign, and Play in the Discourse of the Human Sciences," discusses the impossibility of totalization "not because the infiniteness of a field cannot be covered by a finite glance or a finite discourse, but because the nature of the field—that is, language, and a finite language—excludes totalization" (*WD*, 289). The work of the Oulipo can provide examples of both, and often, at the same time?

The Oulipo have divided their activities into two main areas of inquiry, analytic and synthetic oulipo. Anoulipism is the search for constraints in ancient or contemporary works (the discoveries are described as anticipatory or synchronous plagiarism, and the concept possibly alludes to Borges's essay on the precursors of Kafka (Borges 1970, 234–236) whereas syntholoulipism is dedicated to the discovery and application of new forms. The possibility of the discovery of anticipatory texts suggests an isomorphism with Derrida's interest in texts that test philosophical categories: "[A]s [Derrida's] discussion of Shakespeare's *Romeo and Juliet* . . . indicates, however, this selectivity does not imply an identification of 'modernity' or 'modernism' with the capacity to unsettle philosophic-critical categories . . ." (*AL,* 4). Nevertheless, if, for Derrida, 'certain texts classed as 'literary' have seemed . . . to operate breaches or infractions at the most advanced points"[14] (*Pos,* 69) for a writer like Perec, as cited above, the kinds of writing in which the Oulipo are interested are those that have often been seen as peculiarly *regressive,* the games and diversions of a child or a lunatic, with no obvious *solicitation* of the categories of philosophy and literature. As Perec remarks, "[c]onstraints are treated . . . as aberrations, as pathological monstrosities of language and of writing"—which should perhaps alert any reader of Derrida (and not just on account of some of the responses to formally complex books such as *Glas*), for it is precisely the marginal, that which might be excluded as an "aberration," which on closer reading operates deconstructively on the very demarcations of exclusion. Anoulipism, the autogenealogic activity of demonstrating that there is a *tradition* of "aberrant" writing, reveals the presence of formally constrained works always alongside those texts classically regarded as literature. Rather than being "the last formalist hurrah,"[15] the Oulipian use of formal constraint *unsettles* standard interpretations and understanding of formalist procedures; the constraints are emphatically not separable from "content" in any simplistic binarism. The example of Georges Perec's *La Disparition* (1969, 1994) might serve to illustrate the point: utilizing the simple (meaning not complex, rather than not difficult) constraint of writing a three-hundred-page novel in French without using the letter E, Perec invokes the death of his parents in World War II (his mother died at Auschwitz). The disappearance of the letter (E is pronounced the same as *eux,* or "them") provides the armature for a murder mystery wherein the victims die on the verge of uttering the forbidden E. Perec also includes games of translation, lipogrammatic texts in other languages, versions of famous literary passages. The book *is* the constraint: it would be inconceivable without it. Could any reader think of *Glas* otherwise?

## BANLIEUE

One area of convergence between Derrida and some of the Oulipian texts lies in the question of the boundary or frame, the *parergon.* David Carroll, in *Paraesthetics* (1987, 144–154), discusses the application of the term to the case of literature, addressing the question of "the specificity of literature . . . how it functions and what makes it literary." The use of this concept in the case of the Oulipo raises some problems. On the one hand, as Carroll states, the formalist might claim that it is the use of formal and rhetorical devices which serves to demarcate the literary; on the other hand, it is precisely the *excess* of such devices that has led some critics to question the literariness of certain Oulipian texts. This is a problem that needs to be examined more fully, possibly by relating the work of the Oulipo to the notations and structures, often mathematical, and therefore ostensibly outside the frame of literature, that are involved or invoked in their textual production. However, in a restricted interpretation, or in a more literal analogy with the frame of the painting, there are certain effects played out with the boundary of the text as book, as material object, by various Oulipian works. Harry Mathews's *The Sinking of The Odradek Stadium* and Paul Fournel's *Banlieue* (or *Suburbia*) are two texts that demonstrate this attention to framing: *The Sinking of The Odradek Stadium*, an epistolary novel, the plot (in all senses of the word) of which hinges on destinerrancy, opens with points of suspension[16] and ends with an uncompleted sentence: a refusal of closure. Secondly, in common with several other Oulipian texts,[17] the novel includes an index[18] which, outside the text/novel in its traditional dimensions, loops back into the book as a "random access" device that operates to break linearity.[19] The third device is the use of the running head: the book's title, appearing on the cover and on the top of each page, which only gains a possible significance in the final few pages, and is dependent on the interpretation of a word that might be an error in transcription, a mishearing, a misspelling, or not an error at all. Mathews plays with the materiality of the book and the quirky habits of book production to break the frame of the text, of the act of reading. A more extreme example is Fournel's parodistic tour de force in *Banlieue*. Here, the full armory of framing devices surrounds an *absent* text: the frame *is* the work, or perhaps, in a moment of mirroring, the absent text becomes the parergon of the parergon ("A *parergon* without *ergon*? A 'pure' supplement? . . . A supplement with nothing to supplement, calling, on the contrary, for what it supplements, to be its own supplement?" [*TP*, 302]). From the front cover, through a dedication, footnotes, post-face, index, errata, to the back, complete with blurb and bar code, Fournel examines everything that surrounds and conditions the text.[20] The clue lies in the placement of a definition of *Banlieue* on the second page: the *juridical space* around a town, the extent of authority, is what is at stake here. The question is one of boundary, of what might legitimately be considered as inside or outside, what might cross over, or disrupt this divide.

## ABANIKA TRADITORE

Again and again, the problem of translation, the doing and the thinking of translation, its possibility, its impossibility. In a short text, written in the form of a letter to Georges Perec, and entitled "Abanika Traditore" in French, and "The Dialect of the Tribe" in English. Immediately, the question of the title and the translation of the title emerges. The French title echoes the phrase *traduttore, traditore* (translator, traitor), replacing the first element with the invented word Abanika, the "chief word-chief" of the tribe of the Bactrian tribe; presumably a reader, encountering the invented word in the context of the phrase will already have made a tentative translation: abanika = translator. So the title hints at the process of the story itself. This is of course lost in English: Mathews has replaced the title with a phrase that is another translation, T. S. Eliot's version of Mallarmé's line, "donner un sens plus pur aux mots de la tribu" (which is taken from *Le Tombeau d'Edgar Poe*—and hence alludes to yet another important translation, that of Poe into French by Baudelaire). In both cases then the title acts as a complex commentary on translation itself. The story begins as a response to a request for a festschrift in Perec's honor, and Mathews begins by meditating on translating his friend's work, thence to the act of translation, and thence to the proposition that "translation is a paradigm, an exemplar for writing itself." From this point the text moves into a fictional account of the language of a small tribe in New Guinea:

> [A]n account of the method used by the Pagolak-speaking tribe to translate their tongue into the dialects of their neighbours. What was remarkable about this method was that while it produced translations that foreign listeners could understand and accept, it also concealed from them the original meaning of every statement made. . . . To translate successfully, and not reveal one's meaning? What could be more paradoxical? What could be more relevant?

Mathews then moves on to discuss the function of the abanika or chief-word-chief of the tribe and the realization that the strange transformative powers are inherent in the tribe's language. Mathews writes,

> In a matter of days, I found myself perfectly capable of understanding what the Abanika were saying and perfectly incapable of repeating in other terms . . . The Abanika's declaration, you see, was the very process of transforming language that I expected it to be about. It was not an account of the process, it was the process itself. And how can you translate a process? You'd have to render not only words but the spaces

between them—like snap-shooting the invisible air under the beating wings of flight.

(here the allusion to the *white spaces* of Mallarmé's "Un Coup de Dés" is irresistible). The Abanika's magic changing is the "redirecting of language towards foreign eyes in a way that both provides clarity and suppresses translation's customary raison d'être—the communication of substantive content. You and I may know that such communication is at best hypothetical, perhaps impossible; that translation may, precisely, exorcise the illusion that substantive content exists at all." What Mathews suggests, then, is that the distinction between form and content is illusory, form cannot simply be squeezed dry and extracted of meaning, there is just the process of language itself. As the text continues, the narrator tries to gloss the important terms of the Pagolak tongue, until, finally, there is no recourse but to continue and end in Pagolak itself, the account of the process can only be accounted for in the "original" language, and yet this language is also one in which the recognition of the need for translation, for a "magic changing," is part of the language itself. Mathews's short story resonates with Derrida's work—nearly every translator of Derrida comments on the impossibility of translation, to the extent that several of his texts have appeared in bi- or multilingual editions (*Des Tours de Babel* is the obvious example of English and French texts being placed together)—translators repeatedly stress the irreducibly French idiom and invention of Derrida's texts, coupled with the necessity of this impossibility. Commentaries become themselves the parergon of the texts while addressing their most crucial, inescapable demands: the rhetoric of the translator is imbricated in an act of describing what the translation already fails to do. Derrida's Pagolak, his "magic changing," is a process that resists the extraction of "substantive content," the singular meaning is resisted.[21] Of course in *using* Derrida in this way one risks interrupting the "magic changing" of his work in precisely the way that Mathews has fictionalized.

## PARAGRAMMATOLOGY

> The overwhelming majority of Oulipian works thus far produced inscribe themselves in a SYNTACTIC structurElist perspective (I beg the reader not to confuse this word—created expressly for this Manifesto—with structurAlist, a term that many of us consider with circumspection).
>
> —François Le Lionnais (Motte 1986, 29)

The Oulipian definition of the paragram ("the printer's error consisting of the substitution of one letter for another" [Motte 1986, 200])[22] is not to be confused with the anagrammatic definition proposed by Saussure and taken up by Julia Kristeva. The quotation above, from the first major collective publication of the Oulipo in 1973, seems to nod playfully at the famous paragrammatic term coined by Derrida, *différance*, to mark a written alteration not discernible in speech. Derrida moves from E to A, the Oulipo from A to E, a reversal, a mirroring, which directs attention to the widespread use of a *différance* effect in various Oulipian works. Long before the formation of the group, Raymond Queneau, in *Exercices de style*, produced a book in which a simple set of events is narrated in ninety-nine styles, ranging across dialects and genres, micro- and macrostructural rhetorical devices.[23] Queneau repeatedly plays with written forms and the representation of speech, producing on the one hand hilarious "phonetic" transcriptions of speech which are barely lisible, and on the other, permutional combinations of letters which are lisible (to a degree) but virtually unpronouncable. Across the book there is the supposed "meaning" of the text, a representational narrative (but "narrative" itself is only one the styles Queneau uses . . .) which all but vanishes with repetition, as with each text evaporates the possibility of separating form and content, of writing as mere transcription.The truth of the tale lies not in one account, or several, but dispersed amongst all, elusive, in the spacing.

## CLINAMEN—THE NECESSITY OF CHANCE

If perhaps there is one figure, one concept, that might serve to link Derrida with the Oulipo, it would be that of the *clinamen*, the element of chance in the materialist scheme of Lucretius. Drawn from an Epicurean addition to Democritian philosophy, Lucretius defines the clinamen as the unaccountable swerve that allows the falling atoms to form matter, and is also the basis of free will. Marx wrote his doctoral thesis on Greek materialist philosophy, but the clinamen recurs most notably in Jarry's *Faustroll*, and is subsequently taken up by the "Pataphysicians," and thence to the Oulipo. Others, too, have found the concept alluring—among them Harold Bloom, Claude Lévi-Strauss, and, of course, Derrida (MC, 1–32). If, for Georges Perec, Paul Klee's dictum that "Genius is the error in the system" becomes a means by which the rigidities of constraint might be made to play a little, to allow for "free will," a space for invention, for Derrida too, the clinamen becomes a figure of destinerrancy. Noting that at the very place in the text that the clinamen is introduced into the text of Lucretius, there is an indeterminate reading, voluptas/voluntas (freedom and will/pleasure), Derrida invokes a link between clinamen, freedom, and pleasure, and thence moves to Freud's pleasure principle. The clinamen then may stand for *différance*, and for the moment of invention among the play of constraints: might we allow it to stand for the interpretative swerve that brings Derrida and the Oulipo together, here, as I write, on this page?

## NOTES

Some section headings refer to various texts by members of the Oulipo, either by title or through quotation, which comment, directly or obliquely, in a *supplementary* fashion, on the material that follows. "Country Cooking from Central France: Roast Boned Rolled Stuffed Shoulder of Lamb (Farce Double)," (Matthews, 1980).

*L'Arbre* was an autobiographical project by Georges Perec, uncompleted at the time of his death in 1982 (for an account of the text see Robin 1993, 5–28). The work was intended as a "family history," but one that deliberately fragmented linear reading trajectories, allowing multiple pathways through the text. "The Novel as History" (Mathews 1980) is a brilliant parody of sociohistorical matrices of interpretation, indicating that the network of connections and contexts for any event are potentially infinite, allowing only arbitrary closure, and is a witty warning against exactly the sequential situating that is attempted in the opening sections of this essay.

*Rats who must build* etc. is quoted in Motte (1986, 22).

"Banlieu" is by Paul Fournel, in *La Bibliothèque Oulipienne*, volume III (1990, 183–214) trans. Harry Mathews in *Oulipo Laboratory* (1995).

1. For one account of a crude attack on Derrida, one might consult his dignified and restrained *"Honoris Causa:* 'this is *also* extremely funny,' " (*P . . . ,* 399–419). The letter of protest referred to in the interview is reproduced on 419–421. A rough schematic might oppose Anglo-Saxon to Continental philosophy, and continental continuations of traditions usually associated with modernism to an English rejection of modernist practice (at least with regard to the mainstream press in Britain; there is a crucial issue here of the *politics* of publishing): but there are also resistances within France to be accounted for, as alluded to by Derrida in, for example, *"Honoris Causa . . . ,"* and, in the case of the Oulipo, by the critique of Gérard Genette, among others.

2. I am indebted to Patrick ffrench for allowing me pre-publication access to his brilliant and meticulous account of Tel Quel, *The Time of Theory,* (1995). Although I disagree with his conclusions about the Oulipo, his book points to a much more complex relationship between the two groups than might ini-

tially be thought. For example, ffrench hints at an unacknowledged debt with regard to writers such as Raymond Queneau (listed by Roland Barthes as one of the writers "degree zero"), who contributed to the literary innovations of the *nouveau roman* and Tel Quel (31). He also discusses the complex polemics and rivalries of the time: Jean-Pierre Faye left Tel Quel in 1967, and became involved in founding the review *Change*, alongside contributors such as Jacques Roubaud, who had joined the Oulipo in 1966. The two reviews engaged in various polemical skirmishes; Faye at one point attacking Tel Quel, and by implication Derrida, for their espousal of Heidegger (117 n. 48, 181). See also Jacques Derrida (*Pos*, 103–104 n. 28).

3. The word is taken from the title to Michel Leiris's 1966 collection of essays. A jacket note by Richard Sieburth to the translation explains: "In the vocabulary of venery, *brisées* refer to the broken branches or snapped twigs that indicate the elusive presence of game. . . . For the forester, *brisées* in turn signify boundary markers—branches or stakes planted in the ground to define an area of timber now ready for logging." Michel Leiris, *Brisées: Broken Branches*, trans. Lydia Davies (1989). Elusive trail and tentative boundary might serve as a description of the first part of this essay . . .

4. The question of affinities, I hesitate to write "influences," is, in any case, far broader than suggested here. The relationship between French and American literature, or more narrowly French and American poetics, indicates the complexities involved. For example, Marcelin Pleynet and Denis Roche were published in the magazine *Locus Solus*, edited by John Ashbery, Harry Mathews, Kenneth Koch, and James Schuyler: Pleynet and Roche went on to be associated with Tel Quel, Mathews with the Oulipo. Mathews has translated poems by Roche and Pleynet in *The Paris Review* and in Paul Auster, ed., *The Random House Book of Twentieth Century French Poetry* (1982). *Locus Solus* was named after a novel by Raymond Roussel, a writer admired by, among others, the surrealists, the Collège de Pataphysique, Michel Leiris (who was related to Roussel), Alain Robbe-Grillet, the Oulipo, and Michel Foucault, whose *Raymond Roussel* (1963) was reviewed by Philippe Sollers in *Tel Quel*. Roche and Pleynet published translations of Ezra Pound, Charles Olson, and John Ashbery in *Tel Quel*, while Jacques Roubaud (a member of the Oulipo) has translated many American poets, most notably Louis Zukofsky, and has edited anthologies of translations of American poetry with Michel Deguy; and so on . . . (cf. ffrench, 1995, 52–59); Serge Gavronsky, *Toward A New Poetics* (1994, 33–45).

5. For a full discussion of this question, see Derek Attridge's introduction to Jacques Derrida (*AL*, 1–29).

6. Sources: Keith Beaumont, *Alfred Jarry: A Critical and Biographical Study* (1984); Roger Shattuck, *The Banquet Years* (1968). Jarry's early philosophical encounters thus leap across the Hegelian and existentialist modes of French thought (prevalent from the 1930s to the late 1950s) and anticipate the renewed interest in Nietzsche in the 1960s.

7. Marlena G. Corcoran, "Drawing Our Attention to Jarry, Duchamp, and Joyce: The Manuscript/Art of William Anastasi," *James Joyce Quarterly* 32, 3/4 (Spring/Summer 1995): 659–671. This article discusses the work of William Anastasi, who has spent many years studying *Finnegans Wake*, incorporating and transforming this research into his art. Corcoran quotes Anastasi's belief that "Jarry is an enormous unacknowledged source. According to my reading of *Finnegans Wake*, Joyce retells or recalls various scenes from the life, as well as every novel and theatre piece of the French author." Corcoran suggests that, although many might disagree with Anastasi's evidence and conclusions, one trajectory of Joyce studies, having moved from mythical and Homeric aspects through to Cubist contexts, might project into the possibility of reading Joyce via a Dada genealogy.

8. The College of 'Pataphysics is not an "Alfred Jarry Society," although Jarry's work features regularly in its publications. To date, there have been three major English language collections of 'pataphysical materials: *What Is Pataphysics?* a special issue of the *Evergreen Review* 4, 13 (May-June 1960); *The True, The Good, The Beautiful: An Elementary Chrestomathy of 'Pataphysics*, (1993); *A True History of the College of 'Pataphysics* (1995). The last contains a brief bibliographical guide to texts available in English by various members of the College.

9. Linda Klieger Stillman, *Alfred Jarry* (1983, 39–41). A major English language study with detailed readings of all the principal works. The linking of pataphysics with deconstruction, however delicious, is ultimately unconvincing; although Stillman does emphasise the *affirmative* aspect of deconstruction. Perhaps the attempt to link the two is itself an exercise in Pataphysics. As far as I can tell, there is only one reference to Jarry in Derrida's writings, occurring in a footnote that cites André Bréton's *Les vases communicants*, in which Breton quotes from Jarry's *Le surmâle*. Jacques Derrida, "White Mythology" (*MP*, 222 n. 23).

10. See: *A True History of the College of "Pataphysics."* The brief selection of names reveals obvious links with Surrealism, although many of those involved in the College had only brief links with the movement. Other members included Ionesco, Prévert, Dubuffet, and the Marx Brothers.

11. Jacques Lacan published two articles in *Minotaure*, the most lavish of surrealist magazines: in issue 1, and in issue 3–4 (1933). The magazine was originally to have been edited by Bataille, but was taken over by Breton. Michel Leiris and Marcel Griaule also published important anthropological texts in this first year. See: Dawn Ades, *Dada and Surrealism Reviewed* (1978, 279–293).

12. For a detailed account, see: Vincent Descombes, *Modern French Philosophy*, trans. L. Scott-Fox and J. M. Harding (1980).

13. The history of the Oulipo, its manifestos, and selected works may be found in the following publications: (a) in French: *Exercices de littérature*

*potentielle*, in *Dossiers Acénonètes du Collège de 'Pataphysique*, 17 (1961); *Oulipo*, in *Temps Mêlés*, 66–67 (1964); *La Littérature potentielle: Créations, re-créations, récréations* (1973); *Atlas de littérature potentielle* (1981); *Oulipo 1960–1963*, by Jacques Bens (1980); *La Bibliothèque Oulipienne*—a series of small plaquettes published in limited editions of 150–200 copies. These have appeared since 1974, the first being *Ulcérations* by Georges Perec, and, as of 1995, 74 issues have appeared. They have been collected and reprinted in various forms, most recently as *La Bibliothèque Oulipienne* (1990), 3 volumes, collecting issues 1–52. (b) in English: *Oulipo: a Primer of Potential Literature*, by Warren F. Motte Jr. (1986); *Oulipo, Oupeinpo* in *New Observations* 9 (1994); *Oulipo Laboratory* (1995)—translations of six issues of *La Bibliothèque Oulipienne*, plus two manifestos; *Oulipo Compendium* (1997).

14. The writers specified by Derrida here are Artaud, Bataille, Mallarmé, and Sollers.

15. This somewhat dismissive description of the Oulipo is made by Serge Gavronsky in the introduction to his recent anthology of texts and interviews with contemporary French poets, *Toward a New Poetics* (1994, 45, n. 1). Gavronsky, a distinguished translator and commentator on French poetics has obvious problems with the Oulipian approach to composition, which he finds, citing the Goncourt brothers as precedent, "aesthetically limiting," and continues " . . . the Oulipian experiments . . . are saved only by their humor, their inventiveness, or, in the case of Georges Perec's *W, or The Memory of Childhood*, by a quest for Jewish identity that is deeply felt, for all the stylistic and linguistic juggling" (29). This is misleading. Quite apart from the fact that Perec explicitly problematizes the notion of identity, the "juggling" serves precisely as a means of interrogating the autobiographical as a text of certainty and stability. This kind of critique of the Oulipo is common, where the formal devices are viewed as a diversion from or hindrance to getting at the "real meaning" of a text, rather than as part of the means by which the text generates meaning.

16. The immediate resonances are, of course, the "points de suspension" which form the fulcrum of Perec's *W, or The Memory of Childhood*, and Derrida's *Points de suspension, Entretiens*, a recent collection of interviews.

17. Georges Perec uses an index and appendices in several works, such as *La Vie mode d'emploi* and *Quel petit vélo . . . ?*, but the practice has a long history, the most notorious example perhaps being Boswell's *London Journals*.

18. Geoffrey Bennington's excellent essay "Index" in *Legislations, the Politics of Deconstruction* (1994, 274–295), takes the question of the index as a starting point for a discussion of deictics and iterability in Derrida and Lyotard.

19. Oulipians have other methods for suggesting this. Jacques Roubaud, in *The Great Fire of London*, trans. Dominic di Bernardi (1991), envisages a book that is no longer a book, but rather a huge two-dimensional surface, a wall or huge computer screen, which would contain the text and also mark, perhaps with colored string, interpolations and "bifurcations"—a spatial rather than linear text.

20. Bennington, in "Index," refers on its first page to Gérard Genette's *Seuils*, " . . . a sort of poetics of approaches to books (titles, prefaces, acknowledgements, dedications, cover–notes, etc.) . . . " (1994, 274). In an article on Harry Mathews, Warren F. Motte Jr. discusses " . . . Oulipian poetics, which postulates the mutual complementarity of ludic spirit and serious intent, a tenet which has caused the group some prejudice." A footnote here cites " . . . Genette's *Palimpsestes: La littérature au second degré* (1982, 49–57), wherein Oulipian research is trivialized and reductively compared to the Surrealist *cadavre exquis*." Motte indicates that Noël Arnaud has replied to these criticisms in *Sureau* 1 (1984), 12–18, to which I have been unable to refer. Warren F. Motte Jr., "Permutational Mathews," *Review of Contemporary Fiction* VII, 3 (Fall 1987): 91–99, esp. 93 and 99 n. 3. The debate might revolve around the contest between the *psychoanalytic* orientation of Surrealist practice (automatic writing, exquisite corpse, et al.), and the partial recourse to a *mathematical* model of invention by the Oulipo. The debate is complex however: a recent article by Mathews on the Oulipo appeared in the journal *Lacanian ink* (no. 8, Spring 1994), introduced by a paragraph that suggests that Queneau's links with Lacan might provide the basis of a fertile reading of Oulipian activity. Derrida is useful too: "It is clear that the . . . resistance to logical-mathematical notation has always been the signature of logocentrism and phonologism. . . . A grammatology that would break with this system of presuppositions, then, must in effect liberate the mathematization of language . . . " (*Pos*, 34–35). The whole passage is worth consulting; Derrida argues for the importance of the "non-phonetic" language of mathematics, which I may be reading somewhat reductively for the sake of argument.

21. See Derrida, "Letter to a Japanese Friend," in *A Derrida Reader* (269–277).

22. See also Bernard Dupriez, *Gradus—Les procédés littéraires*, 10/18 (1984): 319–320.

23. Raymond Queneau, *Exercices de style* (1947). *Exercises in Style* trans. Barbara Wright (1958; repr. 1981). In France, a lavish edition appeared in 1963 which utilized unique typefaces for each text, and forty-five exercises drawn or painted by Jacques Carelman, in different visual styles.

# CHAPTER 8

# Structuralism, Biology, and the Linguistic Model

CHRISTOPHER JOHNSON

Derrida's critical engagement with Lévi-Strauss in the 1960s has a sense of urgency and necessity which is symptomatic of a situation in which the human sciences, and amongst them anthropology in particular, seemed to be challenging the traditional position of philosophy in France. The debate around what is commonly called "structuralism" is an aspect rather than the essence of such a context, and to this extent Derrida's engagements with Lévi-Strauss could be seen as the response of philosophy to the "spontaneous" philosophy of anthropological discourse, and by implication a questioning of the discourse of the human sciences in general.[1] The following contribution, rather than being an application of Derrida (in the case of Derrida's work the very concept or practice of "application" is a problematic one), could be seen to constitute an extension of his original critique of the discourse of the human sciences, again focusing on the exemplary figure of Lévi-Strauss. Derrida remarks in *Writing and Difference* that "metaphor is never innocent. It orients research and fixes results" (*WD*, 17). This description could be extended to the case of the different *models* employed (applied) in the texts of Lévi-Strauss.

I will begin with what might be termed a *conjuncture*, the conjuncture of persons, of the disciplines those persons represent, and of the models used in these disciplines: anthropology, biology, and linguistics. This conjuncture is first a historical or, rather, biographical one, that of the meeting between Lévi-Strauss and Roman Jakobson in 1942 at the New School for Social Research in New York. Lévi-Strauss later describes his introduction to Jakobson's work on phonology in the early 1940s as being something of a revelation, giving shape and coherence to his thinking on his own research (1988, 62–63; 1976, 7–9). The application he goes on to make of the linguistic model is now well known. In a first phase, it plays a role in his study of kinship structures, though in his major work on the subject, the *Elementary Structures of Kinship*, the reference to linguistics is in fact relatively limited.[2] The second phase dates from the 1950s, when following his nomination at the École pratique des hautes études in Paris, Lévi-Strauss begins to specialize in the anthropology of religions and extends the linguistic model to the analysis of myth. This is the definitive formulation of the structural-linguistic model and more or less its final application, its final destination in Lévi-Strauss's work. From this point it could be said that Lévi-Strauss is practicing a form of "normal science" within the paradigm he has himself defined. From the *Mythologiques* cycle onwards, it could be argued, nothing significant is added to the paradigm, and there is simply application of the method of analysis elaborated in the earlier, programmatic texts.

It is possible to speculate on what would have been the history and nature of structuralism and indeed of anthropology in France, had the paths of Lévi-Strauss and Jakobson not crossed in New York in 1942, but it is probable that even in the absence of the contingent event of this biographical conjuncture, Lévi-Strauss would have found the conceptual framework for structural anthropology already to hand in a number of contemporary sciences. Thinkers such as Piaget and Serres show that the origins and the development of the structural paradigm are in fact more general than structural linguistics itself. Serres, for example, describes the new paradigm as "neo-Leibnizian," to the extent that it is the concept of the code, of permutation and combination that now seems to predominate in the exact and the human sciences. Whereas in the nineteenth century the dominant concept was energy, formalized in the three laws of thermodynamics, in this century it is information. One of the most striking convergences is in biology, where the discovery of the biochemical basis of heredity encoded in DNA was dependent on concepts originating in linguistics and information theory (Serres 1974, 17–21).

It would be useful here to resume briefly the explanation given by the French biologist François Jacob regarding the role of the linguistic model in biology. According to Jacob, the heuristic value of the linguistic model lies in its ability to account for a number of facts we now know about hereditary processes. First, the formation of a sequence of nucleotides, the basic structural units of DNA, which are distinguished by the permutation of the same sugar molecule with one of the four organic bases. Jacob compares this with the arrangement of letters of an alphabet in a text. Second, the "punctuation" of a given sequence, determining where the reading of its encoded information begins and ends. Third, the concept of "translation": this encoded information is translated (via RNA "messenger") into the appropriate protein structure, which can be viewed as the "expression" of a specific sequence of nucleotides. Finally, there is the phenomenon of genetic mutation, which can be compared to the errors (the additions, deletions, or transpositions) introduced into a text during the process of copying or editing. This concept of mutation is essential to explaining how living organisms adapt to a changing environment. It is only through the random mutations of the elements of the genetic code that new characteristics might emerge at the level of organic form, of morphology. These new characters would then be selected according to their appropriateness to a given environment (Jacob 1974, 195–205).

The intention here is not to question Jacob's account of the use of the linguistic model in his own discipline: this obviously has its place in a specific history of contemporary science, and is a whole subject in itself. What is relevant to the present discussion is the manner in which the bio-linguistic or bio-combinatorial model is disseminated across different disciplines, between the so-called "exact" and "human" sciences.[3] On his own admission, Lévi-Strauss has always maintained a keen interest in developments in contemporary and especially biological science, indeed, he considers it the duty of the human scientist to be generally informed of such developments. His criticism of philosophy, or a certain type of philosophy (personified in the figure of Sartre) is precisely that it has paid insufficient attention to the insights of modern science. For his part, Lévi-Strauss is quick to recognize the importance of the discoveries in biology for the human sciences—though it is significant that he does not absorb the implications of the metaphor of text that, as has been seen, governs Jacob's description of the processes of replication. This is the fundamental difference between Lévi-Strauss's and, for example, Derrida's assimilation of the biological-informational paradigm; but again, this is another subject in itself.[4]

To continue and complicate the preliminary notion of "conjuncture": not only does Lévi–Strauss recognize the importance for the human sciences of contemporary developments in biology, he also actively participates in the interdisciplinary debate on their significance. Characteristic of this convergence of disciplines was the round-table discussion broadcast in 1968, which brought together himself, Jakobson, Jacob, and another biologist, Philippe L'Héritier.[5] Reading through this intriguing encounter of anthropology, biology, and linguistics, it is difficult not to notice the contrast between the behavior of the different participants, or more precisely, between the "human" and the "hard" scientists. Whereas the interventions of the latter are for the most part restricted to description of the advances made in their respective areas of specialization, both Lévi-Strauss and Jakobson are more prepared to speculate on the meaning and more general implications of the apparent convergence of disciplines. In fact, the discussion or debate that is supposed to take place between the different disciplines never properly materializes, though it is significant that while Jacob agrees with Jakobson on the "striking" analogy between genetic and linguistic inheritance, he wonders to what extent the analogy is simply due to the fact that this is the only possible way of producing variety and diversity, of deriving the complex from the simple.[6] A few years later, in 1972, there is a similarly inconclusive exchange between Jacob and Lévi-Strauss.[7]

If the end result of these mediatized dialogues between hard and human science is, perhaps unsurprisingly, a certain noncommunication, then equally unsurprisingly the more restricted dialogue between linguistics and anthropology on the subject of the biological is less inhibited in its range of speculation. In his preface to Jakobson's *Six Lectures on Sound and Meaning*, Lévi-Strauss quotes some of Jakobson's previous reactions to the developments of modern biology. Again, Jakobson draws attention to the striking similarity between biological and linguistic systems, and even speculates on there being a stronger continuity between the two levels, linguistic structures being modelled directly on the genetic code. Lévi-Strauss himself reserves judgment on this point, preferring to defer such speculation until collaborative research between linguists and biologists would have thrown more light on the matter. In spite of this restriction, at the same time he goes on to make what he admits to be the more modest hypothesis on the relationship between linguistic structures and the structures of myths (1976, 14–15). So despite the parenthesis placed around Jakobson's interpretation of the recent developments in biology, the performative effect of the mention of these developments is to give a semblance of scientific validation to Lévi-Strauss's own hypothesis on the formal homology between language and myth, to give the impression of the underlying necessity of this homology, of an essential continuity between the two levels. In fact, the conclusion of his preface to Jakobson goes further than this, proposing three levels of coding: neuropsychological, linguistic, mythical; language is turned toward the body on the one hand and on the other hand toward society and its collective representations (1976, 17–18). Of course, he does not venture so far as to give any indication of the *articulation* between these different levels—neuropsychological, linguistic, more generally the cultural or symbolic. Nor is there any indication of how the systemically distinct levels of the genetic and the neurological might be related. Instead, there is the implicit assumption that interdisciplinary exchange—collaboration between the relevant disciplines, linguists and other specialists—will gradually resolve the problem of articulation, of the *interface* between the different levels. This is perhaps one of the most persistent questions of Lévi-Strauss's work from the *Elementary Structures of Kinship* onward, that is, the question of the articulation between "nature" and "culture," the solution to that is always placed in some future convergence between the exact and human sciences, a horizon which arguably is never reached, or indeed reachable.[8]

Having reviewed the main elements of the conjuncture in question, a conjuncture of individuals, disciplines, and models, in the remainder of this discussion I will be concentrating on the specific example of an early but well-known text by Lévi-Strauss as an illustration of one of the possible *effects* of this conjuncture. The text was commissioned in 1952 by UNESCO on the subject of race and modern science, and is entitled *Race and History*.[9] What is interesting about this text from the point of view of the present discussion is that Lévi-Strauss is brief and elliptical on the question of science itself, but that his exposition depends on the implicit application of scientific models and, more specifically, biological models.

He begins the essay by making the preliminary distinction between race and culture: it is not "race" in the sense of biology or physiology that determines the behavioral and psychological differences observed between human groups, but cultural environment. If, as Lévi-Strauss notes, biological science has shown the concept of race to be redundant, he does see the idea of cultural determinism or rather its corollary, the difference or *diversity* of cultures, as posing a problem. He asks whether cultural diversity is to the advantage or disadvantage of humanity and whether by its nature it holds the possibility of a fundamental inequality between cultures. In order to answer these questions, he suggests that it would first be necessary to make an inventory, not only of the different societies or cultures existing at the present time, but also of all the cultures that would have preceded them in past history. The problem with this is that apart from the limitations of historical analysis as compared to the study of contemporary cultures, many cultures have no written or recorded history, so that even indirect experience of their past is impossible. The most faithful inventory would therefore have to include a number of blank spaces or entries corresponding to unknown or extinct societies, and the number of these blank spaces would inevitably be infinitely greater than those one would be able to fill (325–326).

The concept of the inventory is a recurrent one in Lévi-Strauss's work. When confronted with a given body of data, his habitual response is to establish a table, a frequent point of comparison being the periodic table of the elements. An important aspect of this analogy is the idea of *potentiality*. In the case of Mendeleev's table of the elements, each element that has been discovered has its assigned place in the table, but it is also possible to predict the existence of new, hitherto undiscovered elements. One of the main characteristics of the inventory mentioned in *Race and History*—and this is important for the argument that follows—is precisely the idea of virtuality, of a kind of compossibility, to use the Leibnizian term, that is greater than actuality. In the ensuing sections of Lévi-Strauss's essay, much is made of the fact that Western technological culture represents only a fractional moment in the total history of human culture, and that the industrial and scientific revolutions of the past two or three centuries owe their existence to what he considers to be the no less significant event of the neolithic revolution. This relativizing of the technological achievements of modern culture is apparent in the sections dealing with the neolithic and the more recent technological and industrial revolutions, where the guiding thread of Lévi-Strauss's argument is the concept of *chance*.

He first dispenses with the conventional preconception that the inventions of prehistorical cultures were the result of mere chance discoveries—gifts of nature—and shows that what appear to be the most elementary of technologies actually involve a complex series of operations, and conscious reflection upon these operations. The phrasing of Lévi-Strauss's description of the intentional, reflexive, and directed character of neolithic technology is important, as it is typical of the manner in which he views cultural formations in general: "All these operations are far too numerous and complex to be accounted for by sheer luck. Each one of them taken separately means nothing. It is only by their combination, imagined, willed, and sought by experiment, which allowed success" (349). The subjacent analogy here is clearly a linguistic or informational one: in itself, each operation is meaningless, and it is only the combination of a number of operations that provides the desired result. While the analogy is a rather weak and elastic one, and open to endless qualification, it is nevertheless valuable as an index of how Lévi-Strauss conceptualizes cultural formations (social, symbolic, or technological), which is as *configurations* or *combinations*. It is this notion of the configurational or combinatorial that anticipates and prepares for the introduction of the biological model in the concluding sections of the essay.

To return to the concept of chance: if in a first moment Lévi-Strauss excludes the element of chance from the cultural development of prehistorical societies, at the same time he gives it a central role at another level of determination. In other words, while on the one hand he might grant the privilege of intention and invention to the individual agent, on the other hand he makes the qualification that despite the importance of individual initiative or creativity, this can only be properly realized at specific times and in specific locations (349). So purely individual and psychological factors are not sufficient to explain cultural development, especially of the kind that occurs with what Lévi-Strauss designates as the two great cultural revolutions, the neolithic and industrial-scientific revolutions. Other factors—historical, economic, sociological—have to be present in sufficient concentration to provide a context for individual innovation, and the conjuncture of these factors is too complex to analyze exhaustively in any one case. For this reason, Lévi-Strauss thinks it necessary to have recourse to the notion of probability. He says that the problem of the singularity of technologically "cumulative" cultures, cultures like our own and before it, the neolithic, is a statistical problem, that is, the problem of a relatively more complex "combination" (353). It is at this point that the analogy of the game of roulette is introduced, in which the gambler would have to bet on infinitely long sequences of numbers before winning, and would run the risk of bankruptcy before reaching the required combination of numbers. The solution to this dilemma is to increase the number of players so as to pool resources and thereby increase the probability of a successful combination (354). If one accepts this analogy, what Lévi-Strauss is proposing is that the singular event of cumulative cultures is made more probable if it is understood that these cultures are in fact the result of what he calls a "coalition" of cultures. Only a high level of interaction between a number of different cultures over a long period of time can account for the existence of cumulative civilizations such as our own.[10]

In its simplest formulation, the idea of the cultural coalition seems unobjectionable. It is difficult to refute that prolonged contact and exchange between different cultures does not in any way contribute to a measure of cultural development, though the concepts of "exchange" and "development" would always need qualification, and would probably be impossible to quantify. It is, however, more difficult to argue that the concept of diversity *by itself* can explain the specificity of a cultural formation such as our own—Western technological or "mechanical" culture, as Lévi-Strauss terms it. The weakness of this concept of diversity becomes apparent when he proposes an example illustrating the essential prerequisite, as he sees it, of number and diversity for cultural coalitions to work successfully. The example brings together the Old World at the beginning of the Renaissance and the New World prior to the arrival of the Europeans. Both civilizations, he says, have a high level of contact and interaction between their constituent cultures. The difference is that the cultures of Europe are more highly differentiated, as a consequence of having been in existence and in contact for a longer period of time. The indigenous American cultures, on the other hand, have had less time in which to diverge from one another, and are therefore relatively more homogenous. The test case for this difference in differentiation is the meeting or confrontation of the two civilizations in the fifteenth and sixteenth centuries. Lévi-Strauss suggests that the arrival of the Europeans was so catastrophic for the civilizations of the New World because of their relative cultural homogeneity, which did not permit a sufficiently flexible response to the invading forces:

> Thus, although one cannot say that the cultural level of Mexico or Peru was, at the time of discovery, inferior to that of Europe (we have even seen that in many regards it was superior to it), the various aspects of culture were perhaps also less well formulated. Side by side with amazing successes, the pre-Columbian civilizations are full of failures; they have, as it were, "blanks" in them. They also offer the sight, less contradictory than we may think, of the coexistence of precarious forms and abortive forms. Their rather stiff and weakly diversified organization very likely explains their total collapse in front of a handful of conquerors. The deep cause of it may be sought in the fact that the American cultural "coalition" was established between partners who differed less among themselves than those of the Old World. (356)

Apart from the obvious reductiveness of this explanation from a historical point of view, it could be asked to what extent the concepts of homogeneity and diversity are workable categories for the analysis of cultural difference. Again, how does one quantify, or even qualify, relative cultural homogeneity or diversity? The problem or limitation of Lévi-Strauss's interpretation is that it is clearly predicated on a biological model. Cultures are treated as if they were a collection, or more precisely, a *combination* of genetic traits responsible for the reproduction and survival of a given society. In the present example, the European intrusion is literally like a virus that the "immune system" of the American civilizations would be incapable of dealing with. Like biological groups with a low level of genetic variation, these civilizations would have an insufficient repertory of responses to the external aggression of a highly adaptive culture.[11]

This biological, or rather biologistic, interpretation of intercultural phenomena is not presented as such in *Race and History*. The model is an implicit rather than an explicit one, and it is probably from this rhetoric of implication that the essay derives some of its argumentative force. However, it would be useful here to quote a passage from a later essay by Lévi-Strauss on the same subject, again commissioned by UNESCO and published in 1971, some twenty years after *Race and History*, this time entitled *Race and Culture*. The second essay reproduces many of the arguments of the first, but the passage in question also refers back to the previous essay and makes explicit what was its implicit use of the bio-genetic model. The passage merits quotation in full as it brings together the various concepts I have been working through in *Race and History*:

> Over [twenty] years ago . . . I used the notion of coalition to explain that isolated cultures cannot hope to create by themselves the conditions for a truly cumulative history. For such conditions, I said, diverse cultures must voluntarily or involuntarily combine their respective stakes, thereby giving themselves a better chance to realize, in the great game of history, the long winning series that allows history to progress. Geneticists now express similar views on biological evolution . . . in the history of populations, genetic recombination plays a part comparable to that of cultural recombination in the evolution of the ways of life, the techniques, the bodies of knowledge, and the beliefs whose distribution distinguishes the various societies. (1987, 17–18)

It will be noticed that there is a paradoxical reversal of the direction of reference or causation in this passage. What Lévi-Strauss appears to be saying is that in the twenty years separating the two essays the successive discoveries in genetic science have confirmed his own previous model of cultural development. Whereas, as has been shown, that model was already implicitly biological. *Race and History* was written a few years before the major advances in molecular biology in the 1950s and 1960s, but the necessary elements for Lévi-Strauss's model of cultural interaction and adaptation were already present in neo-Darwinian genetics.

Whatever the problems of influence or precedence, it is evident that by way of the homology suggested between genetic and cultural, Lévi-Strauss is more generally proposing a *stochastic* model of historical change. The genetic recombinations he refers to in *Race and Culture* are the products of random mutation, there is no preprogrammed direction to the process: evolution is teleonomic but not teleological. Nevertheless, in the last section of *Race and History* he argues that the cultural diversity that is the strength of the European coalition must in the long term tend toward homogenization. Again, the metaphor used is that of the game: the longer the game lasts, the greater the tendency toward an equalization of the resources of each player and a reduction in the chances of obtaining a winning combination (358–359). Again, the explicit metaphor of the game is accompanied by a second, implicit analogy, in this instance the thermodynamic or informational concept of entropy. The second law of thermodynamics states that the entropy, that is, the degree of disorder or disorganization of a closed system increases with time. Stated in bio-informational terms and in the closed system of cultural exchange Lévi-Strauss is describing, the intermixing of what at the beginning are a diversity of cultural traits would lead in the long run to an equalization, a flattening out of the initial diversity. The solution to this dangerous but inevitable process of homogenization, he argues, is to actively promote diversity. Normally, the process can be countered in two ways. The first is to diversify the internal structure of a given society, in other words, to introduce hierarchical differences between its constituent groups, leading to the exploitative structure of, for example, our modern industrial societies. The second solution, dependent on the first, is to introduce new players, new partners into the initial coalition of cultures. Historically this is what happened with Western imperialism and colonization (359–360). Whatever reservations one might have concerning this extension of the concept of diversity to structures of hierarchy and subordination, it is clear that Lévi-Strauss's preferred solution to the problem of cultural homogenization is the second option, that is, the opening up of the closed system of cultural exchange—though in the postwar, and what is rapidly becoming the postcolonial context of *Race and History*, the agent responsible for promoting such cultural diversity would not be a colonizing state or coalition of states, but rather the anonymous "international institutions" alluded to in the closing pages of the essay. The mission or responsibility of these institutions would be to oversee the liquidation of obsolete forms of cultural collaboration while selecting others better adapted to present conditions:

> Institutions must first assist humanity and make the reabsorption of these defunct diversities as painless and safe as possible. These diversities are the valueless residues of modes of collaboration which exist as putrefied vestiges and constitute a permanent risk of infecting the

international body. They must be pruned, amputated, if need be, to facilitate the birth of other forms of adaptation. (361)

So if, as was mentioned earlier, the process of cultural recombination described by Lévi-Strauss is a stochastic one, this does not exclude the possibility of a certain agency. Just as in biology artificial selection, and more recently (more powerfully), biotechnology are possible modes of human intervention in the process of evolution, so Lévi-Strauss appears to believe in the possibility of intervention in the sphere of cultural interaction and cultural evolution. The problem is obviously how the "institutions" he refers to might distinguish between the obsolete and the vital, on what criteria the distinction might be made, and indeed *who* would provide the relevant data. It is at this point that the reader can perceive or at least suspect another possible instance of judgment or decision behind these institutions, that of the ethnologist, the ethnologist Lévi-Strauss elsewhere describes as the conscience and consciousness of the West, the witness and mediator of cultures radically different from our own (1984, 509–515; 1978, 31–33).

The literally vital quest for diversity is therefore finally delegated to the ethnologist, but also more specifically and more narrowly still, to the *structural* anthropologist. I say this because the imperative that Lévi-Strauss articulates in the closing lines of *Race and History* is curiously Leibnizian. He says that "we must . . . encourage secret potentialities" held in reserve by history, that "the diversity of human cultures is behind us, around us and ahead of us" (362). This idea of potentiality, of a virtual reality of cultural alternatives, should be related to the repertorial or tabular model of classification discussed earlier, which allowed for the prediction or anticipation of a number of blank spaces in which past or potential configurations could be entered; the potential configurations, it will be remembered, far outnumber actual, existent configurations. As was mentioned earlier, the recourse to the Leibnizian model is frequent in Lévi-Strauss's work, an invariant feature of his version of structuralism. But structuralism, as Lévi-Strauss understands it, is also a humanism, or rather, a "new" humanism that combines the arguments of science with the enlarged vision of humanity offered by the *human* science of anthropology. Not only does Lévi-Strauss criticize the failure of a certain philosophy to learn the lessons of modern science, in texts such as *Race and History* he is also extending the methods and models of structural anthropology to a moral and ethical terrain traditionally occupied by philosophy. This discreet investment and transformation of the old humanism was doubtless in its context a legitimate and necessary gesture, but its mobilization of aspects of modern scientific knowledge needs to be treated with caution. As the preceding analysis has hopefully demonstrated, Lévi-Strauss's explanation of the mechanisms of cultural development juxtaposes a series of combinatorial and relational models, and in their turn these models serve the more general homology between the genetic and the cultural. The term *juxtaposition* is an appropriate one, because the links between the different models are weak links: there is no rigorous explanation, no consistent working-through of their relationship or articulation. More generally, there is the mostly implicit and uncritical assimilation (conflation and confusion) of two qualitatively different levels of organization—the biological and the cultural. In this sense juxtaposition could also be called "bricolage," what Lévi-Strauss defines as science's instrumental and provisional approach to its concepts and models, adopting and discarding them as and when necessary, in the hope that at each stage they will provide a closer approximation to their object (1996, 16–22). Derrida's criticism of the concept of "bricolage" is that it assumes that truth and the instruments or conceptual tools used to reach it are separable, and this is part of his more general criticism of the discourse of the human sciences, a discourse that is not sufficiently critical of its own concepts (*WD*, 284–285). Despite the rhetorical effectiveness of Lévi-Strauss's application of linguistic, informational, and bio-genetic models in *Race and History*, it could be said that it lacks precisely this necessary dimension of critical reflexivity.

## NOTES

1. The relevant texts here are "Structure, Sign, and Play in the Discourse of the Human Sciences," in *Writing and Difference*, 278–293, and "The Violence of the Letter: From Lévi-Strauss to Rousseau," in *Of Grammatology*, 101–140. Full details of these and other works referred to are given in the bibliography.

2. There is only one reference of any substance to Jakobson in the *Elementary Structures*, though his influence from the point of view of methodology is greater than this minimal mention would suggest. In the Introduction to the first edition of the book Lévi-Strauss himself expresses his indebtedness to Jakobson in this respect (*The Elementary Structures of Kinship*, xxvi).

3. Surprisingly, François Dosse's recent history of structuralism makes little reference to the interdisciplinary effect of biology in the 1960s and 1970s (*Histoire du structuralisme*).

4. See the Introduction to my book, *System and Writing in the Philosophy of Jacques Derrida*, 1–11.

5. "Vivre et parler," published in *Les Lettres françaises* 1221 (14 and 21 February 1968), 3–7, 4–6.

6. "Vivre et parler" (14 February 1968), 6. Jacob makes a similar qualification in the article cited above ("Le modèle linguistique en biologie," 199, 203).

7. "François Jacob et Claude Lévi-Strauss face à face," extracts from a televised discussion, published in *Figaro littéraire* 1338 (7 January 1972), 13, 16. The main focus of the discussion is how contemporary biological research has affected our understanding of the relationship between innate and acquired behavior. Inevitably, language is taken as an important example of this, but for the most part the two specialists maintain a polite distance and there is little real debate.

8. On the philosophical problems of Lévi-Strauss's distinction between nature and culture see Derrida, *Writing and Difference*, 282–284.

9. *Structural Anthropology* 2, 323–362. Page references for *Race and History* will henceforth be given in the main text.

10. It should be specified that the analogy used here is not a simple and singular one. The roulette metaphor illustrating the statistical explanation of the emergence of "cumulative" history is in fact combined with a concept of interactive exchange that is visibly derived from Mauss. Lévi-Strauss's assertion that "The exclusive fatality, the unique fault which can afflict a human group and prevent it from completely fulfilling its nature, is to be alone" (356), echoes the conclusion of Mauss's celebrated essay on the gift, where gift exchange is seen as a mechanism for regulating conflict between groups but also a means of avoiding "stagnation and isolation" (*The Gift: The Form and Reason for Exchange in Archaic Societies*, 82).

11. This seems to be an extrapolation on the cultural level of the well-known fact of the decimation of indigenous American populations due to their inadequate immune response to European diseases.

# CHAPTER 9

# French Kissing

*Whose Tongue Is It Anyway?*

JOHN P. LEAVEY JR.

One Tongue in the mouth of the other, a French kiss: such is translation.

To read such a minimalist definition of translation—a French kiss—one would have to know what it is to define translation in one language (whether English or *l'américain*) in terms of or with the designation of another. Translation according to this declaration is not simply *un patin*, but a *French* kiss. The French do not have this possibility, they do not say an American kiss or an English kiss (as they have in other expressions: to take French leave, *filer à l'anglaise*; frenchie, french letter, *une capote anglaise*; or even the notion of "franglais"), and perhaps that is why it would be useful to explore from this impossibility, this lack of the French (what it cannot designate) some limits of the "French contexts of Derrida's thought" and to add, without necessarily gathering together, a fold or two, beyond any opposition of theory and praxis in this addition: applied Derrida.

What in "French kiss" calls for the designation of the other according to the nation? What national warfare is going on here? Now if the kiss is philosophy's, it can be the translation of, in the grossest sense, French philosophy, accused of translating German philosophy, in turn accused of translating Greek philosophy, in turn accused of translating philosophy itself, accused in another tongue of mistranslating itself in its history. In this all-too-brief synopsis of philosophical loves in French kissing, there is already an international assembly of *national philosophies*, of national traits bearing on what cannot be national. And several tongues.

But is the warfare also a warfare among allies, as this term shortly arose after World War I? Tony Thorne in *Dictionary of Contemporary*

149

*Slang* provides two entries of interest: the phrase *French kiss* "appeared in British and American speech shortly after World War I, before which there was, significantly, no equivalent term" (s.v. "French kiss"). The Frenching unit was the "tongue" or "mouth." Under the entry of the verb *french,* Thorne notes that the verb can be shorthand for "engag[ing] in French kissing." Its primary meaning, taken from "the world of prostitution and pornography," is "to perform oral sex." The entry continues:

> The word may refer to cunnilingus or fellatio and derives from the British notion that all forms of "deviant" sexual behaviour are widespread among, if not invented by, the French. This may originate in the widespread accusation of the spreading of venereal disease by foreign neighbours.

A generalization perhaps not simply a tendency of the British, as the Latin *morbus gallicus* "venereal disease" might indicate. And there is, to change the emphasis somewhat, in order to recognize the designation of French by the French, the discussion of the French and the French tongue, of *gallicisme,* of the French on the French, here specifically of Francis Ponge in *Signsponge* (42–45), of what takes "courage"—to write, to deal with improper, unclean words, which means "grabbing," as Derrida says, "the tweezers and treating words between quotation marks, in the first place as a generalized citation for the French tongue." Derrida continues: "I am not pushing things too far when I compare quotation marks to tweezers. He has done it himself, and precisely around the word 'proper' in the expression 'proper name'—'this is done in quotation marks, in other words with tweezers.' " One's tongue's always in another's.

In order to provide some protocols for posing a question of the French of "French kiss," I want to twist together two "words" of Derrida: *plus d'une langue* and *il y a là cendre.* These two words indicate two torsions in Derrida's (con)text and two folds in our plying of Derrida. The first, a risky and risked definition of deconstruction, indicates in one language the insufficiency of any language; the second, one example of the French Derrida is sentenced to write by birth. Both French, both deeply rooted in French, both turn the French against itself, the first calling in its idiom for another language, the second walling itself within its idiom. These two—one a phrase, not "a sentence," a phrase "as brief, elliptical, and economical as a password [*mot d'ordre*]" said "*sans phrase*" (*MPM,* 15; *Mé,* 38), the other a sentence—these two watch "words" can also stand stead as disciplinary: the first, the word, on the margins of philosophy and the breaching of the (national) philosophical mouth and tongue; the second, the sentence, on the bounds of the literary (the *éponge* of Ponge, the *pas* and *sans* of Blanchot, for example). To translate just a bit more, these two French(–) kiss(es).

If I attempt a brief occidental glossophilematology, a phenomenology of disciplined and national kissing, specifically, of French kissing, two bands (a double bind) limit the affair: to kiss (*plus d'une langue*), not to kiss (*il y a là cendre*). Without(,) a third.

## To Kiss—From Literature to Philosophy

One discipline of the kiss, the poetry of the kiss, in which the kiss is both poem and kiss itself, could be said to begin with Joannes Secundus (1511–1536) and his *Basia*. In the first of the two prefatory poems, "De libello basiorum" [This Little Book of Kisses], the kisses are "crafted," the speaker claims to craft the kisses: "I craft the kisses [*basia fingo*]," he says. The kisses are the poems and involve the tongue. In "The Fifth Kiss," both tongues meet: "Et linguam tremulam hinc et inde vibras/Et linguam querulam hinc et inde sugis" ("Basium V") [here and there/your tremulous tongue a vibrato, you/suck my plaintaive tongue now ("The Fifth Kiss")]. "The Eighth Kiss" could be designated as a kiss of tongue and teeth, the tongue that sings of the beloved (and becomes the member tumescent with passion, "ira tumere tanta') and the teeth that "molest" it. This poem, this kiss, asks the beloved why she assaults the very "member" that sings her praise: the poem the kiss the tongue. It begins:

> Quis te furor . . .
> · · · · · · · · · · · · · · · · · · · ·
> Sic involare nostram
> Sic vellicare linguam
> Ferociente morsu?
> ("Basium VIII")

> What madness possessed you,
> · · · · · · · · · · · · · · · · · · · · · · · ·
> . . . to molest my tongue like that
> tearing into it with a
> ferocious bite?
> ("The Eighth Kiss")

The tenth kiss of these kisses, on the uncertainty of the kinds of kisses, includes what the translator F. X. Mathews renders as "soul-kissing": two souls, joined at the mouth, copulate, suck tongue, and diffuse into the foreign body of each other:

Non sunt certa, meam moveant quae basia mentem.

. . . . . . . . . . . . . . . . . . . . . . . . . . . . . . . . . . . . . .

Dulce . . . est . . .

. . . . . . . . . . . . . . . . . . . . . . . . . . . . . . . . . . . . . .

. . . labris querlis titubantem sugere linguam
Et miscere duas juncta per ora animas
Inque peregrinum diffundere corpus utramque . . .
("Basium X")

Kisses that stir my soul have no categories

. . . . . . . . . . . . . . . . . . . . . . . . . . . . . . . . . . . . . .

I love to . . .

. . . . . . . . . . . . . . . . . . . . . . . . . . . . . . . . . . . . . .

. . . suck with moaning mouth the tremulous tongue
that licks my own, our souls diffusing into
the strangeness of each other's flesh, soul-kissing . . .
("The Tenth Kiss")

The strangeness of the body of the other is only explored by the others who follow. These poems in *Latin* attempt to do away with the very other in the hoped-for "hegemony of the Latin."[1] This discipline cedes way to the "vernacular" and the *fingo basia* is translated into one's own tongue in the rise of national literatures.

The kiss is not only the poem, however. It is also the beginning (*der Anfang*) of philosophy, as Derrida, referring to Novalis, reminded me. And of the fragment. In Novalis's 1798 *Preliminary Studies to the Various Collections of Fragments* (*Vorarbeiten zu verschiedenen Fragmentsammlungen*), there are two fragments (74 and 81 [55 and 57 of *Logological Fragments I*])[2] marked for further revision; in them the beginning of philosophy is "the first kiss" (*der erste kuß*):

> . . . Act of self-embrace.
>
> One must never confess [*gestehen*] to oneself that one love's one-self—The secret of this confession [*dieses Geständnisses*] is the life-principle of the self-protective and eternal love. The first kiss in this understanding [*in diesem Verständnisse*] is the principle of philosophy [*das Princip der Philosophie*]—the origin of a new world—the beginning [*der Anfang*] of absolute chronology—this completion of an infinitely growing bond with the self [*Selbstbundes*].
>
> Who wouldn't like a philosophy whose germ is a first kiss? (Novalis 2:329; *Logological I* 58–59 [trans. mod.])

The other marked fragment I want to consider is on the distraction and the distance of reading, of reading about the beginning of philosophy and its musical accompaniment:

I should wish my readers were reading the remark that the beginning of philosophy [*der Anfang der Philosophie*] is a first kiss at the moment when they were listening to Mozart's composition: "Wenn die Liebe in Deinen blauen Augen" being performed with true feeling—if they could indeed sense that they were about to experience a first kiss.

On musical accompaniment to different kinds of meditation, conversation, and reading [*Lectüren*]. (Novalis 2, 331; *Logological I*, 59)

Philosophy begins in a secret love of self-understanding, whose first kiss must be protected against by music (music accompanies what can at best be a presentiment of, in the "vengeful nearness" of, if we read *in der Ahndungsvollen Nähe* in a more contemporary sense), by what distracts the reading of that confession never to be confessed in the growing bonds of self. In the "Fragmentblatt" of 1797, this secret is so secret as to be further proscribed in its revelation—suicide. The "real beginning of all philosophy," Novalis writes, is "*Selbsttödtung*," "the proscribed philosophical act" (Novalis 2:223).[3] Blanchot explains in a fragment in *The Writing of the Disaster*:

> Novalis's affirmation, often misquoted or hastily translated: the true philosophical act is the putting to death of oneself (the dying of the self, or the self as dying—*Selbsttötung*, not *Selbstmord*—the mortal movement of the self—the same—toward the other). Suicide, as this mortal movement of identity, can never be undertaken as a plan or project, because the event of suicide is accomplished within a circle separate from all projects, separate perhaps from all thought or truth, and thus is felt to be unverifiable, indeed unknowable. Any reason one gives for it, however justifiable, seems unsuitable. To kill oneself is to install oneself in the space forbidden to all, which is to say, forbidden to onself. *Clandestinity* . . . (32)

The beginning of philosophy, then, would be the destiny of the secret, a clandestine kiss of self-dying, the dying of self to the other, through the "organ serv[ing] other," the tongue (Novalis 2:377; *Logological Fragments II*, in *Philosophical Writings* 78), and philosophy, "a self-separation and art of binding—a *self-specification* and art *of genesis [Die Philosophie ist eine Selbstscheidungs und Verbindungskunst—eine Selbstspecifications und* Gernationskunst]" (Novalis 2:674)], is that kiss beginning the ever-growing bonds of self, the secret self-embrace in the separation-binding, specification-genesis that is *Selbsttödtung*.

Or, perhaps to translate Novalis into another fragment of today, into a certain French context, in which speech and kiss, as in Novalis, are connected ("the first kiss, the first word of love" [2:354]; or more explicitly: " . . . (speaking) . . . *kiss* . . . the act of embracing" [2:497;

*General Draft*, in *Philosophical Writings* 125]), there is the fragment of Roland Barthes, in which in the *embrasser* (to kiss and also to embrace) the three are intertwined with speech: *"Parler / embrasser."* According to Barthes in his autobiographical *Roland Barthes*, to move to upright posture, for Leroi-Gourhan, is to free the mouth to speak and to kiss. Barthes imagines a "single transgression" of the mouth that leads once again to the body, this time to *"the stammered body"*:

> Let us imagine for this double function, localized in one and the same site, a single transgression, which would be generated by a simultaneous use of speech and kissing: *to speak while kissing, to kiss while speaking.* It would appear that such a pleasure exists, since lovers incessantly "drink in speech upon the lips of the beloved," etc. What they then delight in is, in the erotic encounter, that play of meaning which opens and breaks off: the function *which is disturbed:* in a word: *the stammered body.* (141)

Not said, only implied, the stammered body, reduced to a notable synecdoche of the mouth, is the tongue. And the single transgression then is the French kiss. One tongue in the mouth of the other. Hence, *plus d'une langue*, the first word.

The first of two words: *plus d'une langue.* Derrida is a French philosopher. This supposedly banal statement, however, is not without complication. In the "Ends of Man," a text dated April 1968 in the preamble and signed 12 May 1968, a text prepared for an international philosophical colloquium in New York, Derrida points out that the possibility of such a colloquium "implies that *contrary to the essence of philosophy*—such as it has always represented itself at least—philosophical nationalities have been formed" (*M*, 111; my emphasis). The "political milieu of every international philosophical colloquium," he proposes, is the *"form of democracy"* that "at least" "accommodates" two nonidentifications: nonidentification with the "national philosophical identity" and nonidentification with "the official policies" of the nation (*M*, 113–114). According to the self-represented essence of philosophy, there is the philosopher, the one without language and without nation, there is not the *French* philosopher.

But "philosophical nationalities have been formed." There are French philosophers. Derrida is a French philosopher. Twenty-five years later, in 1992, he still appears to be marking out forms of democratic nonidentification:

> Should I remind you, in addition, that I only ever write in French and that I attach great importance to this fact, as to all problems concerning idiom, natural and national language, traditions of thought, their

filiations and genealogies? But here again, one must go further and point out that things are much more complicated. Because very quickly, and perhaps even from the beginning, this complicity with the "French" or "Parisian" context meant conflict, opposition, rupture, estrangement, a certain uprootedness. (*P. . .* , 416)

So, one might ask, what is Derrida's relation to the French he only ever writes. In a text dated *"9–16 January 1978,"* he asserts in the Translator's Note to "Living On/Border Lines" that "One never writes either in one's own tongue [*langue*] or in a foreign tongue" (101 [modified]). Earlier in the same stereophonic text, still in the stolen translator's note he "sign[s] in advance," he says: "That makes three languages I'm writing in, and this is to appear, supposedly, in a fourth" (76–77). I write only in French, he says, but no one can write only in one's tongue, or a foreign one, so I write in French in several languages.

In 1986, he reiterates his monolingual state: "I have only one language. I don't know any other. Thus I was raised in a monolingual milieu—absolutely monolingual. . . . So, French is my only language." Then the nonidentification, the estrangement: "Nevertheless . . . France was not Algeria; the source, the norm, the authority of the French language was elsewhere. And, in a certain manner, confusedly, we learned it, I learned it as the language of the other—even though I could only refer to one lanaguage as being mine" (*P. . .* , 203–204). He designates French as one of his foreign tongues in the same year, in a note to "How to Avoid Speaking," a note about autobiography:

> for lack of capacty, competence, or self-authorization, I have never yet been able to speak of what my birth, as one says, should have made closest to me: the Jew, the Arab.
> This small piece of autobiography confirms it obliquely. It is performed in all of my foreign languages: French, English, German, Greek, Latin, the philosophic, metaphilosophic, Christian, etc.
> In brief, how not to speak of oneself? But also, how to do it without allowing oneself to be invented by the other? Or without inventing the other? (135–136 n. 13)

Or again in 1991, when he places in proximity the sacrifice and the password of the elliptical definition of deconstruction:

> It so happens . . . then, that I was *born* . . . in the European *preference*, in the preference of the French language, nation, or citizenship. . . . Everything is "drawn" for me from the . . . experience *of* this "preference" that I *have at the same time to affirm and sacrifice.* There is always for me, and I believe there *must be more than one* language [plus d'une *langue*], mine and the other (I am simplifying a lot), and I must try to

write in such a way that the language of the other does not suffer in mine, suffers me to come without suffering from it, receives the hospitality of mine without getting lost or integrated there. (P. . . , 362–363)

In a sacrificial relation to his own tongue, and to quickly summarize the relation to French culture "a sort of Marrano of French Catholic culture" ("I am one of those Marranos who no longer say they are Jews even in the secret of their own hearts, not so as to be authenticated Marranos on both sides of the public frontier, but because they doubt everything, never to go to confession or give up enlightenment, whatever the cost, ready to have themselves burned, almost, at the only moment they write under the monstrous law of an impossible face-to-face . . ." [Cir, 170–171 (mod.)]), Derrida must French kiss in order to write: "We are all mediators, translators" (P. . . , 116). As a philosopher: "Within the so-called philosophic community, the essential adventure has always been a (hi)story of deciphering, translation, interpretive pedagogy, the enigma of a destination" (P. . . 173). But the adventure is always within a natural language: "philosophy is spoken and written in a natural language, not in an absolutely formalizable and universal language" (P. . . , 219; see also 225). If there is a French philosophy—and in all its difficulties and battles, there is—its idiom is "always and only for the other, in advance expropriated (exappropriated)" (P. . . , 227). Plus d'une langue.

## NOT TO KISS—FROM PHILOSOPHY TO LITERATURE

In the other band (the band of autism and mutism, the ban of translation) is the double ring of the two mouths that coyly refuse to kiss: for example, literature and philosophy as contained in one tongue and one mouth.

For philosophy, there is the dream of no translation or of universal translatability. In brief, that would be the dream of the essence of philosophy. Its mouth remains closed around its tongue, teeth clenched to prevent any other tongue from coming in; roof battened down; there is ventriloquism without speech, mumbling, its tongue in its ear, but not of the other: philosophy hears itself speak; thought thinks itself without the other. There is to be no exappropriation. Philosophy will accept a kiss (the ideal) through the ear, but not a French kiss. As long as it does not have to open its mouth, philosophy will kiss. The lips closed will touch another, preferably its own. In order to be woman, as Irigaray points out in This Sex Which Is Not One and Speculum, Of the Other

*Woman,* one lip for philosophy must be distinguished from the other, touching in never touching, top not equaling bottom (mouth, vulva), but both lips refuse the penetration of another tongue. Philosophy's kisser does not open for the woman, only for the kiss of death.

Deconstruction attempts to put the autism of philosophy out of joint. In a note in "Tympan" attached to a term referred to elsewhere as a shorthand to indicate part of the *"general strategy of deconstruction"* (overturning, *renversement*), the tongue suffers some carnage as it breaks open the palate (*la palais*).[4] The obliqueness of the *logos* enables an "ambush" so that the tongue "proliferates *outside*":

> To luxate, to tympanize philosophical autism is never an operation *within* the concept and without some carnage of the tongue [*de la langue*]. Thus it [the tongue] breaks open the roof, the closed spiral unity of the palate. It proliferates *outside* to the point of no longer being *understood*. It is no longer *the* tongue [la *langue*]. (*M*, xv; *Ma*, vii)

The tongue, no longer the tongue in its oblique proliferation through the philosophical palate to the outside of the philosophical mouth, is set in motion by "the bloodiness of a disseminated writing" that "comes to separate the lips, to violate the embouchure of philosophy" and bring the tongueless tongue "into contact with some other code, of an entirely other kind. A necessarily unique event, nonreproducible, hence illegible as such and when it happens, . . . without signature" (*M*, xviii; *Ma*, xii). In brief, writing breaks the second band, the dreamed-of autism, with the force of the French kiss.

Second Word: *Il y a là cendre.* For the other, here literature, there is no translation either. The mouth of literature remains open, tongue at play in a speech so individual, tongue rising and falling as no other, that the word never leaves the mouth: this is the idiom, the poem, the literary.

In December 1971, Derrida sends an *envoi* of dedication, a dedication that scatters the signature and its secrets, "far from the center . . . even their cinder" or sender, and denies the debt as it recognizes it. Writing's debt, the debt of the other, strengthens the letter, which "can always arrive at the other side." But that does not excuse the signer; Derrida signs and returns to that signature many times: *il y a là cendre.* One of the voices in *Feu la cendre* recalls without believing that he confided that this sentence was "in truth his ciphered signature" (51). Like a proper name, this sentence refuses translation; in *Dissemination,* Barbara Johnson does not translate it in its two occurences (171 and 366). Derrida agrees; there are singularity and event in the encryption of this sentence:

> This sentence in itself remains untranslatable. . . . "Il y a là cendre" is not translatable in the play in French of the *là* which in some way carries the whole text. Even before translation, moreover, in the writing of the text itself, the singular little sentence may be encrypted; it may have taken place only once and have been meant only for someone in a singular situation; it is thus effaced. It is carried off, incinerated once again in the word itself. The sentence "Il y a là cendre," which is part of a dedication, linked to a singular event, should not even have been repeated. But it is repeated in the text and, consequently, it is lost or causes to disappear the witnesses themselves once it becomes a sentence. (*P. . .* , 390–391)

Ten years after the *envoi* is sent, a reading begins to impose itself: *Feu la cendre* (1982). This title *Feu la cendre* erases the there (*là*) of the sentence in the drop of the accent (like the circumflex of Genet), but homophonically repeats it. The definite article takes place in another idiomatic phrase: the late cinder, or perhaps another translation, like "Signature Event Context": "Fire She Cinder." *Feu la cendre* is surely as untranslatable as the sentence this title is suspended over. In the dedication that scatters the signature begin to be read Mallarmé and the end of "The Double Session": "The crisis of literature takes place when nothing takes place but the place, in the instance where no one is there to know" (*D*, 285). The passage in *Cinders* reads: "Nothing will have taken place but the place. Cinders there are: Place there is [*Il y a là cendre: il y a lieu*]" (37). In *Cinders* two idioms separated by a colon: both untranslatable. We are warned that they cannot be translated. If the last phrase had continued, *il y a lieu de*, a solution of convenience or opportunity would suggest itself: cinders there are, there is the opportunity that cinders there are takes place, but without witnesses. Or of necessity, as "*Sauf le nom*" indicates: "Passion of, for, the place, again. I shall say in French: *il y a lieu de* (which means *il faut*. 'it is necessary,' 'there is ground for') rendering oneself *there where* it is impossible to go" (59). There is only the necessity of the opportunity for place, its convenience, nothing else. There—place only—at best (the necessity of) an opportunity; at worst, not. One of the voices in *Cinders* says of the opportunity of this sentence: "Discreetly pushed to the side, dissemination thus phrases in five words [*il y a là cendre*] what is destined, by the fire, to dispersion without return, the pyrification of what does not remain and returns to no one" (39). The sentence cannot be translated. If, contrary to that, the sentence *il y a là cendre* is translatable—*Cinders* says it is and provides the translation:

> [T]he cinder is not, is not what it is. It remains *from* what is not, in order to recall at the delicate, charred bottom of itself only non-being

or non-presence. Being without presence has not been and will no longer be there where there is cinder and where this other memory would speak. There, where cinder means difference between what remains and what is, will she ever reach it, there? (39; see also *P. . .* , 322–323)

then translation (*il y a là cendre*) is undermined by the untranslatable (*il y a lieu*): there, the place of cinders. The place of cinders is, exegesis ("education") notwithstanding, nowhere: "the urn of the tongue" (55), "the tomb of a tomb, the monument of an impossible tomb—forbidden, like the memory of a cenotaph, deprived of the patience of mourning, denied also the slow decomposition that shelters, locates, lodges, hospitalizes itself in you while you eat the pieces" (53, 55). In *Glas*, he proposes the word "pyramidal monument (*monumanque pyramidale*)" (34b; see also 240a–241a) that I take, not as he does, to designate the circumflex indicating the dropped "s," a circumflex itself lacking from the name Genet, but the place of the cinder. The nowhere of the no–where place, the late place that was, *feu le lieu*, re-traces "writing in the passion of non-knowledge rather than of the secret."[5] A voice from *Feu la cendre* takes up a variant, as Ned Lukacher points out, of L' Académie Française ("For the defense and illustration of the French language"): "I would say, for the defense and illustration of its own sentence, 'I' the cinder would say that his writing is not interested in knowledge. The raw cinder, that is more to his taste; and the initial consonant matters very little; every word seems to finish with cinder" (75). I would be tempted, then, to read cinder as the gift of the poem: "The gift of the poem cites nothing, it has no title, its histrionics are over, it comes without your expecting it, cutting short the breath, cutting all ties with discursive and especially literary poetry. In the very ashes of this genealogy. Not the phoenix, not the eagle, but the *hérisson*, very lowly, low down, close to the earth" (*P. . .* , 297). The hedgehog.

But such a temptation forgets too quickly the doubleness of writing. There is too much on the cinder to say that there remains the gift of the poem. Too much indicates that there is the philosophical, even if Derrida tries to avoid a "philosophy of cinders." All the work on cinders in French and other tongues in *Feu la cendre* might suggest that Derrida is "trying to bestow a philosophical legitimacy on this word or that word, such as "cinder" for example, to transform it into a philosophical concept." Derrida responds both yes and no to that suggestion:

That is true and false. No doubt, that interests me and I am tempted to take a word from everyday language and then make it do some work as a philosophical concept, provoking thereby restructurations of

philosophical discourse. That interests me . . . at the same time, I re-
strain this movement because to write a philosophy of cinders, to give
to the "cinder" a philosophical dignity, is also to lose it. It is to make
of it precisely something other than what I think it "is" or remains,
since "cinder" cannot be an essence, a substance, a philosophical
meaning. It is on the contrary what ruins philosophy or philosophical
legitimacy, in a certain way. Whence this double gesture that proposes
a philosophical thinking of cinders and shows how "cinder" is that
which prevents philosophy from closing on itself. (*P.* . . , 210)

The cinder ruins philosophy; its taste opens the mouth of philosophy;
cinder is the other in its mouth.

## WITHOUT—WITHOUT A THIRD

French kissing presupposes a sexuality of translation and of philosophy, a sexuality that embraces the French kiss, desires the intromis-
sion of another tongue. Philosophy's kisser opens, for example, in
literature's. Writing can bloody the tongue of philosophy, set the tongue
of philosophy between its teeth and bite clean through, leaving the
dead tongue that Kant desperately calls for, a dead, scholarly tongue,
with no grammatical novelties, with a set lexicon. The kiss of death.
Such are philosophy's secret fear and hope, and so it resists putting its
tongue in the mouth of the other, even in the most passionate kiss (the
other band). If literature can bite the tongue of philosophy (or vice
versa), that would be an untranslatable—event—detached tongues
kissing, mouths agape, teeth bloodied.

Or, the other code of the philosophical tongue can be the cinder on
the tongue—the otherness of the other in the mouth. One tongue in
the mouth of the other—and so more than one, without sacrifice, and
the chance of the kiss.[6] To French kiss can be the bitter taste of the
cinder in the mouth and on the tongue. The last of the animadversions
in *Feu la cendre* is from *The Post Card*, another name for the cinder
("Differing from a letter, a post card is a letter to the extent that nothing of it remains that is, or that holds. It destines the letter to its ruin"
[*PC,* 249]). This fold from a postcard concerns the cindered mouth:

> Before my death I would give orders. If you aren't there, my body is
> to be pulled out of the lake [*lac*] and burned, my ashes are to be sent
> to you, the urn well protected ("fragile") but not registered, in order
> to tempt fate. This would be an *envoi* of/from me which would no
> longer come from me (or an *envoi* sent by me, who would have or-
> dered it, but no longer an *envoi* of me, as you like). And then you
> would enjoy mixing my cinders with what you eat (morning coffee,

brioche, tea at 5 o'clock, etc.). After a certain dose, you would start to go numb, to fall in love with yourself. I would watch you slowly advance toward death, you would approach me within you with a serenity that we have no idea of, absolute reconciliation. And you would give orders. . . . While waiting for you I'm going to sleep, you're always there, my sweet love. (*C*, 74, 76; *PC*, 196)

More than two months earlier, "*15 March 1979*," there is the postcard of the clandestination and the madness of writing in the convulsion of the body, there is what I can only designate as the French kiss without kiss—and I send it without adding another word, only translated:

> I wanted to write you, otherwise, but always with the same foreign language (they don't know how much a language is foreign) . . . and when I write you you continue, you transfigure everything (the transformation comes from behind the words, it operates in silence, simultaneously subtle and incalculable, you substitute yourself for me and right up to my tongue you "send" it to yourself and then I remember those moments when you called me without warning, you came at night at the bottom of my throat, you came to touch my name with the tip of your tongue. Beneath the surface, it took place beneath the surface of the tongue, softly, slowly, an unheard-of trembling, and I was sure that at that second that it was not coming back, a convulsion of the entire body in two tongues at once, the foreign one and the other one. On the surface, nothing, a patient, applied pressure leaving everything in place, forcing no movement of the tongue: and then the tongue is all you hear, and we are alone I believe in receiving its silence. It never says a thing. Because we know how to love it, after our passage, without anything having changed in its appearance, it accepts no longer knowing who it is. It no longer recognizes its own, proper traits, it is no longer the law in its own house, it even has no more words. But for it to consent to this madness, it must be left alone with itself at the moment you enter . . . (*PC*, 183–184)

## NOTES

1. Derrida explores what he calls "*mondialatinisation*," which "names a unique event with respect to which a metalanguage seems inaccessible, even though it remains here, nonetheless, of first necessity" (Derrida's context is the question of religion) ("Foi et savoir: Les deux sources de la 'religion' aux limites de la simple raison," in *La religion*, 42).

2. *Logological Fragments I*, in Novalis, *Philosophical Writings*, trans. Margaret Mahony Stoljar (1997). "This selection is from a manuscript dating from the end of 1797 to mid–1798. Some of the material included was crossed out by Novalis for future revision, other entries (shown by an asterisk) were marked as specially deserving of further work" (171–172, n. 1).

3. *The New Wildhagen German Dictionary* (1965), gives the following for *ächten*: "to send a person to Coventry."

4. The word *palais* opens onto another fold, the fold of Genet in *Glas*: The passage concerns writing "in Oedipus," "*on* Oedipus, mounted on Oedipus, as on a mounting, an easel, a pedestal or a ring. A slab. And the one who mounts—listen to the laughter of the avant-garde and the innovators—knows full well this cavalier operation of the painter, the sculptor, or the jeweler, is no more for Oedipus than against Oedipus, inside him than outside him. And if the Oedipal event was something, it would be what here gives him the force to mount Oedipus, to fuck you, to unhorse you when you want to interpret, judge, decide. You are still inside the *Palais*. In(side) the mother tongue" (81b).

5. "How to Avoid Speaking" (98): "This always presupposed event, this singular having-taken place [what God's name names, 'the trace of the singular event'] is also for every reading, every interpretation, every poetics, every literary criticism, what one currently calls the *œuvre*: at least the 'already-there' (*déjà-là*) of a phrase, the trace of a phrase of which the singularity would have to remain irreducible and its reference indispensable in a given idiom. A trace has taken place. Even if the idiomatic quality must necessarily lose itself or allow itself to be contaminated by the repetition which confers on it a code and an intelligibility, even if it *only occurs to efface itself*, if it arises only in effacing itself, the effacement will have taken place, even if its place is only in the ashes. *il y a là cendre*."

6. Ned Lukacher has astutely pointed out the logic of sacrifice in *Cinders* and its argument against Heidegger, against his "free sacrifice" of historical being to the "truth of Being." Sacrifice, which Heidegger "insists . . . 'tolerates [*duldet*] no calculation, for calculation always miscalculates [*verrechnet*] sacrifice in terms of the expedient and the inexpedient'," in this instance, "provides cover," Lukacher argues, following Derrida, "for the most calculating ideological and psychological investments. Heidegger's sacrifice to the Other lends itself too readily to a calculated sacrifice of the others who do not appear to share the experience of essential thinking" ("Introduction: Mourning Becomes Telepathy," in *Cinders*, 17–18). Lukacher ends his introduction (18):

> She, the Cinder, blocks the path of Heidegger's impossible sacrifice. Heidegger would risk everything on the withheld origin of the "call of conscience" that comes from Dasein's innermost essence, from the being "there." Derrida wants only to take a chance on the Other, to reveal that no sacrifice will succeed in bringing the Other to presence, and to acknowledge that experience of a cinder describes our *ethos*, our "dwelling-place" as human beings. Derrida listens more closely than Heidegger and discerns the almost inaudible call of the Cinder, its strange androgynous intonation. Derrida's recognition or acknowledgement of our debt to the Other purges Heidegger's thinking of its Romantic apocalypticism and thus provides us with a realistic basis on which to rethink and reinvent our relations to others . . . .

*Cinders* is the *for intérieur* of Derrida's oeuvre, where he hears the "lack" that comes like a whisper from the far side of Dasein, from the distant entity beyond Being that holds everything in Being. *Cinders* recounts the emergence of conscience as the recognition of our debt to the Other and to the others. "That is what is owed to the fire, and yet, if possible, without the shadow of a sacrifice." These words from *Cinders* [37] may provide the best clue to translating the enigma of *il y a là cendre*.

CHAPTER **10**

# Translating Istrice

*Derrida's Response from Poetry to the Poem*

Boris Belay

As a prefatory note, let me present you with two signatures, two signature styles: between Heidegger and Derrida, it is not so much a question of content or of form, of course, since these distinctions can hardly be maintained. Let me thus try to attempt to outline a shift in what may fall under the heading of "style." In fact, to make things more simple and more complicated right away, allow me to speak to you, today, about a shift between the poetic and the a-poetic, or maybe between the hermeneutic and the aporetic.

Che Cos'è la Poesia? What is poetry?—between two styles.

Poetic–Hermeneutic Signature

Projective saying is poetry: the saying of world and earth, the saying of the arena of their conflict, and thus of the place of all nearness and remoteness of the gods. Poetry is the saying of the unconcealedness of what is. Actual language at any given moment is the happening of this saying, in which a people's world historically arises for it and the earth is preserved as that which remains closed. Projective saying is saying which, in preparing the sayable, simultaneously brings the unsayable as such into the world. In such saying, the concepts of an historical people's nature, i.e., of its belonging to world history, are formed, for that folk, before it. (Heidegger, *Poetry, Language, Thought*, 74)

A–Poetic–Aporetic Signature.

You will call poem henceforth a certain passion of the singular mark, the signature which repeats its dispersion, each time beyond the *logos,*

a-human, barely domestic, nor reappropriable within the family of the
subject: a converted animal, rolled up in a ball, turned toward the
other and itself—a thing, in other words, and modest, discrete, and
close to the earth, the humility which you surname, thus bearing yourself in the name beyond the name, a catachrestic hedgehog, its spikes
fully out, when this ageless blind thing hears, but cannot see, death
coming. (*"Che Cos'è la Poesia?" Pds*, 307)[1]

Already, you have encountered styles, and probably, the question
of style.

Obviously, these signatures are different, and different from me.

How can they ever be mine, how can I ever cite them, make them
close to what at heart is me, recite them, know them by heart?

How can I ever respond to them, to even one of them? How can
I be responsible to them, and do justice to them? For already the gap
between law and justice has opened: I could easily follow the rule of
the law, the copyright law—as I must—and tell you where these signatures come from: but justice would not be served. There would
remain the question of my response and my responsibility to these
signatures, to what they demand of me—the question of the countersignature to the signature of the other, an other, which of course, is
also another style.

To do justice to it, I must invent a style, invent an other—style:
perform this ever so slight, but impossibly demanding shift, which
welcomes beyond the law.

Let me try, let me begin:

*Che Cos'è la Poesia*? What is poetry?—between two words.

*Che Cos'è la Poesia*? opens with a question about the answer, about
what the answer demands: "Pour répondre à une telle question—*en
deux mots, n'est–ce pas?*—on te demande de savoir renoncer au savoir."
(*Pds*, 303) [To answer (to) such a question—*in two words, isn't it?*—you
are asked to know how to give up knowledge].

What, you may ask, is the origin of this demand multiplied beyond the answer? Why does Derrida abide by it?

On the one hand, as with so many things that he writes, there is
a demand, an order from the outside, one that we could try to hear
again:

"Hello, Mr. Derrida, this is Maurizio Ferraris calling on behalf of
*Poetry* (or *Poesia* in my language). I am calling you because I may have
an order for you. Would you be interested in writing our regular
opening statement which responds to the question, and generally to
the name '*Che Cos'è la Poesia*?' Something short, in two words? As
always, there will be a response to your answer, at the end, but I

cannot tell you where it will come from, that is the rule of *Poesia*. Do you accept?"

Then again, it may not have been so directly, so simply demanding, at least not in Ferraris's words. The fact that Derrida did respond to this call and its demand already implies that the question must have come from a further origin. Indeed, right from the beginning, Derrida feels the force of the demand, he repeats it in his opening statement: "Pour répondre à cette question?—*en deux mots, n'est-ce pas*?" He responds and amplifies it with this further restriction, on the verge of contradiction: to answer to poetry in two words. Why the doubling of the bind? What demands it? And where does the call for a response originate? Is it in *Poesia*, and its editorial board who felt that adding Derrida's signature to theirs would help its cause? Or is it from Poetry, speaking for itself, and calling from one of the prosaic words that echo its name in translation: *Poesia, Poésie, Dichtung*...? Is this why Derrida is ready to put himself in such strictures: to respond to the call of Poetry—a task all the greater since others have attempted it before, others among which the illustrious forefather whose style, opening our question today again, still echoes there and here.

Or is it some other origin, yet, an original moment neither so contingent nor so grandiose, and which would in fact have no precise source, no attributable cause, no traceable origin. Derrida would thus feel a call of a somewhat different nature than that of Poetry itself, one less univocal, following paths less straight, maybe travelling along sideways rather than highways. This call, in fact, would more likely reach him as an appeal, humiliated by the aporetic experience of its event, of its coming to be. But the need to respond, the responsibility would not be any the less, on the contrary: this humble, diffuse and weakened appeal gains, doubles, binding force from its disseminated origin. Its fragility is a sign of its need, of its demand—I, countersigned Derrida, must respond to it, and save it from the danger of its exposure:

> On voudrait le prendre dans ses mains, l'apprendre et le comprendre, le garder pour soi, auprès de soi. (*Pds*, 305)
>
> [One would like to take it in one's hands, to learn it and to understand it, to keep it to oneself, close to oneself.]

This experience of its impossible death demands my response all the more: I must, I must. I must take this fragile, nascent being with me, by me, to defend it against more present forms of being.

And to defend it, in the end—and in its difference—from Being in general, and its call. The fragile appeal must be defended against the momentous claims of the ontico-ontological, even when these are heard on a country path, or in the poet's language? Derrida's responsibility is thus much greater, as it opens itself (on)to a demand whose force remains mostly secret. It requires enough sensitivity for the faint and the humble, where only humility meets humility, the humiliating experience of aporia, the impossible experience.

What is this evanescent being to which, of which Derrida is responding, this call too weak to be an origin?—It is a material being, but small, and close to the ground: shy, it disappears easily, easily forgotten, unheeded. This animal is not caught in hedges but between letters, and words. In fact its materiality consists precisely in this quasi–virtuality of the verb, caught between words and signs, between the letters which make and take its name, between names and the name. Caught between the unnamable and our names for it, it calls out, begs and appeals. It demands to be taken up, by us, close to our heart, otherwise it will not be: the experience of poetry.

Heidegger has been called, he is there throughout Derrida's response. His name is not written, but it is obviously called for. From the beginning: we are reminded of the structure of forgetting and remembering—a-letheia, "in two words, isn't it?"—you are asked to know how to give up knowledge. And to know it well, never forgetting it/Et de bien le savoir, sans jamais l'oublier . . .? And soon hereafter, memory becomes our central thread, guiding us through the labyrinth of this question. What is poetry? It has to do with memory. There, Heidegger's path must be followed: the art of the poet has in its nature the structure of remembering, of letting the forgotten, the covered-over, memories flow back to me, through me. The event of poetry is thus an advent, even if it is the return of something—nothing—whose origins are lost in the play between Lethe and Aletheia. Poetry has to do with allowing for the return of something whose presence is beyond memory, but which demands to be taken up again. Knowledge—present knowledge of the present—can only stand in the way of this openness: protecting, shielding one from the demands that stem from outside of presence. This appeal is thus a threat to presence, for its presence consists precisely in no more than the appeal, which, whether heard or forgotten, is the appeal of the non-present. It calls from outside of the beings that surround me, and yet demands to be responded to as much as they do: its birth already impinges on that which is—and not only, and not least, I.

I . . . am responding to this appeal, it commands me. But this experience is not the call of Poetry, nor the call of Being as it can be uncovered in Poetry. The Earth and the World are not to be unconcealed by this faint appeal. This stuttering begging is unable to be heard by even the commonest of the historical folks, let alone summon the gods out of their remoteness. And as "projective saying," it can barely project itself, clumsily, to me, unsure of its own arrival—it counts on me—hope beyond accounting—for its existence.

No. What is poetry? The question does not demand this. The appeal, frail memory seeking my very core, calls for a different experience: to learn by heart. To learn it, understand it, by my heart, right where it can seek shelter. That is the ground of the question about poetry: to learn by heart. The question does not arise before this appeal is heeded, in all of the required humility and generosity. This openness precedes the question, and in fact dictates it, insofar and exactly as it allows for me to be dictated to. Poetry has to do with this dictation which seeks the shelter of my memory, by my heart. This is why Heidegger haunts these pages more than he is present in them: the question of poetry in *Che Cos'è la Poesia?* is only a promise at this point, a further promise building its gathering momentum on the basis of this an-original frailty. This is why Derrida can cut across Heidegger's *On the Way to Language.* His is an experience that barely dares to scurry through the night, hiding clumsily close to the ground when the scientist, the scholar, and the teacher come treading by: Istrice. "Un coeur là-bas, entre les sentiers ou les autostrades, hors de ta présence, humble, près de la terre, tout bas" (*Pds,* 306) [A heart, down there, between the paths and the motorways, outside your presence, humble, close to the ground, low].

> (And who hasn't ever hit a hedgehog on a highway, and who has even noticed it?)

The experience—aporetic—has now been circumscribed: it is a question of letting it come forth, singularly, to me, to my very heart. Istrice. Strictly speaking, it is thus a movement inward, inward of me, restrained to me, strictly, restricted to this sphere. But it is also restricting of me, because this inwardness of the heart doubles itself into my required openness: I must, I must feel the sharp, intense and piercing responsibility, so strident an appeal it marks my very heart—striated by it. Istrice. Strictly both inward and outward, demandingly hesitant between the two, distressingly aporetic: that is the strictures of the experience, of the crossing across the gap which haunts the present. Istrice is at its root. Not Poetry, but the much more humble and earthly poem.

> Voici donc, tout de suite, en deux mots, pour ne pas oublier. (*Pds*, 304)
>
> [Here then, right away, in two words, so as not to forget.]

This phrase, without verb or subject, circumscribes the poem as best it can. "Here then/Voici donc" presents the injunction, describes the event in its happening; "right away/tout de suite" enforces the urgency of this appeal, its demand; "in two words/en deux mots"— right now, they will be memory and heart— but the economy of the two words carries us throughout; "so as not to forget/pour ne pas oublier" for that is the experience, but also the existence, of the poem: don't you forget it.

This phrase, these two words, "n'est-ce pas déjà cela, le poème?" Derrida asks, "isn't this already the poem?": the promise to learn from the other and to thereby learn of the other, the injunction not to translate from there to here, from this word to mine. Isn't this already the poem, to renounce learning and translation, economies of exchange: even linguistic, and take the other to the letter, as it comes? Again, not as a letter addressed to me, and which should therefore enter into my economy of signs, but rather as a letter sent, and sent to a destination beyond the horizon of calculability. To be learned, it must be taken to the letter, on its own terms, in a grammar that may not be mine. In two words, between yours and mine, the poem demands that the distressing experience of the letter be taken up, and taken to heart.

It is a question of love.

> Le désir du mortel éveille en toi le mouvement . . . de garder de l'oubli cette chose qui du même coup s'expose à la mort et se protège. (*Pds*, 305)
>
> [The mortal's desire awakens in you the motion . . . to guard from forgetting this thing, which thereby both exposes itself to death and protects itself.]

Mortality, yours and mine, can be shared in this experience of the aporia: across it. If I cannot experience your death, nevertheless your mortality—as well as mine—calls out to me. The poem must be saved from its fate, which is also my fate. And we find ourselves tied in this way, bound by this double bind of the double word: not only that fate is inescapable, but also that it is proper. The fate of the poem, its mortality is "what is most its own," yes, and indeed, as such, makes it what it is. But by the same token, and with only a very slight shift, this fate of the poem is mine: not only my mortality, but its death, as I experience it in the "learning by heart." My desire, my attempt to suspend my word and let my heart be shaped by the other, the word of the other—that is the vow of love.

"Tu aimes—garder cela dans sa forme singulière" (*Pds,* 305) [You love—to keep this in its singular form]. Loving the poem, taking it to heart is this singular vow of love: the word that shatters the order of discourse. One word suffices, a long as it is the other word of the other. Yes, yes—responding to the injunction of the shared mortality which separates us/renouncing the protective layers of language and the calculating mechanisms of exchange which hide our shared alterity/translation making way for the name. This animal is catachrestic: it suspends and displaces assignation, but in a radical manner. To do justice to the name of the other, you and I can only found this name anew. The price of its preservation is only to be found in this violent movement of instauration which alone respects the name of the other in what is most proper to it. Here then, two other words for the experience of poetry: love, paternity. But also: loss and property.

Nothing is simple anymore, when I shift from Poetry to the simple poem. Mourning and love, mortal inheritance—these are the impossible desires that now support me. In my heart, I feel the aporetic necessity which commands me. I must, I must take up the other: it made me—mother-tongue, fatherland, you name it? I cannot escape their binding power, nor do I have any desire to. I must love, and love the other. The poem, the poematic experience of the desire for impossible love reminds me of it through its word. Taking it to the letter, I take the other to heart—or rather, again, I let it enter, I open myself to an event which, an-original and an-archic, would not exist without my response. Knowing nothing of its origin, I am nevertheless responsible for its existence. No paradox, here, or only the inescapable paradox: the aporia that, from its groundlessness, founds all responsibility.

> Il a donc lieu, pour l'essentiel, sans qu'on ait à le faire: il *se laisse* faire, sans activité, sans travail, dans le plus sobre *pathos*, étranger à toute production, surtout à la création. (*Pds,* 307)

> [It thus happens, essentially, without one's having to do it or make it: it happens, lets *lets itself* happen, without activity, without work, in the plainest *pathos*, foreign to all production, and above all to creation.]

This formulation of my passion, in its tragic aspects, leads us clearly away from all voluntaristic agency. Responsibility belongs to a different order, and a crucial shift is required to understand it in its utter responsivity. And this shift is required even of that particular hermeneutical attention to poetry to which Derrida is responding here. For Poetry, in the end, will always demand too much gathering, a too active *Versammlung*, too active to do justice, ultimately, to the singular event that founds it. The singular is aporetic—in its essence: it is its essence—how can the poetic ever be responsible to this? What constraints, the poem asks me, will I have to suffer in a discourse about Poetry? My nature plays between the strictly me and what distresses you—will not this language of yours invert this motion? If "Art, as the setting-into-work of truth, is Poetry," can my experience ever be anything but a-poetic?

> Rappelle-toi la question: "Qu'est-ce que . . . ?" (*ti estí, was ist . . . , istoria, episteme, philosophia*). "Qu'est-ce que . . . ?" pleure la disparition du poème—une autre catastrophe. En annonçant ce qui est tel qu'il est, une question salue la naissance de la prose.
>
> [Remember the question: "What is . . . ?" (*ti estí, was ist . . . , istoria, episteme, philosophia*). "What is . . . ?" mourns the disappearance of the poem—another catastrophe. By announcing what is as it is, a question salutes the birth of prose.] (*Pds*, 308)

Between, then, the poetic and the a-poetic, the hermeneutic and the aporetic, the poem, if it is to be taken to heart, to the letter, demands, humbly and haltingly, that I make this shift. From one word to the other, with no programmed transition between the two, I must reinvent the name of the other outside of all systems of exchange. I must reinvent it in what is most proper to it: its name—to give it a name that is to be its own, that does justice to that it is—the impossible.

Between your Name and your name, between your Yes and my Yes, I must protect the impossible from another catastrophe, always possible. The catastrophe is the last event in the poem, the tragic drama: let us, you, I, respond to it in the pregnant silence of the unnamable—barely feeling its heart beat in mine. We must, you, I, invent its singular name, each time anew, syncopated by this rhythm.

Istrice was Derrida's response, in his particular style.

I hereby offer my name for it, another countersignature: irresponsible act of impossible responsibility—to him, to you, to it.

## NOTE

1. All quotations and page references are taken from the French edition of *Points de suspension* and are translated by the author [eds.].

# CHAPTER 11

# Between Barthes, Blanchot, and Mallarmé
## Skia(Photo)–Graphies of Derrida

LAURENT MILESI

"Photographs of myself interest me" (*P. . .* , 196). Could there be an apparently less promising or, precisely, less interesting inaugural statement? Unless, perhaps, one starts reading this interest in photographs of the self, or of Photography, as the articulation of a "difference between," a "being among" or "present," a "taking a part in" (*inter-esse*), at the point when a photograph of Derrida is about to be taken among other French connections and its victim, "neither subject nor object but a subject who feels he is becoming an object," "experience[s] a micro-version of death" and "truly becom[es] a specter" (*CL*, 14). This essay is an inchoate attempt to investigate the intertextual space of this photo-graphic *inter-est* shared between Derrida and Barthes, but also Blanchot, Mallarmé, and Sartre, among others, not so much to claim to show (up) and reveal Derrida fully as, rather, to place his writing in a certain cross-light, to ply between his and others' texts photographically, playing him off against other contemporaries or predecessors, overshadowing him momentarily the better to bring him into focus. Pl(a)ying rather than explicating Derrida, therefore, or opening up a more interesting gap between subject and object and, in the interstices of a reflection on death, time, and the subject / object of photography, sketching "spectrographies" of his writing by catching its haunting motifs in the mesh of intertextual nets, however utopian such a project may eventually prove to be.

When I write "what interests me," I am designating not only an *object* of interest, but the place that *I am in the middle of* and precisely the place that I cannot exceed or that seems to me to supply even the movement by which to go beyond that place or outside of it. (*P. . .* , 67)

## STUDIUM: FRAMING SUSPENSE IN *CAMERA LUCIDA*

Barthes's longstanding engagement with image and photography crystallized in the early 1960s, well before the last *Reflections on Photography* of *Camera Lucida*, with a series of short essays whose continuous reelaboration and adjustment of prior views must be recalled so as to situate Barthes's last "project."

"The Photographic Message" (1961) insists on photography's transmission of "the scene itself, the literal reality" (*IMT*, 17)[1] and already records the uneasy overlap between its denotative "objectivity" and a residual connotative meaning, "at once invisible and active, clear and implicit" (*IMT*, 19). This tension will be redeployed in "Rhetoric of the Image" (1964), a "spectral analysis" of the image's three messages: the linguistic and the iconic, itself divided into the symbolic-cultural (connotative) and the literal (denotative). The semantic plurality of the image will in turn be configured anew in "The Third Meaning: Research Notes on Some Eisenstein Stills" (1970) into the threefold level of the photographic message: direct communication, signification (the symbolic level) or the *obvie*, and the level of *signifiance* which obstinately resists analysis, the *obtus*. Vacillating between presence and absence, this *"obtuse*, supplementary, third meaning" (*IMT*, 64), "the blunting of a meaning too clear, too violent" (*IMT*, 55), captures Barthes's interest by its silent obstinacy (*IMT*, 57) which suspends reading and metalanguage (*IMT*, 61).[2] While the terms of its tentative pinpointing would seem at first sight to run counter to the clarity of connotation (cf. *supra*), hence to the blinding radiance of the future *punctum*, the "blunting" of clear meaning is then supplementally endowed with a "penetrating trait—disturbing like a guest who obstinately sits on saying nothing when one has no use for him" (*IMT*, 57),[3] which uncannily foreshadows the unlocatable incisiveness of the supplementary *punctum* in *Camera Lucida*.

A parallel current in Barthes's reflections on the "essence" of the photographic medium is his continuous preoccupation with its specific temporal dimension. Toward the end of "The Photographic Message" Barthes rejects the equation of the denotative with "the neutral, the objective," and speculates that, if the utopian horizon of pure denotation existed, it would have to be "located" in the trauma, "a suspension of language [and] a blocking of meaning" (*IMT*, 30), which depends on the certainty that the scene really took place: *"the photographer had* to be there" (IMT, 30). The truly traumatic photograph then "is one about which there is nothing to say" (IMT, 31)—the traumatic irony of Camera Lucida will be likewise "to speak of the 'nothing to say' " (CL, 93)—and the real "shock-photo," first "ideologically" (rather than semiotically) dissected in Mythologies and for which the obtus had been obliquely introduced in at least one of its meanings, is one whose obstinate literality surprises the spectator into silence rather than the one that too obviously aims to disturb and "shout" (CL, 41).[4]

This line of thought is taken further in "Rhetoric of the Image," which refines and extends the earlier insights into the necessity of the scene-event in photography. The utopian character of denotation is reaffirmed (IMT, 42) and the temporality proper to the photographic medium made more specific, in terms not of a "being-there" but of "an awareness of its having-been-there." It is at the level of its denoted message or "message without a code" (the famous "slogan" launched in the 1961 study) that one can fully grasp Photography's "real un-reality": the spatial, immediate unreality of the present here, of the illusion of the referent's presence,[5] conjoined with the temporal, anterior reality of a past then, "of the having-been-there, for in every photograph there is the always stupefying evidence of this is how it was," a cela a été which "defeats the it's me" and inaugurates the death of the subject (IMT, 44–45).[6] Whereas, in cinema,[7] "the having-been-there gives way before a being-there of the thing," which keeps open the possibility of its history (IMT, 45), photography can elude history, somewhat paradoxically if one bears in mind a similar emphasis in "The Discourse of History" (1967) and "The Reality Effect" (1968) on what has really taken place both in historical narrative and photography. Although Barthes's changing views of the relation between photography and history cannot be fully explored here,[8] we shall come back to this reality effect which "signif[ies] that the event represented has really taken place," "the enigma of what has been, is no more, and yet offers itself as present sign of a dead thing" (RL, 139, 140), and its relation with photography as an "immediate witness of 'what was here' " (RL, 146).

"The Third Meaning" will firm up this singular temporality of the photographic event by linking it to the more pointed insights afforded by the unnameable trauma of the supplementary obtuse, which "does not yet belong to today's politics but nevertheless already to tomorrow's" (IMT, 62–63).[9] Announcing a similar logic of temporal supplementarity in the later punctum, this "add[ition] to the photograph [which] is nonetheless already there" (CL, 55), this "not yet . . . but nevertheless already," this future or very ancient past, will bear a name in Camera

*Lucida*, at the end of the slow unfolding of the temporality specific to photography: the *interfuit*.

*Camera Lucida*, Barthes's last book, is the narration of a quest in two stages; its architecture is that of a diptych, each of whose panels is organized around a "concept." First, Barthes writes as if he wanted to undertake an objective phenomenological "study" of photography's essence, focusing on what it aims to show, its *obvie*, now called *studium*, despite (or rather because of?) the images being phenomenologically the presence in the referent's absence, an "object-as-nothing" (*CL*, 115).[10] Whether in the *Spectrum*, the little simulacrum emitted by the object (*CL*, 9), or in the contrapuntal experience of the subject's becoming "objectified" by the lens (*objectif*) at the precise instant of the shutter's click, the spectral "return of the dead" essential to every photograph shows forth (*CL*, 9, 13–14; also Derrida, *LDR*, VI) and, with it, its *punctum*, the poignant, puncturing, punctuating moment of inarticulable recognition (*CL*, 26–27), *obtuse* in its resistance to analytic pinpointing, traumatic in its obdurate literality (both *punctum* and trauma having the same etymology of "wound"). *Camera Lucida* is thus a hermeneutic "study in points," a series of twice twenty-four photo-textual vignettes opening with the "frame-photograph" of a *camera obscura* ("Polaroid") from which all human subject is banished, and moving, away from the "pointless study," toward the emblematic absence of the "real" photograph: the "Winter Garden Photograph"— unless the luminous presence of the mother's gaze is captured in the blue-green hues of the "Polaroid" (Price 1994, 165); Barthes's last work, which started as an abortive autobiographical meditation on his mother's photographs, would thus be like the negative of his own *Roland Barthes*, "punctuated three times by the mother's image" ("Barthes puissance trois," 5; my translation). Traumatic, ironically condemned "to speak of the 'nothing to say' " (*CL*, 93) and turning round a blind(ing) spot, Barthes's writing is broken up by token photographs which are as many coverups of the textualization of photography, as is evidenced by such variously concealed "intertextual snapshots," also physically invisible in their original frames, as the photo of Marcel's grandmother by Saint-Loup in Proust's *A la recherche* or, in Sartre's *Psychology of Imagination*, the instancing portrait of his friend Peter. Torn between an objective-phenomenological, then a subjective-experiential writing which eventually spirits away the object of the revelation, Barthes's inquiry "illustrates" the object's nullification, or at best its vacillation between presence and absence, and its own "being-devoid-of-objective." In the contrapuntal structure of its variations "point counter point or point counter study" noted by

Derrida (DRB, 268),[11] the original *point de* (*CC*, 55 [quoted by Derrida], 58, 143) is the performative *"operator"* of a logic of supple-mentarity which had been an attribute of the earlier *obtus*. *Point de photographie*: the *punctum* that, unlike the photograph's artfully studied "shock," punctures me (*CL*, 32), but also the click of the camera pointed at me to "immortalize" me from its objectifying point of view, *point de suspension* in between Life/Death, the paradigm "reduced to a simple click, the one separating the initial pose from the final print" (*CL*, 92),[12] *pas* or *"arrêt"* (cf. *CC*, 122, 142, 165) *de mort*.[13] Thus, for Derrida, the truest photograph is "of someone who puts his hand in front of his face and says: do not take my picture" (*P. . .* , 148).

But the biographical frames of *Camera Lucida* confer a yet more uncanny facet to the "intellectual suspense" that Barthes wanted to preserve about his "hermeneutic thriller" (Lavers 1982, 214) or "mystery novel" (Shawcross 1993, 87),[14] thus honoring *avant la lettre* Derrida's view of photo-stories as "constructions policières" (*LDR*, I).[15] The ironic fate of *Camera Lucida*, if read with the benefit of hindsight, is its suspension between two (series of) deaths, his mother's on 25 October 1977, which left him awaiting his own, "my total, undialectical death" (*CL*, 72), which will happen accidentally soon after these near-ultimate words, but also the book's postmortem beginning on 15 April 1979, one year to the day before the death of Sartre, to whom *Camera Lucida* is dedicated—too many elements of *Unheimlichkeit* which have no doubt cast a spell on the book's critical reception as the gloomy portent of a premature tragic demise. Between life and death, *ob-vie* and *ob-tus*, this suspense points to the chiaroscuro effects or "ombre claire" (*CC*, 169) of the photo-*graphy* of *Camera Lucida*, this "photographic . . . synthesis . . . of another writing of shadow and light, of another *Skia-Photographia*" (*SP*, 24; my translation)[16] in whose shimmering light, reflected in the mixed effects of a subjective and of an objective genitive (like the phenomenological condensation of the material/objective and of the mental/subjective), I shall describe the "obsessions" of Barthes and Derrida.

## PUNCTUM I: THE OBSESSIONS OF BARTHES AND DERRIDA

Added to the overall difficulty of establishing a congruence between the conceptual pairings that traverse Barthes's writing[17] is the ultimately partial correspondence between clear/obscure and *obviestudium/obtus-punctum*. Thus the *studium/ob-vie* "donne envie" (*CC*, 51), yet fails to illuminate, remains dull and obscure, and it is the *punctum*, whose earlier obtuse avatar, on the side of the literal denotative, blunted the clarity of the message, that penetrates with a blinding light, yet kills (*tue*) as it interpellates (*tu*).[18] No matter how fraught with death the shutter's click and photography's *punctum* may have felt for Barthes, the fact that one snapshot enabled the construction of a literary stele to the mother's radiance in order to "resurrect" her (cf. *CL*, 64, 80, 82) in an "imaginary," "utopian"[19] project is enough to unsettle further neat dichotomies. All this may also help to explain why, toward the close of the book, Barthes will claim clarity rather than obscurity, the optical device of the book's title rather than the *camera obscura*, as photography's "real" or symbolic ancestry (*CL*, 106). It is the grace of a truly photo-graphic writing, the light, radiating beyond death, of the mother's gaze that penetrated Derrida (*DRB*, *passim*), which illuminates the obscure dark chamber of the text, turning it into a camera lucida in which, however, the Winter Garden Photograph remains invisible, the only way of enabling the reader/spectator to "experience" at a remove Barthes's revelation: the contemplation of the undivided essence of his mother "*as into herself . . . eternity changes her*" (*CL*, 71), "*telle qu'en elle-même . . .*" (*CC*, 111), a clipped echo of the first line of Mallarmé's "Le Tombeau d'Edgar Poe."

Composed for the erection of a funerary monument to America's *poète maudit*, Mallarmé's poetic homage belongs to a "cycle" of commemorative pieces which were conceived sporadically during a long interim period of literary gestation (from the first major poetic achievements of the 1860s to the climactic *Coup de dés*, 1897), and prefaced by the famous announcement of his death in his letters,[20] the histrionic expression of the poet's groping for a rite of passage that would bring about an ideal, purified conception of himself. In *The Death of Stéphane Mallarmé* Leo Bersani has shown how the different thematic treatments of the poetic self memorialize the personality to which they posthumously refer after the poet's self-proclaimed demise (Bersani, date 19). Similarly, those poems by Mallarmé that, as it were, erect a tombstone through a commemorative writing can be read as gestures of immortalization, in particular his "living homage" to the writer whose fantastical tales summonsed death itself in its unpresentability, as in "The Facts in the Case of M. Valdemar" in which the impossible "*utopic*" (*DRB*, 294) utterance, "*I say to you that I am dead!?*" 'the invention of an unheard-of category . . . ; the *death-life* . . . conceived as . . . nondialectic," so fascinated Barthes that he selected the tale for closer inspection in "Textual Analysis of a Tale by Edgar Allan Poe," where he notes Death's radically traumatic return, less the object of a *revelation* than of a *revulsion* (*SC*, 1988 261–293 [287, 291]).[21]

The beginning of the epitaph-poem to Poe, "tel qu'en lui-même . . . ,"
stalks once more into Barthes's quest for the essential photograph of
the departed mother:

> Ultimately a photograph looks like anyone except the person it repre-
> sents. For resemblance refers to the subject's identity . . . ; likeness gives
> out identity "as itself" [*en tant que lui-même*] whereas I want a
> subject . . . "as into itself" [*tel qu'en lui-même*]. (*CL*, 102–13; *CC*, 160)

The opposition may be read as the counterpart to an earlier fragment
in *Camera Lucida* which had already given a hint of the inadequacy of
a strictly philosophical phenomenological procedure not enriched by
the linguistic-psychoanalytical models of perception of the subject (cf.
Giribone 1982, 12 and Ungar 1983, 143). There the Photograph is

> the absolute Particular, the sovereign Contingency, matte and some-
> how stupid, the *This* (this photograph, and not Photography) [*le Tel
> (telle photo, et non la Photo)*], . . . *tathata* . . . , the fact of being this [*tel*], of
> being thus [*ainsi*], of being so [*cela*]; *tat* means that in Sanskrit and
> suggests the gesture of the child pointing his finger at something and
> saying: *that there it is, lo!* [Ta, Da, Ça!] but says nothing else . . . ; the
> Photograph is never anything but an antiphon of "Look," "See," "Here
> it is" [*ça, c'est ça, c'est tel!*]; it points a finger at certain vis-à-vis . . . (*CL*,
> 4–5; *CC*, 15–16)

In *Empire of Signs* and *A Lover's Discourse*, Barthes had already elaborated the premises of an evolutive reflection on the *tel* whose outcome
in *Camera Lucida* is at once a progress and a partial synthesis and
recasting of those shared echoes and references: the relation to death,
to the supplementarity of place, to obtuse language and to the suspension of judgment, the return of the Sanskrit etymology *tathata* as an
immediate, undevelopable gesture / pointer common to haiku and
Photography (*CL*, 49, also 109; cf. Part 3 *infra*), but also the already
existing gradations between various perceptions of the beloved "as
such" (*comme tel*):

> It's that, it's thus [*ainsi*], says the haiku, *it's so* [*c'est tel*]. Or better still:
> *so!* [Tel!] it says, with a touch so instantaneous and so brief . . . that
> even the copula would seem excessive. . . . Here meaning is only a
> flash, a slash of light . . . ; but the haiku's flash illumines, reveals
> nothing; it is the flash of a photograph one takes very carefully . . . but
> having neglected to load the camera with film. Or again: haiku repro-
> duces the designating gesture of the child pointing at whatever it
> is . . . , merely saying: *that!* [ça!] with a movement so immediate . . . that
> what is designated is the very inanity of any classification of the
> object. (*ES*, 83)[22]

> This first *thus* [tel] is wrong because I leave [it] as an internal point of corruption, an adjective: the other is *stubborn* [entêté]: he still derives from *qualitas*. . . . I shall be like the infant who contents himself with a blank word to show something: Ta, Da, Tat (says Sanskrit). *Thus* [Tel], the lover will say: *you are thus, thus and so, precisely thus.*
>
> Designating you as *thus* [tel], I enable you to escape the death of classification . . . , I want you to be immortal. *As he is* [Tel qu'il est], the loved being no longer receives any meaning . . . ; he is in a sense the *supplement of his own site*. If he were only a site, I might well, someday, replace him, but I can substitute nothing for the supplement of his site, his *thus* [tel]. (*LDF,* 221)[23]

And further on:

> So I accede . . . to a language without adjectives. . . . The language in which the amorous subject then protests . . . is an *obtuse* language: every judgment is suspended.
>
> [. . .]
>
> And what would best resemble the loved being *as he is, thus and so* [tel qu'il est], would be the [writerly] Text, to which I can add no adjective. (*LDF,* 222)[24]

And still in *Empire of Signs*, the deictic pointing at work in the haiku, which designates without saying and thus itself suspends language too (*ES,* 75), had enabled a few pages before to glimpse already—or anew[25]—a reorganization of past and future[26] time as the work from an instant snapshot:

> The haiku never describes; its art is counter-descriptive, to the degree that each state of the thing is immediately, stubbornly [*obstinément*], victoriously converted into a fragile essence of appearance: a literally "untenable" moment in which the thing . . . will pass from one language to another and constitute itself as the memory of this future, thereby anterior. (*ES,* 77)

Against Photography's (cl)aim to immortalize by freezing the subject "as such," but which thus "gives death," mortifies and embalms (*CL,* 11, 14), "states the impossible in the deadest of codes" (*S* 142)—one need only evoke the ritualistic phrase "keep still" (*ne bougeons plus*)— the double echo of Mallarmé's "Tombeau" must not be read only as the conventional sign of a writing that erects a monument "in homage to," like the vision of Benjaminian photography as a "small funerary monument, . . . a grave for the living dead" (Cadava, 1992 90), but as carrying within itself the living testimony of the triumph of death in the "strange voice" of the belatedly recognized poet whose "radiant" grave was fallen from an "obscure disaster" (cf. ll. 4, 11, 12 of Mallarmé's poem), the miraculous uncoupling of Life/Death in a double gesture of "tomberection" (*SNS*, 104–105; *G*, 1b).[27]

Such is the performative interest of the Mallarméan intertext: to enable the passage from the phenomenological "as such"/"as it is" (*tel quel*) even in its complex imbrications with attributes of the *punctum* in earlier texts, to the anagnoristic "as into itself..." (*tel qu'en elle-même*...), stripped of the gloomier note that attends Sartre's use of this shibboleth in *L'Etre et le néant*: "La mort nous rejoint à nous-même, tels qu'en nous-même l'éternité nous a changés" (153).[28] But the point-counterpoint variations on the phenomenal *als/tel* which, despite these earlier and here ultimately refashioned relations with the obtuse, the matte *ça/ainsi* of Photography-as-haiku, the instantaneous illumination of a *satori* (e.g.: *ES*, xi, 4, 74–75; *CL*, 49, 109), supplementarity, the (non) place, death, the suspension of meaning (etc.), still try to "save the phenomena," will need to be supplemented by another operator: the logic of an *als ob* (as if: "comme si") going beyond Vaihinger's *Philosophy of the "as if"*—in which he developed Kant's seminal theory of the necessity of ideational imagination's as if for the reasoned establishment of philosophical reality[29]—for this (unreal) imaginary "resurrection" to meet the real in a u-topia, not merely as the fiction of a figure, a simulacrum (Barthes's *trompe-l'oeil* opening, as if he was going to reinstate phenomenology and a semiotics of the image), or the apotropaic pretenses put up by the living to ward off the dead (DRB, 277, 279):

> The *Als* says the "as such" of holy or profane writing, of writings thus exhibited, but perhaps also the simulacrum of the *als ob* . . . , the fiction or figure (*as if*, comme si) of what appears as such in the retrait of the remark and says itself only according to the image. (SP, 8; my translation)

Yet one should not forget Mallarmé's more personal memorial poem, planned in homage to the dead son and to be titled "Tombeau pour Anatole," which later gave rise to the poignant experiment of *Un Coup de dés*—another of the *punctum*'s etymologies (*CL*, 27; *CC*, 49). Existing in the rhythmical in-betweenness of its blanks and verse in crisis, Mallarmé's interesting *Coup de dés* is punctuated on one of its double pages by the framing repetition of "COMME SI" (as if) casting a series of wild hypotheses at random or to chance ("*destinant au hasard*," to use Derrida's felicitous Janus-faced formula: *MC*, 4).[30] Derrida had already picked up the conjunction of sorts in "The Double Session" (*D*, 264) and, first in the seventh "point" of "The Deaths of Roland Barthes" (DRB, 262; note the Mallarméan frame effect), he will return

to this missing link in the obsessional trajectory from the phenomenal "as such" (en tant que tel, als), or even the metonymic "such
and/or such" (the unsatisfactory photos that fail to yield the whole
essence of the mother), to the anagnoristic "as into herself" (*tel qu'en
elle-même*...) afforded by the Winter Garden Photograph, discovered by chance at the end of the quest. The hypothetical modality of
the *comme si* marks the temporal *point* at which the imaginary inter-
sects with the real: the moment of revelation when Barthes chances
upon a photo of his mother as a child, as it were before her development, which enables him to reverse the inexorable filiation of Time,
as if the mother, whom he had nursed like a child until her death,
was born anew (*CL*, 72). No one has been more able than Derrida to
bring to life this imaginary scene, or, indeed, *ob*-scene since in it
stalks the unpresentable figure of death itself (for if Photography
testifies to the scenes having taken place, its temporal *punctum* is a
reminder of its obscenity, that of intruding death which it harbors
within itself and which yet remains *hors-champ*).[31] His beautiful development will be silently counterpointed with a first selection of
key "points" from *Camera Lucida*:

> I realized that some [photographs] provoked tiny jubilations, as if they
> referred to a stilled center [*centre tu*], ... buried in myself. (*CL*, 16)

> I may know better a photograph I remember than a photograph I am
> looking at, as if direct vision oriented its language wrongly, engaging
> it in an effort of description which will always miss its point of effect,
> the *punctum*. (*CL*, 53)

> The *punctum*, then, is a kind of subtle beyond [*hors-champ*]—*as if the
> image launched desire beyond what it permits us to see.* (*CL*, 59)

> The Photograph is an extended, loaded evidence—as if it caricatured
> not the figure of what it represents ... but its very existence. (*CL*, 115)

> As if: I read these two books one after the other, as if the negative of
> a type of language was finally going to appear and develop before my
> eyes, as if the pace, step [*pas*], style,[32] timbre, tone, and gestures of
> Roland Barthes—so many signatures obscurely familiar... —were all
> of a sudden going to yield me their secret...; as if the unique trait
> were all of a sudden going to appear in full light.... I was dreaming:
> as if the point of singularity, ... as if the insistence of the invariable
> were finally going to be revealed to me as it is in itself [*telle qu'en elle-
> même enfin*]—and in something like a detail. (DRB, 263)

And it was from a detail, that "very locus of signification" which is
precisely what the photograph reveals according Barthes's 1959 study

of "Sept photos-modèles de *Mère Courage*" (17), that, Derrida carries on, "I asked for the ecstasy of revelation, the instantaneous access to Roland Barthes" (DRB, 263).

Related to the nullification of the object in the imaginative consciousness, to the *quasi*-observation of an unreal object arousing quasi-feelings (e.g., *The Psychology of Imagination*, 12, 22, 140), this simulating "as if"[33] of the mental image in the Sartrean imaginary is what Barthes must endeavor to go beyond in order to reach the anagnoristic "truth," despite his initial orientation in Sartre's *L'imaginaire*, to which he owes the "dialectical" overcoming of phenomenological ontology toward an individual experimental psychology capable of taking affect into account (note the respective endings of Sartre's and Barthes's first parts: *CL*, 50 and *The Psychology of Imagination*, 62).

In the excerpt about (the) Photograph(y) as the absolute Particular, "the sovereign Contingency, matte and somehow stupid . . . , in short . . . the *Tuché*, the Occasion, the Encounter, the Real" (*CL*, 4), Barthes resorts to Lacan's conception of the real as Aristotelian *tuché* or chance encounter, as always an essentially missed appointment with what cannot be assimilated in the traumatic experience of the real[34] and which always lies in wait beyond the automaton, "the return, the coming-back [*revenue*], the insistence of the signs," "as if by chance" (Lacan 1977, 53–54).[35] As early as "The Photographic Message" Barthes had underlined the equation between accidental trauma and the real in the deferred temporality of the photograph; as Roger puts it succinctly: "With the *punctum* the hermeneutic value of the *trauma* and the eidetic position of the photographic 'having-been-there' return 'at another place' " (217; my translation). This rite of passage, from the missed encounter with the real—or Photography-as-such to the u-topic meeting point between the imaginary and the real (Barthes's "real unreality"),[36] is precisely the question of writing's other place or scene (its *anderer Schauplatz*) in the project of *Camera Lucida* but also, as we shall see later, in Derrida's homage in "The Deaths of Roland Barthes."

Talking about his fantasmatic longing to inhabit, which "seems to bear me forward to a utopian time, or to carry me back to somewhere in myself," Barthes adds:

> [I]t is as if *I were certain* of having been there or of going there. Now Freud says of the maternal body that "there is no other place of which one can say with so much certainty that one has already been there"? Such then would be the essence of the landscape (chosen by desire): *heimlich*, awakening in me the Mother (and never the disturbing Mother). (*CL*, 40)[37]

A similar inauguration of an impossible place through a utopian writing also presides over the revelation of the essential Winter Garden Photograph (*CL*, 70–71) and the mother's "retrograde" engendering, making of the writing of the photograph a writing of light-as-truth (cf. Derrida, *G*, 108a, 110a) and of resurrection an aletheic erection (Lacoue-Labarthe 1975, 196):

> Ultimately I experienced her . . . as my feminine child. Which was my way of resolving death. If . . . the particular dies for the satisfaction of the universal . . . , I who had not procreated, I had, in her very illness, engendered my mother. Once she was dead . . . [m]y particularity could never again universalize itself (unless, utopically, by writing, whose project henceforth would become the unique goal of my life). (*CL*, 72)[38]

The "critical fortune" of *Un Coup de dés*—an abortive "grave poem" whose "*COMME SI*" redeploys the "tel qu'en elle-même" adapted from "Le Tombeau d'Edgar Poe" in *Camera Lucida*—is precisely to have created such a u-topia for (and through) writing, its famous "Rien n'aura eu lieu que le lieu," which causes a crisis in literature to *take place* according to Derrida in "The Double Session" (*D*, 285[39]). Suspended between twice two deaths and two genres (the planned novel and the critical essay), the writing of *Camera Lucida* can claim to be this u-topia of an "as if" at once scientific and imaginary, founding a "third form" (*RL*, 281), an impossible space that withdraws itself from the all-too-pure binary conceptual pairs "real/unreal" or "real/imaginary" (cf. *RB*, 142):

> It is important for me to act as if I was to write this utopian novel. . . . "As if": is not this formula the very expression of scientific procedure . . . ?[40]

An imaginary dialogue could be set up between the above passage as well as Barthes's interesting definition of his own "dis-placed position" as a writer in 1971 and Anne Berger's hypothesis of a Derridean (non) place, following considerations about the palpitation of the subjective in Derrida's works as being connected with an economy of (non-)mourning, which must be read in the context of his long-sustained desire to write differently, in an "autobiographical" fictional mode:[41]

> That is why I could say that my specific historical position . . . is to be at the rear of the vanguard [à l'arrière-garde de l'avant-garde]: to be in the vanguard is to know what is dead; to be in the rearguard is to love it still: I love fiction [*le romanesque*] but I know that the novel is dead: here is, I think, the exact place of what I am writing. ("Réponses," 102; my translation)

> It would be as if, in a certain way, you knew the place that would allow you to write it [the dream of the book], as if you had found it, and at the same time it were lost to you. (*P. . . ,* 143)

A found-and-lost "point at which here coincides with nowhere," a relationship between the intimacy of the chance of death and the impossibility of an "as if" of the work according to Blanchot in "Mallarmé's Experience" and "The *Igitur* Experience" (1982, 48, 118), this *(non)-lieu* of writing, which we shall take up later in conjunction with Photography's specific temporality,[42] may be deciphered in the cross-light of Derrida's meditation on the pure, yet fragile, inaudible locus in the five obsessional, enigmatic words *"il y a là cendre,"* the spectral haunting of earlier works reduced to / gathered as cinders in *Feu la cendre,* with its own echoes of *Un Coup de dés* (e.g., C 37: "un lieu pur se chiffrât-il"), and, more generally, of the double bind of the (non)-lieu of/in Derrida's writing as a crossing toward such a Mallarméan u-topos: the need to find a place from which to speak and which yet should resist identification in order to preserve the full and problematic plenitude of the voice (*P. . . ,* 135).[43]

## PUNCTUM II: ECSTASIES—"THE VERY LETTER OF TIME"

In the thirty-ninth "point" Barthes dramatically presents the other *punctum*:

> I now know that there exists another *punctum* (another "stigmatum") than the "detail". This new *punctum,* which is no longer of form but of intensity, is Time, the lacerating emphasis of the noeme ("*that-has-been*"), its pure representation. (*CL,* 96)

Barthes's imaginary voyage has uncovered a self-dividing *punctum* and likewise, Photography's lacerating temporal noeme will appear to be made up of several punctuating tempi and rhythms, all metonymic, whose overall movement we shall now try to retrace along with its attendant grammatical tenses, from the aorist, the future perfect/ anterior (*interfuit*), to the final "ecstasy" of Time, through a deferred present.

In "To Write: An Intransitive Verb?" Barthes had recalled the two-fold temporality of Indo-European languages exposed by Benveniste in "The Correlations of Tense in the French Verb:" the system of discourse, suited to the act of enunciation, and the system of history and narrative, appropriate to the recounting of past events without the speaker's intervention, having neither present nor future, and whose specific tense is aorist (or equivalents, like the French preterite or past historic), the tense of "what has taken place" (*RL*, 14–15). Now, this is how the second part of *Camera Lucida* had opened:

> Now, one November evening shortly after my mother's death, I was going through [*rangeai*] some photographs. (*CL*, 63)

The new orientation of the research is marked by this abrupt shift to history's past tense, made possible by the traumatic certainty of the event of the mother's death (Todorov, 1981 327). The real has forced upon Barthes the monumental aorist, which had presided over the explicitly narrative-historical, dated *incipit* of the whole book: "One day, quite some time ago, I happened [*tombai*] on a photograph of Napoleon's youngest brother, Jerome, taken in 1852" (*CL*, 3[44]), and whose acceptance signals the memorialization and the resurrection to come of the dead mother through writing. This "quite some time ago" (before the mother's death) will become transfigured into the book's distant history in the dramatic opening of § 39: "At the time (at the beginning of this book: already far away) when I was inquiring [*m'interrogeais*] into my attachment to certain photographs" (*CL*, 94). The historicization of Photography (*CL*, 30, 64, and 65)[45] is borne out by another temporal contrast which enables Barthes to distinguish it from an act of rememoration or Proustian anamnesis (cf. *CL*, 82)— despite (or, perhaps, because of) the insistence of the writer of *A la Recherche* in Barthes's text (*CL*, 105):

> Not only is the Photograph never, in essence, a memory (whose grammatical expression would be the perfect tense,[46] whereas the tense of the Photograph is the aorist), but it actually blocks memory, quickly becomes a counter-memory. (*CL*, 91)[47]

Yet the "perfect" of recollection will be sublated or "assumed," in a quasi-religious sense, in the more ample movement of Time's ecstasy, as History and even the (photographic) Image have been in Barthes's personal Photograph(y). Barthes owes his revelation to a journey through time back to the first (his "last") photo of the mother as a child, like the Greeks who "entered into Death backward: what they had before them was their past" (*CL*, 71). The (e)motional tug proper to Photography's emphatic *that-has-been* is to pull contrariwise toward the past-as-future; this revulsion or "catastrophe" seen before as a "not yet . . . but nevertheless *already*" (*IMT*, 62–63), here reascribed to the *punctum*, is Death itself:

> [T]he *punctum* [in the photo of the condemned man] is: *he is going to die*. I read at the same time: *This will be and this has been*; I observe with horror an anterior future [or future perfect] of which death is the stake.

> By giving me the absolute past of the pose (aorist), the photograph tells me death in the future. What *pricks* me is the discovery of this equivalent. In front of the photograph of my mother as a child, I tell myself: she is going to die: I shudder... *over a catastrophe which has already occurred.* Whether or not the subject is already dead, every photograph is this catastrophe. (*CL,* 96; cf. also 79)

Taken *before* (while awaiting) the death to which it owes its existence and which *will have taken place* before one sees the snapshot,[48] Lewis Payne's photo is caught in between *pose* and eternal rest (*repos*), in a synthesis that "no longer consists in presenting or representing in the light of the image, in making appear the phenomenal *als* of the *as such* (*phainesthai, phos, phantasma, phantasia*) in the over-exposure or under-exposure of a film surface" (Sp, 24; my translation; cf. also Shawcross 116–117 about the superposition of reality and the past in Photography as a double exposure). In what it holds as truest and most luminous for Barthes, photo-graphy would be an arche-writing that exposes "the *dead time* within the presence of the living present" and defies the "as such" (*comme telle*) invoking the phenomenological experience of a presence (*OG*, 68) through the as if of a future anterior (SPC, 25).[49]

This sliding toward a future-past anterior/perfect (cf. DRB, 264) can be read as an essentially photographic device, in the cross-light of optics and Latin (rather than Greek) tense grammar, as in the *punctum/passatum prossimum* and *punctum/passatum remotum* (historical aorist) which punctuate the opposition between the perfect (of) anamnesis and Photography's historical aorist, but also between the very/too close and very/too far focus of short-sighted/technical and long-sighted/historical-sociological *studies* of Photography—recalling the Nietzschean-Heideggerian dis-tancing (*Dis-Tanz, Ent-Fernung*) often discussed by Derrida—neither of which tackles the photographs that "interest" Barthes (*CL,* 6–7). Between these two tenses and points of view, the vibration of the *punctum* of the whole book suspended between two series of deaths, is tensed in a double *pas de mort* (P, 39): the acceptance of losing the mother twice so as to imaginarily undo one death through another and capture the instant of a mad transient resurrection (*CL,* 71). It is given a name, still in the dead (mother's) tongue in which the conceptualization of the photographic process has been envisaged (cf. *CL,* 81): *interfuit,* perfect of *interesse:*

> The name of Photography's *noeme* will therefore be: "That-has-been," or again: the Intractable.[50] In Latin (a pedantry necessary because it illuminates certain nuances), this would doubtless be said: *interfuit*: what I see has been here, in this place which extends between infinity and the subject, and yet immediately separated (*operator* or *spectator*);

> it has been here, and yet immediately separated; it has been absolutely,
> irrefutably present, and yet already deferred. It is all this which the
> verb intersum means. (*CL*, 77)

Between past and future perfect, recuperating the perfect from the
photographic aorist and deferring the present (see *infra*), the *interfuit*
is this "meantime" that is neither trauma nor repetition/rehearsal
(*répétition*), or both. It recalls the temporal modality of the unconscious
according to Freud and Lacan, the deferred action or *Nachträglichkeit*
of the trauma which must be deciphered as a future anterior re- or
overwriting an earlier memory, whose psychic and optical counterparts would be the delay between event and consciousness, image
and perception (*CL*, 10, 80–81), the photo's take and the light's inscription.[51] A similar bi-directional movement had already inspired the description of the u-topic, traumatic, *heimlich*, maternal place which
Barthes had inhabited/would like to inhabit (*CL*, 40); such is the *après
coup* (*CC*, 87) of the temporal *punctum* in its double articulation, the
intervallic dimension of its supplemental structure, between a pre-
apocalyptic "not yet" and the "always already" of its inscription, which
compresses the present into a (double) impossible utopic point, that of
the missed real where this conjunction/disjunction with the imaginary "takes place," half (real) mourning, half phantasm.

   Doubling back the supplemental (already present, yet superadded)
*punctum* upon itself (cf. *CL*, 55), *Camera Lucida* is a retrospective eluci-
dation of a *nachträglich* experience, as if, in the first part or "study,"
Barthes had not yet discovered the *punctum* of the Winter Garden
Photograph that yielded the jubilant restoration in (and of) the present:
"There she is! (*CL*, 109; cf. 5: *"there it is"*).[52] It is thus a truly photographic development which dramatizes the instant when its author
will be struck by an aletheic light and, by not revealing the Photograph (leaving it as a u-topic image), likewise hopes to puncture or
"photograph" the reader.[53] But thereby, the text, which at once over-
shadows Photography and reveals itself like its process, is the ante-
chamber of death which it will attempt to fight through time's revulsion
and a negotiation of the spectral stalking in the anagnorisis (cf. *infra*),
but on which it will have to close sooner or later, "as if nothing 'in
reality" had happened [*ne s'était passé*]' (*LDR*, XXXIV; my translation).

   Although Barthes's writing has often been celebrated for its modernity, it may also be argued that his last work, between a *will* and
its postmortem effect as a future-perfect *will have been*, is a "spectrog-
raphy" that can be analyzed according to the parameters of postmodernity if the latter is identified, as Lyotard will do after *Camera*

*Lucida,* with the future anterior and a movement in ana—such as ana-mnesis, the "assumption" of its perfect tense, rather than the Orphic gaze looking *back* upon the gift of the spontaneous snapshot (*CL,* 47)—u-topic and unpresentable just like death.[54] This has some affinity with the step backward as a movement forward described by the father of the postmodern avant-garde in American poetry, Charles Olson,[55] for whom history, in his "special view" of it, is no longer turned toward the events of a so-called "historic" past but, once it has been recon-ciled with the natural in the mythological whose tenses are the present and the future, becomes a prospective representation (Olson 1970, esp. 22, 26)—in a first second birth which he called, felicitously for a read-ing of *Camera Lucida,* a "second homecoming":

> [T]here is no "history." (I still keep going back to, the notion, this is (we are) merely, the *second time* (that's as much history as I'll permit in, which ain't history at all. (Olson 1966, 113)

> [H]istory, like religion, myth, and poetry, share the common property that a thing done is not simply done but is re-done or pre-done. It is at once commemorative, magical, and prospective. (Olson 1970, 22)

This historico-temporal catastrophe or "strictly revulsive movement which reverses the course of the thing," caused by the original abso-lute realism of a mad Photography which compels consciousness "to return to the very letter of Time," will finally have a name: *"ecstasy"* (*CL,* 119). Compatible with "the stasis of an *arrest"* at the heart of Photography (*CL,* 91), this truly Heideggerian *ek-stasis* or stepping outside the flux of time opens up the possibility of a personal ontol-ogy of Photography.

The ultimate climax of *Camera Lucida* punctuates the revulsive movement that attends the whole of its orchestration, from phenom-enology to a more personal inquiry, then to the former's return as an "existential" (Sartrean-Heideggerian) reflection on time and being. More than a simple return, this revenance of phenomenology[56] figures the spectral at work in Photography's catastrophic Time, since "It is a proper characteristic of the specter . . . that no one can be sure if by returning it testifies to a living past or to a living future" (*SM,* 99; cf. Mallarmé's "nos spectres futurs" in "Toast funèbre" [*Oeuvres Complètes,* 54–55]). Such is the development of the future *having-been* of Photog-raphy: the spectral as Photography's essence (*LDR,* VI), implying the " 'return of the dead' in the very structure of both its image and the phenomenon of its image" (*DRB,* 281). *Point de mort* as *point du mort,* the *punctum* seems to say "the one who was and will no longer be, who returns [*fait retour*] like that which will never come back [*ne reviendra pas*], who marks the return of the dead to the reproductive image" (DRB, 285); revenance without comeback of the unique anagnorisis as ultimate *punctum* of no return—between spectral haunting and the Sartrean individual defined as "that which can never come back [*ce qui ne revient jamais*]" (1972, 58)—or without returns (*revenus*), according to cinders' aneconomic loss.

Remarking on the literal presence of a photograph's referent at a certain time in the past, Barthes adds that the photograph becomes horrible because it certifies that "the corpse is alive, as *corpse*: it is the living image of a dead thing"; "the photograph's immobility is somehow the result of a perverse confusion between . . . the Real and the Live" (*CL*, 79). This, and the whole emphasis on Photography-as-Death, recalls Blanchot's conception of the image as cadaver in "The Two Versions of the Imaginary" (1982, 254–263), which also develops his view of the lure and unreality of the here, the u-topia of Death, and the alignment of the image with magic (for which see also *CL*, 88):[57]

> Death suspends the relation to place, even though the deceased rests heavily in his spot as if upon the only basis that is left him. To be precise, this basis lacks, the place is missing, the corpse is not in its place. Where is it? It is not here, and yet it is not anywhere else. Nowhere? But then nowhere is here. The cadaverous presence establishes a relation between here and nowhere. [. . .] The corpse is here, but here in its turn becomes a corpse. (1982, 256)[58]

For Blanchot the ultimate meaning of the image is to relegate us, beyond its "life-giving negation of the thing," "to its absence as presence, to the neutral double of the object," to reveal the distance at the heart of the thing, "not the same thing at a distance but the thing as distance, present in its absence, . . . the return of what does not come back [*ce qui ne revient pas*]" (1982, 262, 255–256; cf. DRB, 285, quoted above). "[D]efeat[ing] the *it's me*" (*IMT*, 45), Barthes's Photography or "the living image of a dead thing"[59] is to be read at worst (i.e., before the triumphant, if transient anagnorisis) in relation to the second meaning of Blanchot's deadly image as well as in the light of death as the condition of the sign's very possibility in *Speech and Phenomena*: "I am originally means I am mortal" (54).[60] At the crossroads between phenomenonology and photography-as-phantasmatology, this spectral *revenance* of the sign-as-death (cf. *SM*, 135) shares affinities with but must be demarcated from both Blanchot's "*viens*" at the end of his apocalyptic *Arrêt de mort* (often commented on by Derrida)[61] and the double *pas*[62] of his disaster that always takes place after having taken place, has already taken place outside any place, the trance of the leap outside history placed under the aegis of an eternal return, from the *pas au-delà* of a death approached in "a step-by-step procedure of over-stepping or of impossible transgression" (*ES*, 19). Against Blanchot's disaster of the return whose mark is an always already past immi-nence (let alone the catastrophe of the photography of Benjaminian history anchored in the structure of the *Jetztzeit* [Cadava, 1992 98]) the catastrophe of spectral *revenance* in Barthes is this u-topic ecstasy which defies the spatio-temporal *taking place* with a "not yet . . . always al-ready"—*Point de photographie, pas de mort*—to which the eye can never adjust; *punctum proximum / remotum*: on this side or beyond Photog-raphy-as-death, the unpresentable *punctum* missed by any *studium*. Threading its way between re(-)turn and *revenance*, that of the specter to which one can only say "reviens" (but can one ever say a "*viens*" which is not already somehow a "*reviens*"?),[63] will the writing of *Cam-era Lucida* finally reveal, at the end of this deferred, yet dramatized imminent *present* of the instant, the possibility of the gift of/in Photog-raphy[64] if the condition of a gift is to be without return(s)? And what, then, of Derrida's insistent "returns" ("j'y reviens") in "The Deaths of Roland Barthes"?

In the light of the unpresentability of death and of Photography's impossible present—"what I see . . . has been absolutely, irrefutably present, and yet already deferred" (*CL*, 77)—how can "the very letter of Time" be given; how can the *punctum* both give time and be(ing)? Unlike time, which can be apprehended only in the modality of a present to which past and future are articulated as a present-that-was and a present-to-come, the gift is what presents itself and yet cannot be made a present (of). And should the gift be ever possible, the present of time itself would not; it is impossible for time to be given as present, for the present to be given. (Whereas, for Blanchot, on the contrary, time can be given inasmuch as it is not mine.)[65] The gift is never (a) present, it "gives its self without ever presenting itself, let alone rep-resenting itself" (*Sp*, 24, my translation; cf. also *G*, 80; *GT*, 28 and *passim*; *MPM*, 147; *P*, 67; and also *JD*, 188–203).

Yet there is, at least etymologically, one "letter of Time" that can be given: the date or data littera,[66] the letters given as the very first words of a letter to indicate the space-time coordinates of writing (*Sh*, 17). Of this primary date, which he sometimes indicates with reveal-ing meticulosity (e.g., *ES*, 91, linked to death; cf *supra*), Barthes notes that it belongs to the photograph . . . because it . . . allows me to compute life, death. . . . I am the reference of every photograph, and this is what generates my astonishment in addressing myself to the fundamental question: why is it that I am alive *here and now*? (*CL*, 84)

Barthes speculates about the photograph's given letter or dative date as a marker of life and death, and toward the close of the French original, in counterpoint to the historical date of Napoleon's half-brother which had opened the book, the dates framing the beginning and end of its composition will be indicated, just before returning to the intractable reality (*CC*, 184). "Like an accident and like death, [the date] seems to be imposed from the outside" (*DRB*, 291), writes Derrida about his own desire to date his homage to the friend (14–15 September 1980), against a citational background from Blanchot's *L'Amitié*, thus perhaps marking the spectral *revenance* of the gift as impossible return, the singular encounter but also the incineration in the future anterior of anniversaries to come, "that remainder without remainder one calls ash," this holocaust at the heart of each date (*SPC*, 4, 8, 19, 27, 35, 40, 43, 50). A last rather than first dat(iv)e, then, its deferred *present*, also dated (past) toward the future, spells an imminent death, but also the end of the utopian resurrection, when the *camera lucida* will close for ever on a deadly *camera obscura* . . .

## BETWEEN *S/P*: DERRIDA'S INTEREST

The *studium* is that very wide field . . . of various interests . . . ; it is the same sort of vague . . . interest. (*CL*, 27)

Having thus reviewed the *docile interests* [sages] which certain photographs awaken in me . . . (*CL*, 40)

"Docile" [*sages*] photographs (those invested by a simple *studium*). (*CL*, 49)

[T]he relation to some unique and irreplaceable referent *interests* us and animates our most sound [*sage*] and studied readings. (*DRB*, 290)

Docile, studied *interests*: between Barthes's Photography and Derrida's *Post Card* (originally published also in 1980), thus between s(tudium) and p(unctum), Socrates and Plato, two scenes of filiation in reverse, an interest at the heart of the double bind of Derrida's homage in "The Deaths of Roland Barthes." The critical instant of a punctual, intractable decision, of a fatal click, Derrida decides to write (on) Barthes's plural deaths/dead (*morts*; *DRB*, 259), despite the double impossible choice "given" to him in such circumstances, those of a celebration which turn death and the dead person into a pretext, an excuse for one's own writing. Derrida would have wanted "to avoid, and thus to spare him, the double wound of speaking of him, here and now, as one of the living *or* one of the dead" (DRB, 270)—following the "click" of this occasion, a disjunctive and conjunctive "or"—and contemplates two equally untenable options, two betrayals that would be radically opposed if they were not conjoined in the common failure of a "studious" "pointless" enterprise (DRB, 271): 1) The duty yet also the murderous temptation to quote mimetically, let the other speak contrapuntally or speak as if one were the other (*"comme lui"*), not to say anything oneself (but this excess of fidelity opens a posthumous debt and thus "returns to death. It points to death, sending death back to death," condemning the gift to death (DRB, 271); 2) The desire to substitute one's discourse for the other's, the traumatic re-/ over-writing which thereby negates and suppresses him through a study speculatively adding more death to death—what is also involved when one reads *Camera Lucida* "critically" and thus kills the *punctum*, destroys the imaginary. Can Derrida, then, reproduce Roland Barthes's "tel qu'il fut pour moi" ("Les morts de Roland Barthes," 1987 293), "what took place" during their chance encounters? Derrida hardly dares envisage "the ecstasy of revelation, the instantaneous access to Roland Barthes" as he was in himself (*tel qu'en lui-même . . .* ), unless in a (waking) dream (DRB, 263; quoted *supra*). Faced with the necessity and the impossibility of the gift, with its specific nature on this occasion, how does Derrida solve this double bind? What will his posthumous solution have been?

By reading together, for the first time, both Barthes's first and last books—*Writing Degree Zero* and *Camera Lucida* (DRB, 262)—Derrida locates his homage within a framework capable of keeping in sight the *punctum* in Barthes's Photo-graphy: the "first" photo of the mother as a child, the last that Barthes cast his eyes on. Between *s* and *p*, "The Deaths of Roland Barthes" will neither quote blindly or scandalously, nor impose a ritual studied discourse, but attempt to negotiate the chance intersections, half imaginary half real, between twice two writings and signatures (Barthes's and Barthes's with Derrida's), in sum a new double session[67]—also Barthes's blind spot, "what he couldn't see in his writing" (DRB, 291)—such as the protagonists' initials in the scene of inverted filiation played out in *The Post Card*, between *phi*losophy and *psycho*analysis.[68] Derrida will disseminate these shared variations, point-counter-point or point-counter-study,[69] opening up speculation both as the flickering of being: the Wolf Man's initials

Serge Pankejev, *Wespe* (wasp) shorn of its wings (*Espe*), spectral, *n'S-ce Pas*? (cf. Sp, 24),[70] and, hence, of the *fort da* in "Speculate—on Freud," and also as an essentially photographic operation in metaphysics, rewriting the Cartesian cogito (*LDR*, XVI)[71] into a more suspensive "I am mortal, therefore I am." Provided, however, that this speculation is not (self-) reflexive, absorbed in its own mimesis, but that it enables reflection to take place—another point of encounter, between the un–Hegelian tain of the Derridean mirror and Barthes's undialectical Photography, "a denatured theater where death cannot 'be contemplated,' reflected and interiorized; or again: the dead theater of Death, the foreclosure of the Tragic, exclud[ing] all purification, all *catharsis*" (*CL*, 90; cf. also 31-32).[72] The climactic irony of the "Tragic" in *Camera Lucida* is the subtraction of the tragic, the impossibility of its resolution in catharsis, of the trauma's purge and purification. In "The Deaths of Roland Barthes," which at this point I wish to read alongside *Cinders*, purification gives way to pyrification, the dissemination of a plural, speculative writing (not specular, mimetic, still auto-affected in its homage), between Barthes and Derrida, in their mixed inter-esting obsessions—but also a spectral writing, haunted by the *différance* of an insistent "j'y reviens" in homage to the "viens" that can no longer be proffered to the demised. Warding off photography which, in the blind spot of time when the im-mortalising snap*shot* is taken, punctures the subject as an object both absent and past (both being opposed to "present"),[73] Derrida's commemorative piece, plying between two plural writing agencies, gropes for "that additional vision [*supplément de vue*] which is in a sense the gift, the grace of the *punctum*" (*CL*, 45) in Barthes's "experiential" writing—also the radiance of the mother's gaze, her "air" or "intractable supplement of identity, what is given as an act of grace" (*CL*, 109)—as a way of offering a living homage, in a utopic venue whose "interest" can then perhaps meet the ever-receding horizon of an impossible gift.

To conclude? One should especially not decide (on) a postmortem, return a crisp verdict after a patient dissection—such as: *Camera Lucida* is Barthes's most poignant book and "The Deaths of Roland Barthes" one of Derrida's most moving testimonies. Simply, perhaps, to confess one last interest and return to the studious strategies of this presentation, between an avowed quotation from *Camera Lucida* and what will remain an exappropriated echo, as a homage:

> A detail overwhelms the entirety of my reading: it is an intense mutation of my interest. (*CL*, 49; cf. also 47)

"Like them" and in between them, I have tried to look for the acute freshness of a reading in relation to detail.

## NOTES

The following abbreviations for the works of Roland Barthes have been used throughout this essay. Full details are provided in the Works Cited.

| | |
|---|---|
| CC | LaChambre claire |
| CL | Camera Lucida |
| ES | Empire of Signs |
| ET | The Eiffel Tower and Other Mythologies |
| FDA | Fragments d'un discours amoureux |
| FS | The Fashion System |
| GV | The Grain of the Voice |
| IMT | Image Music Text |
| LDF | A Lover's Discourse: Fragments |
| NCE | New Critical Essays |
| PT | The Pleasure of the Text |
| RB | Roland Barthes |
| RF | The Responsibility of Forms |
| RL | The Rustle of Language |
| SC | The Semiotic Challenge |
| SFL | Sade Fourier Loyola |
| S/Z | S/Z |
| WDZ | Writing Degree Zero |

1. This essay and the two companion pieces on the visual-photographic medium have also been translated in *The Responsibility of Forms*.

2. Cf. also "The Discourse of History" and "The Reality Effect," *RL*, 127–140 and 141–148, for the resistance of the "concrete real(ity)" to meaning. The direct collusion of referent and signifier in those concrete details, which expels the signified from the sign, anticipates and can be mapped on to Kristeva's "vréel" (true-real) in psychotic discourses; see Kristeva and Ribette, 1979 11–35 (also in Moi, 1986 216–237).

3. This awkward guest is what the Romans called *umbra* or shadow (see n. 16 *infra*). For the persistence (the French original says "entêtement," or obstinacy) of the thing to *be there*, see also *The Pleasure of the Text*, 46, and "The Image" (1977; *RL*, 350–358): "Stupidity does not suffer. . . . Hence, it *is there*, obtuse as Death" (*RL*, 351).

4. Cf. also *The Eiffel Tower*, 73: "the only true shock-photos . . . should be the news-agency photographs, where the fact, surprised, explodes in all its stubbornness, its literality, in the very obviousness of its obtuse nature"; and later in *Sade Fourier Loyola* [*SFL*], 134, about stubborn language without supplement, the major utopia of poetry.

5. For which see also Derrida's photo-graphic development of Marie-Françoise Plissart's silent photo-novel, *Lecture de Droit de regards* [*LDR*], XI, XXXIV, XXXV.

6. The "thèse d'irréalité," posited by the imaginative consciousness, had been put forward by Sartre in *L'Imaginaire. Psychologie phénoménologique de l'imagination* (232 in the original; translated as "hypothesis of unreality" in *The Psychology of Imagination,* 212), to which *Camera Lucida* will later pay a homage (*L'Imaginaire* had already been acknowledged in a passing footnote in *The Fashion System*, 4, n. 24).

7. Barthes increasingly affirmed his own view of cinema's aesthetic inferiority to photography owing to the former's rhythmic dimension, which invalidates any attempt to experience the equivalent of Photography's temporal *punctum* and thus bars our access to the imaginary; see e.g., *GV*, 359; *RB*, 84; *CL*, 55, 78. Thus the *photogramme* (still) allows the combination of those assets specific to the two sister arts while eliminating their (especially cinema's) flaws: the obtuse third meaning lies at the core of the "specific filmic (the filmic of the future)," which Barthes detects in the cinematic *still* rather than in the film in movement, "neither the simple photograph nor figurative painting . . . since they lack the diegetic horizon" (*IMT*, 66). See also Benjamin 1992, 231, for a transposition of the opposition between stillness and unarrestable rhythm to painting and film.

8. Some of the textual contradictions are discussed in the light of his 1951 essay "Michelet, l'Histoire et la Mort" in Lombardo (1989, 138ff.), who rightly singles out resurrection as the pivot of the long-deferred convergence between (Michelet's) History (-as-resurrection of forgotten great men) and Barthes's final "assumption" of History within his last "epiphanic" encounter with Photography in *Camera Lucida* (see below). A closer affinity between the photographic event and History provides the focus for Walter Benjamin's two important essays "A Short History of Photography" and "Theses on the Philosophy of History" (1992, 245–255); see Cadava's excellent study, esp. the following opposition: "photography escapes history when history orients itself toward a 'history of photography' rather than a 'photography of history' " (110), and, for parallels with Barthes, n. 47 *infra*. History's unrepresentability according to Benjamin (Cadava, 1992 102) can be related to death (cf. n. 29 *infra*).

9. Cf. also: "I myself experience this slight trauma of signifiance faced with certain photo-novels: *'their stupidity touches me'* (which could be a certain definition of obtuse meaning). There may thus be a future—or a very ancient past—truth" (*IMT*, 66, n. 1).

10. Similarly, in *The Psychology of Imagination*, Sartre had conceived of the mental image, as opposed to perception, as *"a certain way an object has of being absent within its very presence"* (81); cf. esp. 10-13, about the object's nothingness as posited by the imaginative consciousness.

11. The translators' "against" is here emended to "counter," more suggestive of the "contrapuntal" nature of *Camera Lucida* (DRB, 285, 286).

12. Cf. also *A Lover's Discourse*, 12. Note Derrida's 1976–1977 seminar on "Life Death" (*La vie la mort*), part of which was included in "To Speculate—on Freud" (cf. *P. . .*, 52). The affinities of this pulsating tension between life and death with painting's so-called "still life" and the cinematic still could be further developed in the light of Barthes's remarks on photography's *"immobilité vive"* (CC, 81), which immortalizes a *Tableau vivant* into what Nabokov has called a "frozen stillicide" (*Pale Fire*, 1985 l. 35 of the poem). Cf. also CL, 31–32, and RB, 68: " 'as if alive' means 'apparently dead.' "

13. We shall come back to Derrida's readings of Blanchot, in particular of *L'Arrêt de mort* (lit.: *Death Sentence* but also the stoppage of death), in "Pas" and "Living On: Border Lines," as well as to his lecture on *L'Instant de ma mort* delivered at the University of Turin in January 1995, soon after the publication of Blanchot's short *récit*.

14. See *GV*, 358; in the second of two interviews "On Photography," dating from 1977 and 1979, i.e., one year before and after his mother's death respectively. Though Barthes's answers to questions about his last project should not be taken as the warrants of later fulfilled intentions, they usefully point to a first-level reading of *Camera Lucida*: the phenomenological (Sartrean) method, the work's drift toward a specific photograph linked to death (cf. already *GV*, 356), correspondences between photos and textual moments, etc.

15. Cf. also RB, 19 (mistranslated as "official") and RF, 196 about the photograph as the objective, authentic proof of identity in our detective universe.

16. *Skia*: shadow, shade (also in painting), the Romans' uninvited guest or *umbra*, the shades to which Ulysses paid a visit, Ulysses' and Barthes's dead mothers; see LDF, 113, for a prophetic note which could warrant the classically gloomier reading of *Camera Lucida* as the narrative of a *Nekuia*, of a sojourn among shades without return (*Nostos*). Cf. also PT, 32: "There are those who want a text (an art, a painting) without a shadow. . . . The text needs its shadow: this shadow is a *bit* of ideology, a *bit* of representation, a *bit* of subject: ghosts, pockets, traces, necessary clouds: subversion must produce its own chiaroscuro," and Derrida's beautiful evocation of the prisoners in Plato's cave, who never "stretch out their hands towards the shadow

(*skia*) or the light (*phôs*), towards the silhouettes or images that are drawn on the wall" . . . "do not venture out with outstretched hands in the direction of this *skia*- or *photo*-graphy, their sights set on this shadow- or light-writing" (*MB* 15).

17. Some of which, like pleasure (like) versus *jouissance* (love) can be aligned with the "ghost" (DRB, 284) of the last Barthesian dyad (cf. *CC*, 50–51).

18. Different conceptions of light, shock, and "shout" versus "cry" (*CL*, 41, 109) would have to be fully retraced here.

19. The drift of the argument hopes to recharge positively the fundamentally negative or, at least, ambivalent category of the "imaginary" for Barthes, for whom it referred to stereotyped images imposed on a subject from the outside, hence its frequent translation as "image reservoir" and "image-system" (e.g., *PT*, 33–35; *SFL*, 49; *RB*, 105–106; *LDF*, 132–133; *GV*, 208–209). The same goes for our preference of utopia to atopia, despite Barthes's own privileging of the latter (e.g., *RB*, 49), as being more likely to point to the impossible ideal place or (*non-*)*lieu* of such a positive "imaginary" sketched by the writing of *Camera Lucida*, which cuts across a distinction between the non-space of atopia and the ideal space of utopia. For the latter, see Silverman 1994, 132, and also 128, where he contrasts too sharply—and without involving a discussion of *Camera Lucida*—Sartre's imaginative consciousness and Barthes's "image system," despite his project later in the book, in accordance with its general framework, to map out the interstitial space of "photobiographical textuality" (151–61), such as in the "autobiographical" *Roland Barthes* (128–29).

20. "Je suis mort," "je suis parfaitement mort," to Théodore Aubanel (16 July 1866) and Henry Cazalis (14 May 1867) respectively (Mallarmé, *Correspondence*, 1959 222, 240).

21. About the impossibility of saying, "I am dead," see also *RL*, 280, and the first English version of Barthes's lecture at the Johns Hopkins Conference in 1966, omitted in later texts (Macksey and Donato, 1970 143); the point was picked up in the ensuing discussion by Derrida who questioned the possibility of establishing a neat distinction between discursive time and historical time because of the movement of temporality that both retains and effaces the present of enunciation (155–156; for Barthes's use of Benveniste's opposition, see Part 3.). Set against Barthes's awaiting of his "total, undialectical death" (*CL*, 72) after losing his mother, and bearing in mind this earlier fascination with Valdemar's utopic statement and invention of an impossible, nondialectic category, Derrida's remarks in "No Apocalypse, Not Now" about the dialectizable, because symbolizable, work of death, including one's own, can be read as a radicalization of Barthes's "borderline" thinking and experiment in *Camera Lucida*, esp.: "my own death as an individual . . . can always be anticipated phantasmatically, symbolically too, as a negativity at work—a dialectic of the work, of signature, name, heritage, image, grief" (28: fifth missile/missive).

22. For the thesis of the "thusness" (*ainsité*) or magical phenomenality of the instant/snapshot in the haiku-as-photographic-writing, see Comment, 184–193 (and 111–129 on photography). The trajectory of the present essay—from the *"tel"* to the *"tel qu'en elle-même"* and to the *"comme si"* supplementing the *"c'est ça!/ainsi!"*—developed for the most part before my reading of Comment's excellent study, can therefore be seen as an attempt to refocus his simpler equation between Photography's revelation or essential illumination and what would be the reinscription of a pure ontological phenomenality.

23. Cf. the original *Fragments d'un discours amoureux* [*FDA*], 262–263: "Tel II").

24. Cf. also *FDA*, 263: "Le langage obtus."

25. Cf. "The Third Meaning," also from 1970, which juxtaposes the photocinematic still and the haiku; *IMT*, 62.

26. See also *GV*, 211, for Barthes's conception of the photograph-like haiku as "the essential, musical future of the fragment, its form of becoming," characterized by its "matteness" which "engenders no sense, but at the same time . . . is not non-sense."

27. Using the following extract as a touchstone: "the photograph of the missing being . . . will touch me like the delayed rays of a star" (*CL*, 80–81), a parallel could be drawn (to be touched up later) with Blanchot's *The Writing of the Disaster*, especially the fragment on Sade, but applicable to Poe, which can be read as an oblique gloss on Mallarmé's "Tombeau": "henceforth without radiance: dark he wheels, the star of disaster, vanished as he wished it, in the anonymnous tomb of his renown" (45). Blanchot refutes the critics' condemnation of the French poet as obscure, a position that can be aligned with Barthes's interested use of the *camera lucida* versus *obscura* in order to evoke his mother's clear gaze and the searing radiance of the Winter Garden Photograph; see Blanchot, "La Poésie de Mallarmé est-elle obscure?" (*Faux pas*, 1943 126–131) and "Mallarmé and the Art of the Novel," in particular: "Mallarmé the obscure gave brilliance, as if it were something tangible and clear, to what could only be expressed in the total absence of expression" (in Holland, 1995 45).

28. The subtlety of the double syntactical articulation has not been rendered in the translation (cf. *Being and Nothingness*, 1956 169).

29. See also the "Kant Notices" in Lyotard 1988, 124, 131, 133, 135, and 170; therefore another logic of the *quasi* (one of the equivalents of the Germanic *als ob*), related to Jankélévitch's "primary" philosophy of the "almost," which allows one to glimpse the unthinkable quality of the instant as a nonlocatable, a/utopic, a/uchronic almost-nothing, a "point" such as Barthes's *punctum* provided one problematizes the former's indivisible nature since, as we shall see, Barthes's supplemental *punctum* is at once unique (anagnoristic) and (at least) double, composed of its own metonymic counterpoint(s), as ambivalent as

Photography itself (e.g., *CL*, 45, 49: about the haiku). See Jankélévitch 1954, 71–76, 160–164, 208–218, and 1980, 1:54–60 (and, e.g., 2:24, 161, for the two sides of the "as if," the first one being akin to the "simulacrum" in Derrida's "Sauver les phénomènes" mentioned below). Let us note finally that Barthes's wariness of the photographic medium in his earlier writings had to do with such an analogical structure of quasi-identity (cf. "Rhetoric of the Image," *IMT*, 36) characteristic of the image, also understood as a superficial construction of the other.

30. At this point, a more patient study should relate Derrida's substitution of chance/accident and *destinerrance* for destination/destiny in the domains of psychoanalytic transference and philosophical transmission, to the accidental event of the anagnorisis in *Camera Lucida* (cf. *CL*, 27).

31. See Lacoue-Labarthe (1979, 203–207), who echoes both Freud and Lyotard. In his *Philosophie première*, Jankélévitch comments likewise on death's unrepresentability (50) as well as on the necessary attempt at representing it to oneself, as does Blanchot (also echoing Freud) in *The Writing of the Disaster* (118), where the thesis of death's atopia must be related to the absence of a "passage" (but also of passive, past, *pas*; *passim*): "in death nothing comes to pass and . . . death itself does not pass" (70).

32. With its etymological kinship to stylet or "point" (*pointe*), the word carries a trace of Barthes's *punctum* and cannot be understood without reference to Derrida's 1978 study of Nietzsche's sharp stylistic *spurs*. Another interstitial development, via Perec's short piece "Still life, style leaf," could be the starting point of a reflection on the network of allusions that tie together still (life) and style-as-*punctum* in Barthes and Derrida.

33. E.g.: "People have often proceeded as if the image were at first constructed on the model of a perception"; "This does not prevent us from reacting to the image as if its object were before us; we will see later that it is possible for us to attempt to react to an image as if it were a perception" (*The Psychology of Imagination*, 11, 13). In the discussion of Barthes's 1966 lecture "To Write: An Intransitive Verb?" Richard Macksey had reminded him, in connection with "Rhetoric of the Image," of the Peircean conception of the photograph as "a 'quasi-predicate' composed by the 'quasi-subject,' light" (Macksey and Donato, 1970 154–155).

34. Unless the real be the letter of death which is some day or other destined to us all (Žižek 1992, 20–22), even if the date is both assigned (necessary) and undesignated (random); Cf. Blanchot, *The Writing of the Disaster*, 47–48. In *Le Je-ne-sais-quoi et le Presque-rien*, Jankélévitch comments: "It all occurs as if destiny removed the date of death from us so as to divert us from going deeper into its nature" (2:23: § "Mors certa, hora incerta;" my translation).

35. For an excellent analysis of the figures of the trauma, itself a figure of writing, see Brown, 1992 236–184 (esp. 279–283, on *ah!*, *c'est áa!*, *áa a été!*, and *tel!*).

36. As Lombardo notes (1982, 85; also 1985: 119–122), the Lacanian imaginary is displaced toward the Sartrean imaginary, since photography diverts

the process of identification by showing something absent, as well as toward the Lacanian real, described elsewhere as "the unavoidable *res*: death" (Lombardo 1989, 133; Jankélévitch's *res universa* or *res nostra* in his *Philosophie première*, 54). Cf. also Blanchot in *The Writing of the Disaster*: "the real is real inasmuch it excludes possibility—because, in other words, it is impossible. The same can be said of death and, still more accurately, of *The Writing of the Disaster*" (64); "If death is the real, and if the real is impossible, then we are approaching the thought of the impossibility of death" (121; for the real as impossible, see esp. Lacan 1991, 143). One should follow up Barthes's scattered references to the Lacanian imaginary and show that, far from being systematically evacuated, especially in his constructions of an autobiographical (*RB*) or amorous (*LDF*) subject: e.g., "Réponses," 99; *GV*, 282–283 (interview about *LDF*; after a recall of Vico's image of the spirals of history in which things do not return in the same place), it is, rather, made more complex and elusive in the last reflections on the image through the increasing (re-)anchoring in Sartrean phenomenology.

37. This sensitivity of a circular/hermeneutic homecoming to a (utopian) place "where we have not yet been" (Schmidt, 1990 76) will be developed later in conjunction with the future perfect of postmodern temporality. The traumatic reality of the irremediably lost maternal place can also be the meaning of the trauma of *signifiance* if the latter is understood as the "semiotic" (in a Kristevian, semanalytical sense), the pre-linguistic period of bodily drives in which the infant is in intimate identificatory relationship with the mother (cf. Burgin, 1986 84).

38. A longer study should trace the political, literary implications of Barthes's "utopia," its relationship with "atopia" or "atopos" (e.g., *PT*, 23; *RB*, 49; see also n. 16 *supra*), the quality of the loved being in its unnameable "brilliant originality" (*LDF*, 34–36), its opposition to the funereal properties of adjectives (*CL*, 70; *RB*, 43, 68; *LDF*, 221–222, quoted above) which are "those doors of language through which the ideological and the imaginary come flowing in" (*PT*, 14; cf. also *GV*, 174 and "The Grain of the Voice," *RF*, 268). For an excellent, condensed discussion of adjective, utopia, and imaginary, see Moriarty, 1991 174. For the notions of imaginary and utopia in Barthes, see respectively Ulmer (1980) and Knight (1991) (as well as Wiseman, 1989 136–192, about utopia and temporality, about which more anon).

39. See also the opening propositions in his short presentation of Mallarmé in *Tableau de la littérature française AL*, 111).

40. "*Longtemps, je me suis couché de bonne heure. . . .*" (*RL*, 277–290 [289]). Compare with Dandieu's judgment, echoed by Nabokov in his lecture on Proust, "The Walk by Swann's Place" (1913), that "the whole enormous work [*A la Recherche du temps perdu*] . . . is but an extended comparison revolving on the words *as if*—" [Nabokov, *Lectures on Literature*, 208]. Barthes's 1978 lecture on Proust's *A la Recherche* insists on the symbolic role of initiation of the mother's mourning in Proust for Barthes's own work that postdates the death of his own mother (but also the death of the narrator's grandmother [*RL*, 287]

whose photo plays a crucial role in Proust's text), and the relationship it in-augurates between the forced discovery of death's incontrovertible reality and a new practice of writing or "third form" (*RL*, esp. 284 ff.) which Barthes had already been groping for from the early 1970s and which can therefore be related to the "third meaning" in the similarly titled essay, also from 1970. No doubt influenced by an intensification of references to Proust at the time of Barthes's ultimate reflections on photography, and perhaps by a convergence of experiences between Barthes's anagnorisis and the scene of the photograph of Marcel's grandmother in *A la Recherche*, among other things—let us also recall that Barthes was preparing a course on Proust and the novel for the Collège de France before his untimely death—critics have often tended to overstress, beyond textual ambiguities or even disclaimers, the role of the Proustian quest and anamnesis in the elaboration of the book's *punctum*.

41. See, e.g., Salusinsky (1987 esp. 22–23).

42. Thus, the third form of *A la Recherche* rests on the disorganization of Time (*RL*, 281), "a temporal distortion of the *already* and of the *not yet*, the beginning and the end of the adventure, the opening and the clausula of the work" (Marty, 1982 747; my translation).

43. Also, much of " 'There is No One Narcissism' (Autobiophotographies)" (*P. . .* , 196–215; about Derridean writing and thinking as an attempt to cross toward such an ungraspable Mallarméan u-topos, see Steinmetz, 1994 199, n. 17). J. Hillis Miller too has evoked such an insidious (non-) place of/in Derrida's writing, always ready to crypt itself from the reader's gaze and exceeding the resources of a joint topo-nymy, -logy, -graphy (Miller, 1995 esp. 296–297). Start-ing from "How To Avoid Speaking," a longer study would be needed in order to tease out, as far as is utopically possible, the relations between Derrida's ceaselessly affirmative moves (beyond [his writing about] denegation), the figures of the *quasi(ment)*, the "desert" or utopian (*non*)*lieux* of/in his writing (such as the Platonic *khora*) and the (not) taking place of deconstruction evoked for, e.g., in "Some Statements and Truisms . . . ," 93 (see also n. 59 infra).

44. Analogous to the historical portrait of Charles VIII in Sartre's *Psychol-ogy of Imagination* (24).

45. History as the span in the mother's life *before* Barthes's birth, hence the Winter Garden Photograph.

46. As opposed to the imperfect, the counter-anamnesic tense of memory's lure, "the tense of fascination [which] seems to be alive and yet . . . doesn't move: imperfect presence, imperfect death: neither oblivion nor resurrection. . . . This Theater of time is the very contrary of [Proust's] search for lost time; for I remember pathetically, punctually, and not philosophically, discursively" (*LDF*, 217).

47. Compare with Moriarty, 1991 199: "the first person of the past historic functions as a kind of verbal photograph, coupling together the here-and-now and the then?" As Lombardo rightly notes (1982, 85; 1989, 137), Barthes seems

to recant his earlier view in *A Lover's Discourse* that "the nature of the photograph is not to represent but to memorialize [*remémorer*: i.e., to recollect]," in a passage bearing also on the belated imaginary reconstruction of the traumatic event of love at first sight—*coup de foudre*; cf. *CL*, 45 about the lightning-like *punctum*—experienced in the present but conjugated/spoken in the past: an "*anterior immediacy*" (*LDF*, 193–4).

48. As was the disquieting antecedent of the photo of General Nogi and his wife on the eve of carrying out their suicide, premeditated after the emperor's death, and whose caption reads: "They are going to die, they know it, and this is not seen" (*ES*, 92–93).

49. Cf. also, the as ifs of "No Apocalypse, Not Now," 20, within a logic of the "not yet, always already"; also, *Aporias*, 75: 'The impossibility of existing or of *Dasein* that Heidegger speaks of under the name of 'death' is the disappearance, the end, the annihilation of the *as such* [comme tel], of the possibility of the relation to the phenomenon as such or to the phenomenon of the '*as such*' ". Perhaps one should, unlike Howard, resist the lure of a hasty translation of Barthes's *être-là* by *Dasein* in "The Image" (*RL*, 351) as the Heideggerian relation between Dasein, presence, death and a phenomenological *als* only partly overlaps Barthes's position on the thing's obtuse "being-there" (*être-là*) which insists as such but also as death does (cf. n. 3 *supra*).

50. A synonym for Stupidity in *PT*, 19, which takes us back to the obtuse and which, in the wakening of the "intractable reality" of the mad Photograph, closes *Camera Lucida* (*CL*, 119).

51. See also Benjamin's "A Small History of Photography," 243 (as well as "The Work of Art in the Age of Mechanical Reproduction," 1992, 230), for an analogous parallel between the revulsive temporality of the optical unconscious revealed by Photography and that of pulsions brought to light in the psychoanalytic unconscious. For Freud's and Benjamin's overlapping views of psychical processes as being indissociable from photographic reproducibility, see Cadava, 1992 105–106, who reminds us that for Benjamin in "On Some Motifs in Baudelaire," the photographic camera "gave the moment a posthumous shock" (1992, 171). Other Barthesian statements in Cadava's study of the Benjaminian views of history and photography include the following: "the photographic event reproduces, according to its own faithful and rigorous *rigor mortis* manner, the posthumous character of our lived experience" (89); "[the photograph] belongs to the afterlife of the photographed. It is permanently inflamed by the instantaneous flash of death" (92)—see also Coquio 1993, esp. 202–204 (focused on *CL*). Produced by the eternalization of the shutter's instant click in the time-lagged perception of the image, this posthumous shock must be envisaged in relation to the differential structure of an optical unconscious in the gaze as well as to the *nachträglich* dimension of psychical, especially traumatic, experience.

52. The "trauma's trauma" in the supplemental *punctum* would then perhaps be the abolishing twist to its very supplementarity, the subtraction of

a "(no) more" (*plus de*) in the operation "There she is!" . . . "So, yes, so much and no more" (*CL*, 109; cf. *CC*, 167–168), which confers upon it its instantaneous immediacy, (n)either in default (n)or in excess, not unlike the Text which one recognizes as a "that's it (for me)!" (cf. *PT*, 13).

53. The invisible, unrepresentable *punctum* of the Winter Garden Photograph works as an apotropaic gesture (cf. Sarkonak, 66): to avoid the mechanical, deindividualizing reproducibility of the experiential object and of its unique referent. Yet one must take care not to collapse Barthes's demarche with Benjamin's position, in "The Work of Art in the Age of Mechanical Reproduction," according to which reproduction signifies the traumatic loss of identity. Such a hasty conflation would miss the crucial opposition between the analogical identity/resemblance and the essential "air" as "intractable supplement of identity" (*CL*, 109; also 102–103, quoted above), an opposition that is necessary to the miraculous articulation between the reality of *ça-a-été* and the truth of *c'est ça!* (*CC*, 176; *CL*, 113) in the transcending *punctum* (unlike *CL*, 12: "the Photograph is the advent of myself as other: a cunning dissociation of consciousness from identity").

54. See also Wiseman's conclusions, esp. 189–191, in which she relates the debate on postmodernism in architecture to the temporal ecstasy provoked by Barthes's Photography. In Shawcross's critical epilogue (133–143), Barthesian Photography, the witness to an unclassifiable "avant-garde," seems to escape Lyotard's approach to both modern *and* postmodern (re-) presentation—while drawing a blank on the latter's specific temporality according to him—as well as the Habermasian modernity of a future having already started and whose attempt at dechronologizing the "new" and the "modern" Wiseman recalls. Without falling prey again to the oversimplified views of a Photography judged postmodern whenever it parodically constructs its self-reflexivity (e.g., Hutcheon, *passim*), this brief development will endeavor to argue for Barthes's postmodernity through his redeployment of an "ecstatic" temporality at work in history against mere feelings of a pure nostalgia for a lost past.

55. Cf. *Call Me Ishmael*, 14: "Melville went back, to discover us, to come forward." His celebrated critique of Pound's system of writing as "a structure of mnemonics raised on a . . . nostalgia" (Seelye, 1991 98) must be understood in relation to the conception of a retrograde (literary) history reared on recollections and *ubi sunt*.

56. As Derrida puts it in *Specters of Marx*, "and what is a *phenomenology* if not a logic of the *phainesthai* and of the *phantasma*, therefore of the phantom?" (*SM*, 122).

57. For Benjamin, the quasimagical power of photography was related to its validation of the here now, and not of a here then, whereas in Sartre the magical link between an image and its original was predicated upon the encounter between a past there and a present here (*The Psychology of Imagination*, 24–25).

58. Another essay, "L'expérience de Proust," about the image as presence–absence, is quoted in *CL*, 106 (Blanchot 1959, 25). In this essay, Blanchot identifies the space of the Proustean imaginary in the patient staging of lost and found time in *A la Recherche*, or what we have called Barthes's dramatization of the instant in *Camera Lucida* (cf. § "Aussitôt quoique peu à peu" and esp. 28; see, also in *Le Livre à venir*, "La Rencontre de l'imaginaire" [1959, 9–19]).

59. A distant phenomenological echo of the "present sign of a dead thing" in "The Discourse of History" (1967; *RL*, 140).

60. The passage, on 60–61 of the French original, is acknowledged in a footnote of Barthes's "Textual Analysis of a Tale by Edgar Allan Poe" (*SC*, 287), excerpted by Derrida (*DRB*, 292–293), who, as a modest gift of homage, leaves out Barthes's acknowledgment (*Speech and Phenomena* also alludes to Poe's tale: 97). (In his preface to the 1971 edition of *Essais critiques*, Barthes had underlined in retrospect the impact of Derrida's three 1967 books, alongside the work of *Tel Quel* and Kristeva, in the case against a naive belief in the critical possibilities of the sign [8]; see also his 1972 "Lettre à Jean Ristat" in the special Derrida issue of *Les Lettres françaises*.) Parallels between Barthes and Derrida on writing, voice, signature, etc. as spectral return and death are too uncannily numerous to be teased out here. Let us briefly mention: first, in *Writing and Difference* (orig. also 1967): "Death strolls between letters. To write, what is called writing, assumes an access to the mind through having the courage to lose one's life, to die away from nature" (71), and, almost at random, these four later developments: "When I sign, I am already dead" (*G*, 19b, about Genet's "The Man Condemned to Death"); *SPC*, 58, for the link between the spectral *revenance* of the mark or re-mark and the experience of mourning and death; (*LOBL*, 103), about living on (neither life nor death) as the status of writing, mark or trace; *Signéponge*, 108 about the "signature of the dead man." On the Barthesian side, see *RB*, 68: "the voice is always *already* dead," and 168: "I am speaking about myself as though I were more or less dead"; and finally, about the relation between death and writing, e.g., *Writing Degree Zero*, 45: "The Novel is a Death"; *New Critical Essays*, 44, about writing as the beginning of death; and, indirectly, *LDF*, 78, about the obtuse nature of writing (cf. n. 3 *supra*).

61. Let us recall that *L'Arrêt de mort* is the narration of an incredible survival during World War II; cf. LOBL, 135 and 138, about living on as "phantom revenance"? For Derrida's comments on Blanchot's "viens," see esp. *On a Newly Arisen Apocalyptic Tone in Philosophy* (*ONAATP*, 162, 165, 166). Blanchot's *récit* was recently recalled to our attention by the publication of *L'Instant de ma mort*, a terse but remarkable account, also set during the war, whose significance did not escape Derrida, who lectured on it at the University of Turin soon after its appearance. This dramatization of the ecstatic fork in time and consciousness when the narrator's preordained death was miraculously stayed and the instant was turned into a perpetual suspension (*instance*; cf. 19), offers

a poignant equivalent to Barthes's dramatization of the instant in the suspensive writing of *Camera Lucida*, with its division between the narrator's (Barthes's) conceptions of his mother's recent demise and of his own prospective death. Derrida highlighted how the instant of one's death is always such a pending imminence, at once necessary and impossible, and how the narration, with its split narrative agencies, straddles this utopia of the survivor's impossible testimony to "his own" death (my thanks to my friend Carmen Concilio for those indications); compare with Poe's emphasis on the precariousness of this situation in the Valdemar story. About this other double *pas au-delà* of death's dual structure of necessity and impossibility, cf. esp. *L'Instant de ma mort* (17): "As if the death outside him could from now on only bump against the death within him" (my translation). A longer study would need to examine more rigorously the complex links between Blanchot's passive affirmation of death, the Derridean belief in an originary *yes* and in the sign-as-death, and, running counter to his challenge of his mother's demise, Barthes's placid anticipation of his own end.

62. As in P (32, also 57): "dans tout récit de Blanchot, il y va de ce pas," echoed in a discussion of death and translation in *Aporias* (6, 37).

63. Cf. already in *The Post Card* (10), about the return of revenants, the hypothesis that "there have ever been, from the first 'come' ['*viens*'], but revenants"? Here again, these tentative remarks should be firmed up in the context of Derrida's insistence on the mark's iterability, and in particular the iterability of the "yes" (such as Molly Bloom's) in "Ulysses Gramophone: Hear Say Yes in Joyce" [U]—starting "*Oui Oui*" (U, 27), the diacritic on *ouï-dire* (hearsay [yes]) testifying to the "originary" division (cf. also U, 43, 69–70: reactive repetition inherent to the yes of the signature or of the gift; 60: "*yes* always appears as a *yes, yes*"; 63: recall of the *yes, yes* in the beginning; etc.)—but especially in "Nombre de oui" where Derrida envisages the ontologico-transcendental *quasi-analytics* of a yes as an "originary" repetition marked by the structural necessity of forgetting, the "second" *yes* being "as if the 'first' were forgotten, past enough to demand a new initial yes" (649, my translation; for the recall of the *yes, yes*, cf. also P, 90 and *EO*, 13–14). Cf. Clark's comments in conjunction with the trajectory of a (double) "Pas" from "Viens" to "Viens/Oui, oui," which informs Derrida's hypothesis of a hymen between the two women and narrations of Blanchot's *récit*: "If reading for Blanchot is a mode of saying 'yes' to the work—a form of step back into its imaginary space—it is not surprising that Derrida's *Pas* affirms the reading of Blanchot as a double 'yes' " (130–131).

64. Following the example of the gift, retrospective and to himself, of enthralling images unnameable like *puncta* (cf. *CL*, 51) and inviting the imaginary, with which Barthes had opened his autobiophotographical composition (*RB*, 3).

65. Cf. *The Writing of the Disaster*, about giving according to the time of the other, which is "the unrepresentable representation of a time without present and always returning" (89).

66. Note also *CL*, 43 about the dated fashion touching Barthes. *Datum* is also the unattested etymology of the French for playing dice (*dé*); compare the

inter-play on *dé*, finger *doigt*, from *digitum*, and pointing in Mallarmé (cf. *D*, 269, n. 68: finger [datum, digitum], etc.) and in Barthes, for whom pointing is opposed to definition (*SFL*, 62: image is deictic, designates, does not define; *Fashion System*, 303: the (fashion) photograph "points to [meaning] with its finger"; S/Z, 62: "The connotative signified is literally an *index*: it points but does not tell"; cf. also Halley).

67. See, on both sides of the *faux pli* of the double session of *Dissemination*, between as spacing, articulation, interval, and the double half (*mi-*) in "Mimi(que)" (*D*, 222, n. 36; 227-228, quoting a letter from Sollers). See also *P. . .* , 188, on the calculated necessity to invent a new tone and adapt one's style to the other's signature (as in DRB, 263, quoted supra).

68. That is, from Ph [*Feu*], "which one can indifferently call *phainesthai* or *phos*, phenomenon, phantasm, phantom or photography"—drawn from JD's fantasized scene between C[amille] and C[laude], which we shall spell indifferently *C[hambre] C[laire]* (*LDR*, XXI; my translation)—to PS (or SP), including even perhaps the late (*feu*) Jean-Paul Sartre, (a)live and dead / lying low (ici gît/[J]PS), and his *L'Imaginaire: Psychologie phénoménologique* de l'imagination, all as "signature[s] paraphée[s]" (SP, 24), initialled beforehand by Barthes and, especially, Derrida (cf. *Speech and Phenomena, Positions, Spurs, Signsponge*, "Speculate—On Freud," *Specters of Marx*, "Sauver les Phénomènes," etc.). In the P.S. of *Positions*, Derrida had already noted the self-disseminating polysemy of the letter *s* (96).

69. Just as he will pluralize the deaths/dead (*morts*) and disseminate them like ashes, this "remainder without remainder" (*P. . .* , 208) of writing's disaster on such an unspeakable occasion; compare with *The Writing of the Disaster*: "When all is said, what remains to be said is the disaster. Ruin of words, demise writing . . . : what remains without remains (the fragmentary)" (33).

70. Between philosophy and psychoanalysis: one should here also retrace the interweavings of the motif, between René Major (esp. *Rêver l'autre* and *Lacan avec Derrida*) and Jacques Derrida (*The Post Card*, "Sauver les phénomènes," etc.).

71. Cf. Steinmetz (1994 179), framing a quotation from *LDR*, XVI: "Every metaphysical 'speculation' is of an essentially 'photographic' nature and engages 'the writing of appearing [*du paraître*], of apparition and of appearance'—of apparition which is nothing but an appearance—'the brilliance of the *phainesthai* and of light, *photography*' " (my translation). See also DRB: "Ghosts: the concept of the other in the same, the *punctum* in the *studium*, the dead other alive in me [*le tout autre mort vivant en moi*]. This concept of the photograph photographs all conceptual oppositions, it traces a relationship of haunting which perhaps is constitutive of all logics" (267).

72. See Moriarty (1991 239, notes 22, 25) about theatricality and death in connection with photography. About Benjaminian photography as a dislocation, from within, of the possibility of reflection, see Cadava (1992 93).

73. Cf. Sartre's *Being and Nothingness* (1956 176).

# Notes on Contributors

**Boris Belay** is a doctoral student at the State University of New York at Stonybrook, and has worked under Derrida's supervision. His research focuses on the place and influence of Georges Bataille's political reflections in contemporary French thought.

**John Brannigan** is Head of Irish Studies at the University of Luton, where he also lectures in the English Department. He is author of *Beyond the Angry Young Men* and *Cultural Materialism and New Historicism* (1998), and has published articles on Tennyson and Cultural Materialism. He has co-edited *Applying: to Derrida* (1996). He is currently working on a book on British Literature from 1945 to the present.

**Christopher Johnson** is lecturer in French at Keele University. He was a Junior Research Fellow at Trinity College, Cambridge, and in 1992 was a Visiting Fellow at the Humanities Research Institute of the University of California, Irvine. He is author of *System and Writing in the Philosophy of Jacques Derrida* (1993), and is at present preparing a book on Lévi-Strauss and French anthropology. He is currently general editor of the journal *Paragraph*.

**John P. Leavey Jr.** teaches at the University of Florida. He is the author of *Glassary*, the translator of *The Archeology of the Frivolous*, and, with Richard Rand, the translator of *Glas*.

**Ian Maclachlan** is a Lecturer in French at the University of Aberdeen, having previously taught at the Universities of Oxford and Leicester. He has translated texts by Maurice Blanchot and Roger Laporte, and is the author of the forthcoming study *Roger Laporte: the Orphic text*. He is currently working on a study of time and literary value in contemporary French literature and philosophy.

**Jessica Maynard** teaches in the Department of English at King's College, London, where she is completing work on her doctoral dissertation. She is currently researching into discourses of terror and terrorism in nineteenth- and twentieth-century fiction, and representations of the city.

**Laurent Milesi** received his Ph.D. from Oxford University and currently teaches English and American Literature and Critical Theory at Cardiff University of Wales. He is the author of *The "Litteral" of Language in Finnegans Wake*, and is working on a study of Freud's concept of *nachträglichkeit*, and a study of the trope of the dance(r) as a (self-) representation of writing in twentieth-century poetry and theory.

**Ruth Robbins** is a lecturer in literary studies at the University of Luton. She has research interests in late-nineteenth-century literature and has published articles on Hausman, Wilde, and Vernon Lee. She is co–editor of *Victorian Identities: Social and Cultural Formations in Nineteenth–Century Literature* (1995) and *Applying: to Derrida* (1996).

**Michael Syrotinski** received his Ph.D. from Yale University, where he studied with Derrida. He has taught at Illinois State University, and currently teaches Contemporary French and Francophone Literature and Culture at the University of Aberdeen. He has published numerous articles in these fields, is author of *Defying Gravity: Jean Paulhan's Interventions in Twentieth Century French Intellectual History* (forthcoming), co-translator of Derrida's *Politics of Friendship*, and has translated and edited a collection of Paulhan's short stories for the University of Nebraska Press.

**Michael Temple** is a lecturer in French at Queen Mary and Westfield College, London. He is the author of *The Name of the Poet: Onomastics and Anonymity in the works of Stéphane Mallarmé*. He is currently working on a further study of Mallarmé, as well as projects involving Jean-Luc Godard and Serge Gainsbourg.

**Burhan Tufail** has taught at the University of North London and at Queen Mary and Westfield College. His research interests include American Literature and contemporary French writing.

**Julian Wolfreys** has taught at the universities of Luton and Dundee. He is the author of *Being English: Narratives, Idioms and Performances of National Identity from Coleridge to Trollope* (1994), *The Rhetoric of Affirmative Resistances: Dissonant Identities from Carroll to Derrida* (1997), *Writing London: the Trace of the Urban Text from Blake to Dickens* (1998), and *Deconstruction • Derrida* (1998). He is editor of *The Derrida Reader: Writing Performances* (1998), and is co-editor of *Victorian Identities: Social and Cultural Formations in Nineteenth-Century Literature* (1995), *Applying: to Derrida* (1996), *Literary Theories: A Case Study in Critical Performance* (1996), and *Re: Joyce – Text • Culture • Politics* (1997).

# Works Cited

*A True History of the College of 'Pataphysics.* London: Atlas Press, 1995.

Ades, Dawn. *Dada and Surrealism Reviewed.* London: Arts Council of Great Britain, 1978.

Arendt, Hannah. *The Origins of Totalitarianism* (1966). San Diego and New York: Harcourt Brace and Co, 1979.

Artaud, Antonin. "The Theatre of Cruelty: First Manifesto." In *The Theatre and Its Double.* London: Calder, 1993.

Attridge, Derek, ed. Jacques Derrida. *Acts of Literature.* New York: Routledge. 1992.

Auster, Paul, ed. *The Random House Book of Twentieth Century French Poetry.* New York: Random House, 1982.

Bannet, Eve Tavor. *Postcultural Theory: Critical Theory after the Marxist Paradigm.* New York: St Martin's Press, 1993.

Barthes, Roland. "Barthes puissance trois," *Quinzaine littéraire* 205 (1–15 mars 1975): 1–5.

Barthes, Roland. "Lettre à Jean Ristat," *Les Lettres françaises* (29 March 1972).

Barthes, Roland. "Réponses," *Tel Quel* 47 (1971): 89–107.

Barthes, Roland. "Sept photos-modèles de Mère Courage," *Théâtre populaire* 35 (1959): 17–32.

Barthes, Roland. *A Lover's Discourse. Fragments.* Trans. Richard Howard. Harmondsworth: Penguin, 1990.

Barthes, Roland. *Camera Lucida: Reflections on Photography.* Trans. Richard Howard. London: Vintage, 1993.

Barthes, Roland. *Empire of Signs.* Trans. Richard Howard. London: Jonathan Cape, 1983.

Barthes, Roland. *Essais critiques.* Paris: Seuil, 1971.

Barthes, Roland. *Fragments d'un discours amoureux.* Paris: Seuil, 1977.

Barthes, Roland. *Image Music Text.* Essays selected and trans. Stephen Heath. London: Fontana, 1977.

Barthes, Roland. *La Chambre claire: Note sur la photographie.* Paris: Seuil, 1980.

Barthes, Roland. *New Critical Essays.* Trans. Richard Howard. New York: Hill and Wang, 1980.

Barthes, Roland. *Roland Barthes*. Paris: Seuil, 1975.

Barthes, Roland. *Roland Barthes*. Trans. Richard Howard. New York: Hill and Wang, 1977.

Barthes, Roland. *S/Z*. Trans. Richard Miller. Preface by Richard Howard. Oxford: Blackwell, 1990.

Barthes, Roland. *Sade Fourier Loyola*. Trans. Richard Miller. London: Jonathan Cape, 1977.

Barthes, Roland. *The Eiffel Tower and Other Mythologies*. Trans. Richard Howard. New York: Hill and Wang, 1979.

Barthes, Roland. *The Fashion System*. Trans. Matthew Ward and Richard Howard. London: Jonathan Cape, 1985.

Barthes, Roland. *The Grain of the Voice. Interviews 1962–1980*. Trans. Linda Coverdale. London: Jonathan Cape, 1985.

Barthes, Roland. *The Pleasure of the Text*. Trans. Richard Miller. London: Jonathan Cape, 1976.

Barthes, Roland. *The Responsibility of Forms: Critical Essays on Music, Art, and Representation*. Trans. Richard Howard. Berkeley and Los Angeles: University of California Press, 1985.

Barthes, Roland. *The Rustle of Language*. Trans. Richard Howard. Oxford: Blackwell, 1986.

Barthes, Roland. *The Semiotic Challenge*. Trans. Richard Howard. Oxford: Blackwell, 1988.

Barthes, Roland. *Writing Degree Zero*. Trans. Annette Lavers and Colin Smith. London: Jonathan Cape, 1967.

Baudelaire, Charles. *Oeuvres Complètes*. Ed. Claude Roy and Michel Jamet. Paris: Bouquins Robert Laffont, 1980.

Beaumont, Keith. *Alfred Jarry: A Critical and Biographical Study*. Leicester: Leicester University Press, 1984.

Beckett, Samuel. *Proust* (1931). New York: Grove Press, 1980.

Bénabou, Marcel. "Rule and Constraint." Trans. Warren F. Motte Jr. In *Oulipo: A Primer of Potential Literature*. Ed. Warren F. Motte, Jr. Lincoln: University of Nebraska Press, 1986.

Benjamin, Walter. "A Small History of Photography." In *One-Way Street and Other Writings*. Trans. Edmund Jephcott and Kingsley Shorter. London: Harcourt Brace Jovanovich, 1978, 240–257.

Benjamin, Walter. *Illuminations* (1955). Ed. and int. Hannah Arendt. Trans. Harry Zohn. London: Fontana, 1992.

Bennington, Geoffrey, and Jacques Derrida. *Jacques Derrida*. Paris: Seuil, 1991.

Bennington, Geoffrey, and Jacques Derrida. *Jacques Derrida*. Chicago: Chicago University Press, 1993.

Bennington, Geoffrey. *Legislations: The Politics of Deconstruction*. London: Verso, 1994.

Benveniste, Emile. *Problems in General Linguistics*. Trans. Mary Elizabeth Meek. Coral Gables: University of Miami Press, 1971.

Bersani, Leo. *The Death of Stéphane Mallarmé*. Cambridge: Cambridge University Press, 1982.

Blanchot, Maurice. "The Ease of Dying." Trans. Christine Moneera Laennec and Michael Syrotinski. In *Progress in Love on the Slow Side: Récits by Jean Paulhan*. Lincoln: University of Nebraska Press, 1994, 122–142. Original French "La Facilité de mourir," *Nouvelle Revue Française* 197 (May 1969): 743–764.

Blanchot, Maurice. *Faux Pas*. Paris: Gallimard, 1943.

Blanchot, Maurice. *L'Arrêt de mort*. Paris: Gallimard. 1948.

Blanchot, Maurice. *L'Instant de ma mort*. Montpellier: Fata Morgana, 1994.

Blanchot, Maurice. *Le Livre à venir*. Paris: Gallimard, 1959.

Blanchot, Maurice. *The Space of Literature*. Trans. and int. Ann Smock. Lincoln: University of Nebraska Press, 1982.

Blanchot, Maurice. *The Work of Fire*. Trans. Charlotte Mandell. Stanford: Stanford University Press, 1995.

Blanchot, Maurice. *The Writing of the Disaster*. Trans. Ann Smock. Lincoln: University of Nebraska Press, 1986.

Borges, Jorge Luis. *Labyrinths*. Trans. D.A. Yates and J.E. Irby. Harmondsworth: Penguin, 1970.

Bowie, Malcolm. *Mallarmé and the Art of Being Difficult*. Cambridge: Cambridge University Press, 1978.

Breton, André, and Philippe Soupault. *The Magnetic Fields*. Trans. David Gascoyne. London: Atlas Press, 1985.

Breton, Andre. "Declaration of January 27, 1925." In *The History of Surrealism*. Ed. Maurice Nadeau. London: Plantin Publishers, 1987.

Breton, André. "Manifesto of Surrealism 1924." In *Manifestoes of Surrealism*. Trans. Richard Seaver and Helen R. Lane. Michigan: University of Michigan Press, 1972.

Brown, Andrew. *Roland Barthes: The Figures of Writing*. Oxford: Clarendon, 1992.

Burgin, Victor. "Re-reading *Camera Lucida*." In *The End of Art Theory: Criticism and Postmodernity*. Basingstoke: Macmillan, 1986, 71–92.

Cadava, Eduardo. "Words of Light: Theses on the Photography of History," *Diacritics* 22, 3–4 (1992): 84–114.

Carroll, David. *Parasthetics: Foucault, Lyotard, Derrida*. London: Methuen, 1987.

Chénieux-Gendron, Jacqueline. *Surrealism*. Trans. Vivian Folkenflik. New York: Columbia University Press, 1990.

Cixous, Hélène. *Three Steps on the Ladder of Writing*. Trans. Sarah Cornell and Susan Sellers. New York: Columbia University Press, 1993.

Clark, Timothy. *Derrida, Heidegger, Blanchot: Sources for Derrida's Notion and Practice of Literature*. Cambridge: Cambridge University Press, 1992.

Cohen, Margaret. *Profane Illumination: Walter Benjamin and the Paris of Surrealist Revolution*. Berkeley: University of California Press, 1993.

Comment, Bernard. *Roland Barthes: vers le neutre*. Paris: Christian Bourgois. 1991.

Connor, Steven. *Theory and Cultural Value*. Oxford: Blackwell, 1992.

Coquio, Catherine. "Roland Barthes et Walter Benjamin: image, tautologie, dialectique." In *Barthes après Barthes: Une actualité en questions*. Actes du colloque international de Pau. 22–24 novembre 1990. Textes réunis par Catherine Coquio et Régis Salado. Pau: Publications de l'Université de Pau, 1993, 195–208.

Corcoran, Marlena G "Drawing Our Attention to Jarry, Duchamp, and Joyce: The Manuscript/Art of William Anastasi," *James Joyce Quarterly* 32, 3–4 (Spring/Summer 1995): 659–671.

Crow, Christine M. *Paul Valéry and the Poetry of Voice*. Cambridge: Cambridge University Press, 1982.

Crow, Christine M. *Paul Valéry: Consciousness and Nature*. Cambridge: Cambridge University Press, 1972.

Deguy, Michel. *Donnant Donnant*. Paris: Galilée, 1981.

Deguy, Michel. *Given Giving: Selected Poems of Michel Deguy*. Trans. Clayton Eshelman. Int. Kenneth Koch. Berkeley: University of California Press, 1984.

Derrida, Jacques. " 'As if I Were Dead': An Interview with Jacques Derrida." In *Applying: to Derrida*. Ed. John Brannigan, Ruth Robbins, Julian Wolfreys. Basingstoke: Macmillan, 1996.

Derrida, Jacques. " 'This Strange Institution Called Literature': An Interview with Jacques Derrida." In *Acts of Literature*, 33–75.

Derrida, Jacques. "At this Very Moment in this Work Here I Am." Trans. Ruben Berezdivin. In *Re-Reading Levinas*. Ed. Robert Bernasconi and Simon Critchley. Bloomington: Indiana University Press, 1991, 11–51.

Derrida, Jacques. "Biodegradables: Seven Diary Fragments." Trans. Peggy Kamuf. *Critical Inquiry* 15 (Summer 1989): 812–873.

Derrida, Jacques. "Circonfession." In Geoffrey Bennington and Jacques Derrida. *Jacques Derrida*. Paris: Seuil, 1991.

Derrida, Jacques. "Circumfession." In Geoffrey Bennington and Jacques Derrida. *Jacques Derrida*. Trans. Geoffrey Bennington. Chicago: University of Chicago Press, 1993.

Derrida, Jacques. "How to Avoid Speaking: Denials." Trans. Ken Freiden. In *Derrida and Negative Theology*. Eds. Harold Coward and Toby Foshay. Albany: State University of New York Press, 1992, 73–142.

Derrida, Jacques. "Les morts de Roland Barthes." In *Psyché: Inventions de l'autre*. Paris: Galilée, 1987, 273–304.

Derrida, Jacques. "Like the Sound of the Sea Deep Within a Shell: Paul de Man's War." In *Responses: On Paul de Man's Wartime Journalism*. Ed. W. Hamacher, N. Hertz, T. Keenan. Lincoln: University of Nebraska Press, 1989, 127–164.

Derrida, Jacques. "Living On: Border Lines." Trans. James Hulbert. In *A Derrida Reader: Between the Blinds*. Ed. Peggy Kamuf. New York: Harvester Wheatsheaf, 1991.

Derrida, Jacques. "Living On: Border Lines." Trans. James Hulbert. In Harold Bloom et al. *Deconstruction and Criticism*. New York: Seabury Press, 1979, 75–176.

Derrida, Jacques. "Mallarmé." In *Tableau de la littérature française. vol. III: Mme de Staël à Rimbaud*. Paris: Gallimard. 1974. Trans. Christine Roulston as "Mallarmé." In Attridge, ed. *Acts of Literature*. 110–127.

Derrida, Jacques. "My Chances/*Mes Chances*: A Rendezvous with Some Epicurean Stereophonies." Trans. Irene E. Harvey and Avital Ronell. In *Taking Chances: Derrida, Psychoanalysis, and Literature*. Ed. Joseph H. Smith and William Kerrigan. Baltimore and London: Johns Hopkins University Press, 1984, 1–32.

Derrida, Jacques. "No Apocalypse. Not Now (full speed ahead, seven missiles, seven missives)." Trans. Catherine Porter and Philip Lewis. *Diacritics* 14,2 (1984): 20–31.

Derrida, Jacques. "Nombre de oui." In *Psyché: Inventions de l'autre*. Paris: Galilée, 1987, 639–650.

Derrida, Jacques. "Of an Apocalyptic Tone Recently Adopted in Philosophy." Trans. John P. Leavey Jr. *Oxford Literary Review* 6, 2 (1984): 3–35. New trans. by John Leavey Jr. *On a Newly Arisen Apocalyptic Tone in Philosophy*. In *Raising the Tone of Philosophy*. Ed. Peter Fenves. Baltimore: John Hopkins Press, 1993. 117–171.

Derrida, Jacques. "Pas." In *Parages*. Paris: Galilée, 1986, 19–116.

Derrida, Jacques. "*Sauf le nom (Post-Scriptum)*." Trans. John P. Leavey Jr. In Jacques Derrida. *On the Name*. Ed. Thomas Dutoit. Stanford: Stanford University Press, 1995, 35–85.

Derrida, Jacques. "Sauver les phénomènes: pour Salvatore Puglia," *Contretemps* 1 (1995): 14–25.

Derrida, Jacques. "Shibboleth: For Paul Celan." Trans. Joshua Wilner. In *Word Traces: Readings of Paul Celan*. Ed. Aris Fioretos. Baltimore and London: The Johns Hopkins University Press, 1994, 3–72.

Derrida, Jacques. "Some Statements and Truisms about Neologisms, Newisms, Postisms, Parasitisms, and Other Small Seismisms." Trans. Anne Tomiche. In *"The States of 'Theory": History, Art, and Critical Discourse*. Ed. and int. David Carroll. Stanford: Stanford University Press, 1990, 63–94.

Derrida, Jacques. "The Deaths of Roland Barthes." Trans. Pascale-Anne Brault and Michael Naas. In *Continental Philosophy I: Philosophy and Non-Philosophy since Merleau-Ponty*. Ed. Hugh J. Silverman. New York: Routledge, 1988. 259–296.

Derrida, Jacques. "The Time of a Thesis: Punctuations." Trans. Kathleen McLaughlin. In *Philosophy in France Today*. Ed. Alan Montefiore. Cambridge: Cambridge University Press, 1983, 34–50.

Derrida, Jacques. "Ulysses Gramophone: Hear Say Yes in Joyce." Trans. Tina Kendall and Shari Benstock. In *James Joyce: The Augmented Ninth. Proceedings of the Ninth International James Joyce Symposium. Frankfurt 1984*. Ed. Bernard Benstock. Syracuse: Syracuse University Press, 1988, 27–75.

Derrida, Jacques. "Un entretien avec Jacques Derrida: Heidegger, l'enfer des philosophes," *Le Nouvel Observateur*, 6–12 novembre 1988.

Derrida, Jacques. *Aporias*. Trans. Thomas Dutoit. Stanford: Stanford University Press, 1993.

Derrida, Jacques. *Cinders*. Trans. Ned Lukacher. Lincoln: University of Nebraska Press, 1991.

Derrida, Jacques. *De l'esprit: Heidegger et la question*. Paris: Galilée, 1987.

Derrida, Jacques. *De la Grammatologie*. Paris: Editions de Minuit, 1967.

Derrida, Jacques. *Dissemination*. Trans. and int. Barbara Johnson. Chicago: University of Chicago Press, 1981.

Derrida, Jacques. *Feu la cendre*. Paris: Des femmes, 1987.

Derrida, Jacques. *Given Time: I. Counterfeit Money*. Trans. Peggy Kamuf, Chicago: University of Chicago Press, 1992.

Derrida, Jacques. *Glas*. Trans. John P. Leavey Jr. and Richard Rand. Lincoln: University of Nebraska Press, 1986.

Derrida, Jacques. *Khôra*. Paris: Galilée, 1993.

Derrida, Jacques. *L'autre cap*. Paris: Editions de Minuit, 1991.

Derrida, Jacques. *La carte postale*. Paris: Flammarion, 1980.

Derrida, Jacques. *La dissémination*. Paris: Seuil, 1972.

Derrida, Jacques. *La problème de la genèse dans la philosophie de Husserl*. Paris: Presses universitaires de France, 1990.

Derrida, Jacques. *La Voix et le phénomène: Introduction au problème du signe dans la phénoménologie de Husserl*. Paris: Presses universitaires de France, 1967.

Derrida, Jacques. *Lecture de Droit de regards*. Paris: Minuit, 1985.

Derrida, Jacques. *Mal d'archive*. Paris: Galilée, 1995.

Derrida, Jacques. *Marges de la philosophie*. Paris: Minuit, 1972.

Derrida, Jacques. *Margins of Philosophy*. Trans. Alan Bass. Chicago: University of Chicago Press, 1982.

Derrida, Jacques. *Memoires, for Paul de Man*. Rev. ed. Trans. Cecile Lindsay, Jonathan Culler, Eduardo Cadava, and Peggy Kamuf. New York: Columbia University Press, 1989.

Derrida, Jacques. *Mémoires, pour Paul de Man*. Paris: Galilée, 1988.

Derrida, Jacques. *Memoirs of the Blind: The Self-Portrait and Other Ruins*. Trans. Pascale-Anne Brault and Michael Naas. Chicago: University of Chicago Press, 1993.

Derrida, Jacques. *Of Grammatology*. Trans. Gayatri Chakravorty Spivak. Baltimore: Johns Hopkins University Press, 1976.

Derrida, Jacques. *Parages*. Paris: Galilée, 1986.

Derrida, Jacques. *Points . . . : Interviews, 1974-1994*. Ed. Elisabeth Weber. Trans. Peggy Kamuf et al. Stanford: Stanford University Press, 1995.

Derrida, Jacques. *Politiques de l'amitié*. Paris: Gallimard, 1994.

Derrida, Jacques. *Positions*. Paris: Editions de Minuit, 1972.

Derrida, Jacques. *Positions*. Trans. Alan Bass. Chicago: University of Chicago Press, 1981.

Derrida, Jacques. *Psyché. Inventions de l'autre*. Paris: Galilée, 1987.

Derrida, Jacques. *Signéponge/Signsponge*. Trans. Richard Rand. New York: Columbia University Press, 1984.

Derrida, Jacques. *Specters of Marx: The State of the Debt, the Work of Mourning, and the New International*. Trans. Peggy Kamuf. Int. Bernd Magnus and Stephen Cullenberg. New York and London: Routledge, 1994.

Derrida, Jacques. *Speech and Phenomena and Other Essays on Husserl's Theory of Signs*. Trans. and int. David B. Allison. Preface by Newton Garver. Evanston: Northwestern Uniersity Press, 1973.

Derrida, Jacques. *Spurs: Nietzsche's Styles/Eperons: Les styles de Nietzsche*. Int. Stefano Agosti. Trans. Barbara Harlow. Chicago: University of Chicago Press, 1979.

Derrida, Jacques. *The Ear of the Other: Otobiography, Transference, Translation*. Ed. Christie McDonald. Trans. Peggy Kamuf. Lincoln and London: University of Nebraska Press, 1985.

Derrida, Jacques. *The Other Heading: Reflections on Today's Europe*. Trans. Pascale-Anne Brault and Michael Naas. Int. Michael Naas. Bloomington: Indiana University Press, 1992.

Derrida, Jacques. *The Post Card: From Socrates to Freud and Beyond*. Trans. Alan Bass. Chicago: University of Chicago Press, 1987.

Derrida, Jacques. *The Truth in Painting*. Trans. Geoff Bennington and Ian McLeod. Chicago: University of Chicago Press, 1987.

Derrida, Jacques. *Writing and Difference*. Trans. Alan Bass, London: Routledge and Kegan Paul, 1978.

Descombes, Vincent. *Modern French Philosophy*. Trans. L. Scott-Fox and J. M. Harding. Cambridge: Cambridge University Press, 1980.

Dosse, François. *Histoire du structuralisme*. 2 volumes. Paris: Editions la Découverte, 1991 and 1992.

Dupriez, Bernard. *Gradus-Les procédés littéraires*. Paris 10/18 (1984): 319–320.

Ellmann, Maud. "Spacing Out: A Double Entendre on Mallarmé," *Oxford Literary Review* 3, 2: 22–31.

Fédier, François. *Heidegger: anatomie d'un scandale*. Paris: Robert Laffont, 1988.

Felman, Shoshana, and Dori Laub. *Testimony: Crises of Witnessing in Literature, Psychoanalysis, and History*. London: Routledge, 1992.

ffrench, Patrick. *The Time of Theory*. Oxford: Oxford University Press, 1995.

Foucault, Michel. *Raymond Roussel*. Paris: Gallimard, 1963.

Fournel, Paul. "Banlieue." In *La Bibliothèque Oulipienne*. Vol. III. Paris: Seghers, 1990. Trans. Harry Mathews. *Oulipo Laboratory*. London: Atlas Press, 1995.

Freud, Sigmund. "Screen Memories" (1899). In *Complete Psychological Works Vol III*.

Frey, Hans-Jost. *Studies in Poetic Discourse: Mallarmé, Baudelaire, Rimbaud, Hölderlin*. Trans. William Whobrey. Stanford: Stanford University Press, 1996.

Fry, Christopher M. *Sartre and Hegel: The Variations of an Enigma in "L'Etre et le néant."* Bonn: Bouvier, 1988.

Galindo, Martha Zapata. *Triumph des Willens zur Macht, Zur Nietzsche-Rezeption im NS-Staat*. Hamburg: Argument, 1995.

Gasché, Rodolphe. *The Tain of the Mirror*. Bloomington: Indiana University Press, 1987.

Gascoyne, David. "Introduction." In Breton and Soupault. *The Magnetic Fields*.

Gavronsky, Serge. *Toward A New Poetics*. Berkeley: University of California Press, 1994.

Genette, Gérard. "Le bonheur de Mallarmé." In *Figures I*. Paris: Seuil, 1961.

Genette, Gérard. "Valéry and the Poetics of Language." In *Textual Strategies: Perspectives in Post-Structuralist Criticism*. Ed. and int. Josué V. Harari. London: Methuen, 1979.

Genette, Gérard. *Mimologiques*. Paris: Seuil, 1976.

Genette, Gérard. *Palimpsestes: La Littérature au second degré*. Paris: Seuil, 1982.

Giribone, Jean-Luc. "Les phénomènes . . . et le reste," *Communications* 36: "Roland Barthes" (1982): 7–17.

Grondin, Jean. *Sources of Hermeneutics*. Albany: State University of New York, 1995.

Halley, Michael. "Argo Sum," *Diacritics* 12 (1982): 69–79.

Heller, Gerhard. *Un Allemand a Paris*. Paris: Seuil, 1981.

Henry, Michel. *C'est moi la vérité: Pour une philosophie du christianisme*. Paris: Seuil, 1996.

Holland, Michael, ed. *The Blanchot Reader*. Oxford: Blackwell, 1995.

Hume, David. *Treatise of Human Nature* (1738), Book I, Part IV. Ed. L. A. Selby–Bigge. Oxford: Clarendon Press, 1978.

Husserl, Edmund. *Cartesian Meditations: An Introduction to Transcendental Phenomenology*. Trans. Dorion Cairns. The Hague: Martinus Nijhoff, 1960.

Husserl, Edmund. *L'origine de la géometrie*. Trad. et int. Jacques Derrida. Paris: Presses universitaires de France, 1974.

Hutcheon, Linda. *The Politics of Postmodernism*. London: Routledge, 1989.

Irigaray, Luce. *Speculum: Of the Other Woman*. Trans. Gillian C. Gill. Ithaca: Cornell University Press, 1985.

Irigaray, Luce. *This Sex Which is Not One*. Trans. Catherine Porter with Carolyn Burke. Ithaca: Cornell University Press, 1985.

Jacob, François. "François Jacob et Claude Lévi-Strauss face à face," *Figaro littéraire* 1338 (7 January 1972), 13; 16.

Jacob, François. "Le modèle linguistique en biologie," *Critique* 322 (March 1974): 195–205.

Jacob, François. "Vivre et parler" (with Philippe L'Héritier, Roman Jakobson, and Claude Lévi-Strauss), *Les Lettres françaises* 1221 (14 and 21 February 1968): 3–7.

Janicaud, Dominique. *Le tournant théologique de la phénoménologie française*. Combas: Editions de l'Eclat, 1991.

Jankélévitch, Vladimir. *Philosophie première: Introduction à une philosophie du "presque."* Paris: Presses universitaires de France, 1954.

Jankélévitch. Vladimir. *Le Je-ne-sais-quoi et le Presque-rien*. Paris: Seuil, 1980.

Joannes Secundus (Jan Everaerts). *The Kisses of Joannes Secundus*. Trans. F. X. Mathews. Kingston, Rhode Island: The Winecellar Press, 1984.

Johnson, Christopher. *System and Writing in the Philosophy of Jacques Derrida*. Cambridge: Cambridge University Press, 1993.

Kafka, Franz. *Wedding Preparations in the Country and Other Posthumous Prose Writings*. Trans. Ernst Kaiser and Eithne Wilkins, with notes by Max Brod. London: Secker and Warburg, 1973.

Kamuf, Peggy. "Introduction: Reading Between the Blinds." In *A Derrida Reader*. xiii–xlii.

Kaplan, Louis. *Laszlo Moholy-Nagy: Biographical Writings*. Durham: Duke University Press, 1995.

Knight, Diana. "Roland Barthes in Harmony: The Writing of Utopia," *Paragraph* 11 (1988): 127–142.

Knight, Diana. "Roland Barthes: Structuralism Utopian and Scientific," *News From Nowhere* 9 (1991): 18–28.

Kofman, Sarah. "Ça Cloche." Trans. Caren Kaplan. In *Derrida and Deconstruction*. Ed. Hugh J. Silverman. London: Routledge, 1989.

Kojève, Alexandre. *Introduction à la lecture de Hegel*. Paris: Gallimard, 1947.

Kristeva, Julia, and Jean-Michel Ribette, eds. *Folle vérité: vérité et vraisemblance du texte psychotique*. Paris: Seuil, 1979.

Kristeva, Julia, *La révolution du langage poétique*. Paris: Seuil, 1973.

Lacan, Jacques. *Ecrits*. Paris, 1966.

Lacan, Jacques. *Ecrits: A Selection*. Trans. Alan Sheridan. London: Tavistock/ Routledge, 1977.

Lacan, Jacques. *Le Séminaire: Livre XVII: L'envers de la psychanalyse 1969–1970*. Texte établi par Jacques-Alain Miller. Paris: Seuil, 1991.

Lacan, Jacques. *The Four Fundamental Concepts of Psychoanalysis*. Trans. Alan Sheridan. London: Hogarth Press, 1977.

Lacoue-Labarthe, Philippe. *The Subject of Philosophy*. Ed. and Foreword Thomas Trezise. Trans. Thomas Trezise et al. Minneapolis: University of Minnesota Press, 1993.

Lacoue-Labarthe, Philippe. *Typography: Mimesis, Philosophy, Politics*. Int. Jacques Derrida. Ed. Christopher Fynsk. Trans. Christopher Fynsk et al. Cambridge: Harvard University Press, 1989.

Lacoue-Labarthe, Philippe, and Jean-Luc Nancy. "Entretiens sur Roger Laporte," *Digraphe* 18/19 (1979): 175–203.

Lacoue-Labarthe, Philippe. "Typographie," In *Mimesis—des articulations*. Ed. Sylviane Agacinski et al. Paris: Aubier–Flammarion, 1975, 165–270.

Lacoue-Labarthe, Philippe. *Le Sujet de la philosophie (Typographies 1)*. Paris: Aubier–Flammarion, 1979.

Laporte, Roger. " 'Les 'blancs' assument l'importance,' " *Les Lettres françaises* 1429 (1972): 5.

Laporte, Roger. "Bief," *L'Arc* 54 (1973): 65–70.

Laporte, Roger. "Nulle part séjournant." In *Les Fins de l'homme: à partir du travail de Jacques Derrida*. Ed. Philippe Lacoue-Labarthe and Jean-Luc Nancy. Paris: Galilée, 1981, 201–208.

Laporte, Roger. "Roger Laporte au bord du silence." Interview conducted by Jacques Derrida. *Libération*, 22 December 1983: 28.

Laporte, Roger. *"Souvenir de Reims" et autres récits*. Paris: Hachette, 1979.

Laporte, Roger. "Une double stratégie." In *Ecarts: quatre essais à propos de Jacques Derrida*. Lucette Finas et al. Paris: Fayard, 1973, 208–264.

Laporte, Roger. *Carnets (extraits)*. Paris: Hachette, 1979.

Laporte, Roger. *Etudes*. Paris: P.O.L., 1990.

Laporte, Roger. *Quinze variations sur un thème biographique*. Paris: Flammarion, 1975.

Laporte, Roger. *Une Vie*. Paris: P.O.L, 1986.

Lavers. Annette. *Roland Barthes: Structuralism and After*. London: Methuen, 1982.

Le Lionnais, François. "Second Manifesto." In *La Littérature potentielle: Créations, re-créations, récréations*. Paris: Gallimard, 1973. Trans. Warren F. Motte Jr. *Oulipo*. Ed. Motte.

Lechte, John. *Fifty Key Contemporary Thinkers*. London: Routledge, 1994.

Leiris, Michel. *Brisées: Broken Branches*. Trans. Lydia Davies. San Francisco: North Point Press, 1989.

Lejeune, Philippe. *Le Mémoire et L'Oblique: Georges Perec autobiographe*. Paris: P.O.L., 1991.

Lévi-Strauss, Claude. *De Près et de loin*. Odile Jacob: Paris, 1988.

Lévi-Strauss, Claude. Preface to Roman Jakobson. *Six Leçons sur le son et le sens*. Paris: Editions de Minuit, 1976.

Lévi-Strauss, Claude. *Structural Anthropology 2*. Trans. Monique Layton. Harmondsworth: Penguin, 1978.

Lévi-Strauss, Claude. *The Elementary Structures of Kinship*. Trans. J. H. Bell, J. R. von Sturmer and R. Needham: Boston: Beacon Press, 1969.

Lévi-Strauss, Claude. *The Savage Mind*. Trans. Rodney Needham. Oxford: Oxford University Press, 1996.

Lévi-Strauss, Claude. *Tristes tropiques*. Trans. John and Doreen Weightman. Harmondsworth: Penguin, 1984.

Lévi-Strauss, Claude. *The View from Afar*. Trans. Joachim Neugroschel and Phoebe Hoss. London: Penguin, 1987.

Llewelyn. John. "Derrida, Mallarmé, and Anatole." In *Philosophers' Poets*. Ed. David Wood. London: Routledge, 1990, 93–110.

Lombardo, Patrizia. "Le dernier livre." *L'Esprit créateur* XXII,1 (1982): 79–87.

Lombardo, Patrizia. *Edgar Poe et la Modernité: Breton, Barthes, Derrida, Blanchot*. Birmingham, Ala.: Summa, 1985.

Lombardo, Patrizia. *The Three Paradoxes of Roland Barthes*. Athens, Ga., and London: University of Georgia Press, 1989.

Lucretius. *De Rerum Natura*, Book II, 251. Quoted by Marx in *Notebooks on Epicurean Philosophy*. In Karl Marx and Frederick Engels, *Collected Works*. London: Lawrence and Wishart, 1975. Vol I: Karl Marx: 1835–43.

Lukacher, Ned. "Introduction: Mourning Becomes Telepathy." In Derrida, *Cinders*, 1–18.

Lyotard, Jean-François. *The Differend. Phrases in Dispute*. Trans. Georges Van Den Abbeele. Manchester: Manchester University Press, 1988.

Macksey, Richard, and Eugenio Donato, eds. *The Language of Criticism and the Sciences of Man: The Structuralist Controversy.* Baltimore and London: Johns Hopkins University Press, 1970.

Magné, Bernard. "Les Sutures dans *W ou le Souvenir d'Enfance,*" *Cahiers Georges Perec* No 2, textuel 34/44, 1988.

Magné, Bernard. "Transformations of Constraint," *The Review of Contemporary Fiction* 13, 1 (Spring 1993): 111–123.

Major, René. *Lacan avec Derrida: Analyse désistentielle.* Paris: Mentha, 1991.

Major, René. *Ràver l'autre.* Paris: Aubier Montaigne, 1977.

Mallarmé, Stéphane. Correspondence. Vol. I: 1862–1871. Ed. Henri Mondor. Paris: Gallimard, 1959.

Mallarmé, Stéphane. *Oeuvres complètes.* Ed. Henri Mondor and G. Jean–Aubry. Paris: Gallimard, 1945.

Mallarmé, Stéphane. *Poésies.* Ed. Bertrand Marchal. Paris: Gallimard, 1992.

Marty, Eric. "L'assomption du phénomène," *Critique* XXXVIII (423–4: 1982): 744–752.

Mathews, Harry. *Country Cooking and Other Stories.* Providence: Burning Deck, 1980.

Mauss, Marcel. *The Gift: The Form and Reason for Exchange in Archaic Societies.* Trans. W.D. Halls. London: Routledge, 1990.

Mehlman, Jeffrey. " 'Response' to 'More on Writing and Deference,' " *Representations* 18 (Spring 1987): 162–164.

Mehlman, Jeffrey. "Blanchot at *Combat.*" In *Legacies of Anti-Semitism in France.* Minneapolis: University of Minnesota Press, 1983.

Mehlman, Jeffrey. "Deconstruction, Literature, History: The Case of *L'Arrêt de mort.*" In *Proceedings of the Northeastern University Center for Literary Studies,* Volume 2. 1984, 33–53.

Mehlman, Jeffrey. "Perspectives on De Man and Le Soir." In *Responses: On Paul de Man's Wartime Journalism.* 324–333.

Mehlman, Jeffrey. "Writing and Deference: The Politics of Literary Adulation," *Representations* 15 (Spring 1986): 1–14.

Melville, Herman. *Moby Dick.* (1851) Harmondsworth: Penguin, 1984.

Miller, J. Hillis. *Topographies.* Stanford: Stanford University Press, 1995.

Moi, Toril, ed. *The Kristeva Reader.* Oxford: Blackwell, 1986.

Mondor, Henri. *Autres précisions sur Mallarmé et inédits.* Paris: Gallimard, 1961.

Mondor, Henri. *L'Histoire d'un faune.* Paris: Gallimard, 1948.

Montaigne, Michel de. *Essais III.* Int. Alexandre Micha. Paris: Garnier-Flammarion, 1969; *The Essays of Michel de Montaigne.* Trans. and ed. M. A. Screech. Harmondsworth: Allen Lane, 1991.

Moriarty, Michael. *Roland Barthes.* Cambridge: Polity, 1991.

Motte Jr., Warren F. "Permutational Mathews." *Review of Contemporary Fiction* VII, 3 (Fall 1987): 91–99.

Nabokov, Vladimir. *Lectures on Literature.* Ed. Fredson Bowers. Int. John Updike. London: Picador, 1983.

Nabokov, Vladimir. *Pale Fire.* New York: Vintage, 1989.

Nancy, Jean-Luc. *The Inoperative Community.* Ed. Peter Connor. Foreword Christopher Fynsk. Trans Peter Connor et al. Minneapolis: University of Minnesota Press, 1991.

Norris, Christopher. *Derrida.* London: Fontana, 1987.

Novalis (Friedrich Philipp von Hardenberg). *Das philosophische–theoretische Werke.* Ed. Hans-Joachim Mähl and Richard Samuel. Vienna: Carl Hanser, 1978.

Novalis. *Philosophical Writings.* Trans. and ed. Margaret Mahony Stoljar. Albany: State University of New York Press, 1997.

Olson, Charles. *Call Me Ishmael.* New York: Grove Press, 1947.

Olson, Charles. *Selected Writings of Charles Olson.* Ed. Robert Creeley. New York: New Directions, 1966.

Olson, Charles. *The Special View of History.* Ed. and int. Ann Charters, Berkeley: Oyez, 1970.

Paulhan, Jean. "Manie." In *Les Cause célèbres.* (1944) Paris: Gallimard, 1982, 137–139.

Paulhan, Jean. *Alain, ou la preuve par l'étymologie. Oeuvres complètes.* Vol. 1. Paris: Editions du cercle du livre précieux, 1966.

Paulhan, Jean. *Braque le patron. Oeuvres complètes* Vol. 5, 11–41.

Paulhan, Jean. *Correspondance Jean Paulhan–Francis Ponge 1923–1968.* Vol. 2. Edition critique annotée par Claire Boaretto. Paris: Gallimard, 1986.

Paulhan, Jean. *De la paille et du grain. Oeuvres complètes.* Vol. 5, 313–406.

Paulhan, Jean. *Les Fleurs de Tarbes, ou la Terreur dans les Lettres* (1941). Paris: Gallimard, 1971.

Perec, Georges. Interview in *L'Arc*, quoted by Marcel Benabou, "Perec's Jewishness," *Review of Contemporary Fiction* 13, 1 (Spring 1993).

Perec, Georges. *Je Suis Né.* Paris: Editions du Seuil, 1990.

Perec, Georges. *La Disparition*. Paris: Denoël, 1969; *A Void*. Trans. Gilbert Adair. London: Harvill, 1994.

Perec, Georges. *W ou un Souvenir d'Enfance*. Paris: Editions Denoël, 1975. *W or the Memory of Childhood*. Trans. David Bellos. London: Collins Harvill, 1989.

Poe, Edgar Allen. *Selected Writings*. Ed. David Galloway. Harmondsworth: Penguin, 1967.

Price, Mary. *The Photograph: A Strange Confined Space*. Stanford: Stanford University Press, 1994.

Queneau, Raymond. *Exercices de style*. Paris: Gallimard, 1947. *Exercises in Style*. Trans. Barbara Wright. New York: New Directions, 1981.

Richard, Jean–Pierre. *L'univers imaginaire de Stéphane Mallarmé*. Paris: Seuil, 1961.

Robin, Régine. "Un projet autobiographique inédit de Georges Perec: *L'Arbre*," *Le Cabinet d'amateur* 1, 1. (Spring 1993): 5–28.

Roger, Philippe. *Roland Barthes: Roman*. Paris: Grasset. 1986.

Rose, Jacqueline, and Juliet Mitchell, eds. *Feminine Sexuality: Jacques Lacan and the "Ecole Freudienne."* New York: Norton, 1985.

Roubaud, Jacques. *The Great Fire of London*. Trans. Dominic di Bernardi. Elmwood Park: Dalkey Archive, 1991.

Rousset, Jean. *Forme et signification: essais sur les structures littéraires de Corneille à Claudel*. Paris: Corti, 1962.

Royle, Nicholas. *After Derrida*. Manchester: Manchester University Press, 1995.

Safranski, Rüdiger. *Ein Meister aus Deutschland: Heidegger und seine Zeit*. München: Hanser, 1994.

Salusinsky, Imre. *Criticism in Society*. New York: Methuen, 1987.

Sarkonak, Ralph. "Roland Barthes and the Spectre of Photography," *L'Esprit créateur* XXII, 1 (1982): 48–68.

Sartre, Jean-Paul. *Being and Nothingness: A Phenomenological Essay on Ontology*. Trans. and int. Hazel E. Barnes. New York: Washington Square Press, 1956.

Sartre, Jean-Paul. *L'Etre et le néant. Essai d'ontologie phénoménologique*. Paris: Gallimard, 1943.

Sartre, Jean-Paul. *L'Imaginaire. Psychologie phénoménologique de l'imagination*. Paris: Gallimard, 1940.

Sartre, Jean-Paul. *The Psychology of Imagination*. London: Methuen, 1972.

Scherer, Jacques. *Grammaire de Mallarmé*. Paris: Nizet, 1977.

Schmidt, Dennis J. "Circles—Hermeneutic and Otherwise: On Various Senses of the Future as 'Not Yet.' " In *Writing the Future*. Ed. David Wood. London: Routledge, 1990, 67–77.

Schürmann, Rainer. "Que faire à la fin de la métaphysique?" *Cahiers de l'Herne: Heidegger*. Ed. Michel Haar. Paris: Editions de l'Herne, 1983.

Seelye, Catherine, ed. *Charles Olson and Ezra Pound: An Encounter at St. Elizabeths*. New York: Paragon, 1991.

Serres, Michel. *Hermès III. La traduction*. Paris: Editions de Minuit, 1974.

Shattuck, Roger. "What Is 'Pataphysics?" *Evergreen Review* 4, 13 (May-June, 1960).

Shattuck, Roger. *The Banquet Years*. New York: Harcourt, Brace and Co., 1958. Rev. ed. New York: Random House, 1968.

Shattuck, Roger. *The Innocent Eye*. New York: Farrar Strauss Giroux, 1984.

Shawcross, Nancy M. "The Intertexts of *La chambre claire*: Barthes, the Photograph, and the Interstice of Time." Unpublished Diss. Rutgers State University of New Jersey: New Brunswick, 1993. Ann Arbor: University Microfilms International, 1993.

Silverman, Hugh. *Textualities: Between Hermeneutics and Deconstruction*. New York: Routledge, 1994.

Sollers, Phillipe. "Littérature et totalité." In *Logiques*. Paris: Seuil, 1968.

Spiegelberg, Herbert. *The Phenomenological Movement: A Historical Introduction*. The Hague: Martinus Nijhoff, 1982.

Steinmetz, Rudy. *Les Styles de Derrida*. Brussels: De Boeck, 1994.

Stillman, Linda Kleiger. *Alfred Jarry*. Boston: Twayne, 1983.

Syrotinski, Michael. "Some Wheat and Some Chaff: Jean Paulhan and the Post-War Literary Purge in France." *Studies in Twentieth Century Literature* 16, 2 (Summer 1992): 247–263.

Temple, Michael. *The Name of the Poet: Onomastics and Anonymity in the Works of Stéphane Mallarmé*. Exeter: University of Exeter Press, 1995.

*The True, the Good, the Beautiful: An Elementary Chrestomathy of 'Pataphysics*. London: Atlas Press, 1993.

Thorne, Tony. *Dictionary of Contemporary Slang*. London: Bloomsbury Publishing, 1990.

Todorov, Tzvetan. "Le dernier Barthes." *Poétique* 47: "Roland Barthes" (1981): 323–327.

Ulmer, Gregory L. "The Discourse of the Imaginary," *Diacritics* 10 (1980): 61–75.

Ungar, Steven. *Roland Barthes: The Professor of Desire*. Lincoln: University of Nebraska Press, 1983.

Vaihinger, Hans. *The Philosophy of the "As if": A System of the Theoretical, Practical, and Religious Fictions of Mankind*. Trans. C. K. Ogden. London: Kegan Paul. Trench. Trubner & Co. 1924.

Valéry Paul. *Poems*. (Bilingual ed.) Trans. David Paul. London: Routledge and Kegan Paul, 1971.

Valéry, Paul. *Cahiers*, 29 vols. Paris: C.N.R.S, 1957–1961.

Valéry, Paul. *Charmes ou poèmes*. Ed. Charles G. Whiting. London: Athlone Press, 1973.

Valéry, Paul. *Paul Valéry: Œuvres*. Ed. J. Hytier, 2 vols. Paris: Bibliothèque de la Pléiade, vil. 1, 1975, vol. 2, 1977.

Wills, David. *Self De(con)struct: Writing and the Surrealist Text*. Townsville, Queensland: James Cook University of North Queensland, 1985.

Wiseman, Mary Bittner. *The Ecstasies of Roland Barthes*. London: Routledge, 1989.

Wood, David, ed. *Philosophers' Poets*. London: Routledge, 1990.

Wood, David. *Philosophy to the Limit*. London: Routledge, 1990.

Žižek, Slavoj. *Enjoy Your Symptom!: Jacques Lacan in Hollywood and Out*. London: Routledge, 1992.

# Index